The Color of Crime

Critical America

GENERAL EDITORS: Richard Delgado and Jean Stefancic

The Color of Crime was originally published in 1998. For a complete list of titles in the series, please visit the New York University Press website at www.nyupress.org.

The Color of Crime

Second Edition

Katheryn Russell-Brown

NEW YORK UNIVERSITY PRESS

New York and London

NEW YORK UNIVERSITY PRESS
New York and London
www.nyupress.org

Library of Congress Cataloging-in-Publication Data
Russell-Brown, Katheryn, 1961–
The color of crime / Katheryn Russell-Brown. — 2nd ed.
p.   cm. — (Critical America)
Includes bibliographical references and index.
ISBN-13: 978-0-8147-7617-9 (cl : alk. paper)
ISBN-10: 0-8147-7617-5 (cl : alk. paper)
ISBN-13: 978-0-8147-7618-6 (pb : alk. paper)
ISBN-10: 0-8147-7618-3 (pb : alk. paper)
1. Discrimination in criminal justice administration—United States.
2. Crime and race—United States. 3. African American criminals.
4. Racism—United States. 5. White criminals.   I. Title.
HV9950.R87 2008
305.8—dc22   2008023336

New York University Press books are printed on acid-free paper,
and their binding materials are chosen for strength and durability.
We strive to use environmentally responsible suppliers and materials
to the greatest extent possible in publishing our books.

Manufactured in the United States of America

c 10 9 8 7 6 5 4 3 2 1
p 10 9 8 7 6 5 4 3 2 1

To my twin delights, Sasha and Louis

Contents

Acknowledgments

I never imagined when I signed the contract for *The Color of Crime* in 1995 that the book, which was published in 1998, would have a second edition. As the tenth anniversary of its publication approached, I was excited to have a chance to revisit, rethink, and rewrite some of the material.

I would not have been able to undertake this second look at my first book without the help of many people. First, thank you to Richard Delgado for giving me an opportunity to write for New York University Press's wonderful Critical America series. *The Color of Crime* is in exceptional company. Both of my editors, Niko Pfund, the first time around, and Ilene Kalish, the second time around, offered incisive critical commentary on early drafts and were skilled at gently prodding me to complete the manuscript.

The University of Florida's Levin College of Law made it possible for me to conduct research and hire students.

I was fortunate to have superb research assistance from a number of U.F. students, including graduate students Amanda Moras and Maura Ryan and law students Katherine DeBriere, Oshia Gainer, and William MacQueen. Their thoughtful questions, comments, and edits have greatly improved the text.

A number of colleagues, including Angela Davis, Shaun Gabbidon, Sherrilyn Ifill, Eric Miller, Kenneth Nunn, Imani Perry, and Andrew Taslitz, offered feedback on various ideas, concepts, and themes.

To my husband, parents, all of my family, and each of my friends, from the bottom of my heart, thank you.

Introduction

> In the heart of any individual, family, community or society,
> memory is of fundamental importance. It is the fabric of identity.
> At the heart of every oppressive tool developed by the apartheid
> regime was a determination to control, distort, weaken, even erase
> people's memories. . . . The struggle against apartheid can be typi-
> fied as the pitting of remembering against forgetting.
>
> —Nelson Mandela[1]

Memory is a funny thing. We like to believe that our memories are an accurate reflection of the way things were. When it comes to
historical memory, however, the truth of the matter is often fleeting, distorted, and incomplete. As it turns out, to tell the truth about the past
is not so easy a task. Our collective memories are clouded in myths, in
silences, and with a stubborn insistence to put on a happy face.

On issues involving race and crime, we consistently wring our hands,
point fingers, and cover our eyes. Whether it is racial profiling, capital
punishment, police brutality, rising incarceration rates, Barry Bonds, O. J.
Simpson, or racial hoaxes, as a society, we are loathe to invoke the country's racial record. Our ever-ready attempts to run interference between
the past and present reduce our racial history to a disembodied mass of
curious data. The United States' racial history and its impact on the justice system, however, do not go away simply because we ignore them. The
proverbial tree that falls in the forest while no one is present does make a
sound—a loud, crushing one. Luckily there are many people who seek to
give history its due weight in analyses of contemporary conditions. Count
me in.

Ten years have passed since I wrote the first edition of *The Color of
Crime*. I am pleased that I have had the opportunity to continue this research in the form of a second edition. Each of the chapters has been

1

updated and rewritten. For the chapter on racial hoaxes (the most popular one), I have included data on twenty-five new hoax cases, raising the total number to ninety-two. There are also two brand new chapters. One examines how the deviance associated with Black skin "bleeds" into other areas, including the images associated with certain names (e.g., "Black-sounding" names) and accents and how all of this is directly tied to racial disproportionality in the criminal justice system. The other new chapter makes the case for race and crime literacy. Two appendices are included. Appendix A reprints the Traffic Stops Statistics Study Act (proposed congressional legislation that would require police to gather race data at each traffic stop), and appendix B offers a brief summary of each racial hoax case.

Issues of race and justice persist. The iceberg's tip includes cases such as the Jena Six, the Duke lacrosse Team, Amadou Diallo, Sean Bell, James Byrd, and the aftermath of Hurricane Katrina. The *criminalblackman* is still alive. Curator Thelma Golden has wryly observed that the African American male is "one of the greatest inventions of the twentieth century."[2] Barry Bonds and Michael Vick remind us that Black men continue to be the public face of deviance. O. J. Simpson returned to the front pages in 2007, and once again the media went O. J. wild. Because race issues continue to be portrayed in hues of Black and White, this book focuses on African Americans.

For many years, academics have pushed to move race analyses beyond the well-entrenched Black-White dichotomy. Part of the difficulty in making assessments more inclusive is that groups of color cannot be accurately discussed as a single entity and then compared with Whites. Each racial group has had a unique experience with the American criminal justice system. For instance, Native Americans, from their early encounters with Whites, had their land stolen and were stripped of their language and lineage. A complex and contorted tripart legal system exists to adjudicate Indian legal affairs. In contemporary times, American Indians, who make up less than 1 percent of the U.S. population, have the highest rates of victimization. Although there are some common themes of racial oppression across Blacks, Latinos, Asians, and Native Americans, the way the criminal law has been used to marginalize each group is notably distinct. Latinos, the largest U.S. minority group, have disproportionately high rates of arrest and incarceration. They acutely face the interrelated issues of immigrant rights and racial profiling. Asian Americans, approximately 4 percent of the U.S. population, are typically cast as being involved in human trafficking or gang-related offenses. Given these distinctions, lumping Blacks, Latinos, and Asian Americans together, when discussing crime, though desirable in theory, is problematic. More research must be devoted to each of these racial groups. To this end, work on Latinos by professor Ramiro Martinez is particularly impressive, as is work on American Indians by professor Marianne Neilsen.

The primary and unapologetic focus for this text is on the relationship between African Americans and the U.S. criminal justice system. In various instances, however, references are made and data is presented regarding other racial groups.

I wrote *The Color of Crime* to answer the many unanswered questions I had about race, as a law student and later as a graduate student. I went to law school hoping to learn about the intersections between law, race, and justice. Likewise, when I returned to graduate school for a doctoral degree in criminology, I presumed that my studies would focus in part on how and why race matters in the administration of justice. In both instances, I was frustrated with the slim pickings of assigned readings and the infrequent and uninformed discussions on these seminal issues. Beyond addressing my own queries, this book's modest objective is to offer students and interested others a richer and fuller backdrop with which to understand and critique the workings of today's criminal justice system. I have written the second edition to continue this—my academic expedition.

Chapter 1, "Media Messages," looks at how Native Americans, Asian Americans, Latinos, and Blacks are portrayed by the media, including television and movies. As the chapter details, when it comes to people of color, it is the best of times and the worst of times. Today there are more faces of color that appear on situation comedies and dramas, but the substance of these roles raises interesting questions. The discussion identifies some remarkable trends in these portrayals, including how some minority groups (e.g., Native Americans and Asian Americans) are rarely seen or heard but are discussed without being at the table.

Chapter 2, "The Skin Game," illuminates the issues raised in chapter 1, specifically, how the racialized media images of Black skin have become embedded within the American fabric. It traces how the widely accepted perception of Black skin as a representation of deviance manifests itself in popular culture and ultimately in the criminal justice system. The discussion of various forms of racial assaults, including microaggressions and macroaggressions, identifies some of ways that Blackness is interpreted and talked about publicly. The chapter details how race is "found"—via

"Black-sounding" names and accents—and used as a way to marginalize and block access to the mainstream.

Chapter 3, "History's Strange Fruit," sets out the historical role of race in the development and operation of the U.S. criminal justice system, from the slave codes to Jim Crow legislation. This history is used to determine which operating principles are necessary for a racially fair criminal justice system. These "fairness principles" lay the groundwork for the book's assessment of whether the criminal justice system is racially biased.

Chapter 4, "Discrimination or Disparity?" offers a detailed look at Black involvement in the criminal justice system. It examines how racial discrimination is understood and assesses the value of traditional tools of analysis. The chapter also takes a close look at the relationship between Black men, the law, and the police and considers why this relationship continues to be a problematic one.

Chapter 5, "Are We *Still* Talking about O. J.?" looks back at the Simpson criminal case and details why the case was so racially charged—how the case tapped our greatest fears and hopes about race and crime. The chapter examines "Black protectionism" as the reason for the steadfast support that Simpson received from African Americans. The media treated the case as a "Black v. White" issue, to the exclusion of Latinos, Asian Americans, and Native Americans, even though together these three racial groups total almost one-fifth of the nation's population.

Chapter 6, "Racial Hoaxes," examines cases involving a false allegation of crime against someone based on his or her race. Some of the more well-known cases include Jennifer Wilbanks ("the runaway bride"), Susan Smith, Charles Stuart, and the Duke lacrosse case. False allegations of crime, particularly against Black men, are not as uncommon as we might hope. The chapter evaluates the phenomenon of racial hoaxes and details more than ninety cases, concluding that perpetrators should be subject to greater criminal penalty.

Chapter 7, "White Crime," examines how crime committed by Blacks is labeled "Black crime," yet crime by Whites is not accorded a similar race label. The chapter considers crimes that would fall within the category of "White crime." It also considers whether racial labels should be attached to crime and, if so, which crimes it should encompass. The chapter concludes with a critique of professor James Q. Wilson's argument that White racism is caused by high rates of Black crime.

Chapter 8, "Race Literacy," makes the case that there is an identifiable body of material that is required for a working knowledge of race and crime issues. This progressive extension of professor E. D. Hirsch Jr.'s arguments for a "cultural literacy" rests on university president Judith Shapiro's writings on "sociological illiteracy." The chapter identifies important names, terms, phrases, and concepts that should be considered part of this body of knowledge.

The Color of Crime is devoted to remembering. The task of remembering is work indeed. As Nelson Mandela cautions, vigilance is required to fight against practices that dismiss or disappear histories. Through an analysis of cases, ideological and media trends, issues, and practices that resonate below the public radar, this text "remembers" race. *The Color of Crime* acknowledges and explores the tacit and subtle ways that deviance is systematically linked to people of color, particularly African Americans.

A Note on Racial Terminology

Throughout the book, I capitalize both "Black" and "White" when used as a racial reference. I use "Black" and "African American" interchangeably. "Latino" is the preferred term for people of Spanish descent, but when I refer to research that uses another racial term, such as "Hispanic," I use that term.

1

Media Messages

The medium is the message.

—Marshall McLuhan[1]

Pick a mass medium. Any medium. Television, radio, newspaper, the Internet, magazines, or books. Any one of them. Each one has its own power and its own unique ability to make us see the world through the eyes of its recorder. Irrespective of the mass medium you examine, however, the messages about race are fairly uniform. Here are some media "race-isms":

- Native Americans are rarely featured in news stories or seen in the media more generally, including movies and situation comedies.
- Asian Americans are infrequently featured in news stories and are sometimes represented as media players (e.g., anchors and pundits).
- Latinos are regularly discussed as news topics, are featured as entertainers and athletes, and are infrequently shown as having a seat at the media table.
- Blacks are regularly seen as subjects and reporters of the news, as entertainers and athletes, and are frequently portrayed as media players.
- Whites are the predominant face of the news and are featured in every aspect of news production, as owners, producers, and subjects.

This may appear to be an unfairly harsh portrait of how race is represented today. After all, a lot has changed in the past thirty years. So much ground has been gained in recent years. People of color are regularly featured on television, in sitcoms, dramas, movies, and commercials. Although this is true, there has not been as much progress as we might imagine and not in as diverse a way as we might think. This chapter looks at the mainstream representations of Native Americans, Asian Americans, Latinos, and African Americans.

Native Americans

Challenge yourself to name Native Americans who have recently been featured in the news. Push yourself to name a few prominent Native Americans. If you are unable to come up with any names, how about a recent news or feature story involving Native Americans? As part of a class exercise, I ask my students to describe the images they have of various groups by race. When asked about Native Americans, typical responses include, "spiritual," "alcoholic," "noble," and "gambling." Except for the latter, these descriptions represent decades, even centuries-old stereotypes of Native Americans. Further, most students have a hard time naming any well-known Indians; some have mentioned writer and filmmaker Sherman Alexie or former congressman Ben Nighthorse Campbell. Most of my students indicate that they do not know any Native Americans personally. Their impressions have been formed primarily by the media and what they have "heard"; thus, they are not based on any real exchanges or interactions with American Indians.[2]

A 2004 Justice Department study reported that American Indians were two times as likely to be victims of violent crime (e.g., rape, aggravated assault, and robbery) than African Americans. They are also the most likely to be victims of interracial crime—harmed by someone who is not Native American. Little of the press attention that is focused on Native Americans addresses issues of crime and violence.

The primary media talk about Native Americans centers on gambling casinos or the issue of using Indian names and symbols for athletic teams and mascots. Professional sports teams' names, such as the Washington Redskins and the Atlanta Braves (including their mascot and the "Tomahawk chop" hand signal), have been challenged as offensive and racist. "Redskin" refers to the early practice of hunting and killing Indians and offering their scalps as proof for the payment of a bounty.[3] The repeated presentation of these images is acutely problematic, especially when we consider that there is little in the popular press that serves as a counterbalance.

Another underlying feature of the media stories involving Native Americans is that they live away from the mainstream—the suggestion is that they live away from the rest of "us." This distance supports the idea that American Indians are somehow different. In 2007, Nike introduced "Nike Air Native N7," a shoe specifically designed for Native Americans. The shoe features feathers and arrowheads.[4] There was a good deal of debate about whether this marketing campaign exemplifies cultural sensitivity, crass capitalism, or something else. In some ways it furthers the belief that American Indians are separate from everyone else. This is notable considering that approximately one-fourth of American Indians in the United States live on reservations.

In the 2000 census, more than two million people identified themselves as Native Americans, less than 1 percent of the total U.S. population. Due to high rates of intermarriage between American Indians and Whites, it is not always readily discernible who is a Native American. Neither that fact nor their relatively small population size, however, diminishes concerns about media coverage. Notably, there are numerous groups that are a small fraction of the population yet are visible in the mass media.

Asian Americans

As media representations go, Asian Americans, who represent 4 percent of the U.S. population, fare slightly better than Native Americans. There are only a handful of fairly well-known Asian American female celebrities, including actresses Sandra Oh (*Grey's Anatomy*), Lucy Liu (*Charlie's Angels*), journalists Ann Curry (NBC's *Today Show*), Julie Chen (*CBS Morning News*), Parminder Nagra (*ER*), Lisa Ling (*National Geographic*), and Betty Nguyen (CNN news anchor). Kimora Simmons, a model and entrepreneur, who has biracial roots (Black and Asian), appears to identify herself as African American.[5]

Asian American men are even scarcer in the media than Asian American women. Dr. Sanjay Gupta, a neurosurgeon and CNN medical reporter, is one of the more prominently featured Asian American men. Best-selling author and physician Deepak Chopra is also familiar to many in the United States. Garrett Wang (*Star Trek Voyager*), Kal Penn (*Harold and Kumar Go to White Castle*), and Masi Oka (*Heroes*) may be familiar to moviegoers and TV watchers, but they do not have broad name recognition.

Golf phenomenon Tiger Woods and actor Keanu Reeves are one-half Asian. Although Woods has spoken openly of his Thai heritage, it appears that many people recognize him as an African American. Regarding Reeves, it does not appear to be common knowledge that he has Asian roots. This adds an interesting twist to the issue of how race is portrayed in the media. In order for someone to represent a particular racial group, their race has to be known. Though they are citizens of other countries, martial artists Jackie Chan and Jet Li and basketball player Yao Ming are Asian males who are recognized by U.S. audiences.

In the sixty-year history of television there has been only one television show about an Asian American family. In the mid-1990s, comedian Margaret Cho, who is Chinese, starred in the situation comedy *All-American Girl*. The show lasted one season. In the 1960s and 1970s, Asian Americans on television were routinely portrayed in stereotypical subservient roles, for instance, Mrs. Livingston, the maid on *The Courtship of Eddie's Father*. Arguably one exception was Don Ho in the 1970s television series *Hawaii Five-O*.

In 2007, Yul Kwon won the top prize on the reality television show *Survivor*. He says that he chose to take part in the show to alter the profile of Asian American men. The son of Korean immigrants, Kwon said, "I didn't see people like me on television when I was growing up. I wanted America to see Asian Americans as they truly are."[6]

There are very few Asian American men who are visible in the mainstream media, either as entertainers or media players. The way that Asian Americans gain visibility is through news stories. When groups are not represented as media players or entertainers, they are primarily shaped by news portrayals. In 2007, the Asian American man who perhaps received the most news attention was Cho Seung-Hui. He was the troubled young man who was responsible for the Virginia Tech massacre that resulted in thirty-two deaths.

The dearth of Asian American representations also does something else. It suggests that "Asian American" has a monolithic meaning. This one-box-fits-all category reduces Asians to one massive group and obscures the fact that in addition to China, Japan, and Korea, there are numerous Asian countries, including Vietnam, Cambodia, Indonesia, Singapore, Malaysia, Thailand, Taiwan, Laos, India, and Pakistan. These countries are not interchangeable. Other racial groups are also treated as racial monoliths. Blacks, for instance represent the African Diaspora, which includes many countries (e.g., Africa, Caribbean nations, South America, and the United States).

There are two common media representations of Asian Americans. The women are routinely drawn as the exotic objects of sexual desire. This character typically comes with a host of other attributes: petite physique, sexual aggressiveness, and docility. Asian American men are typically portrayed as smart, techno-savvy geeks. This character, the flipside personality of the Asian American woman, is often a sidekick who is sexually undesirable, a workaholic, and decidedly not hip. He does not get the girl. Both of these characterizations are Hollywood-inspired fictions.

In addition to these portrayals, Asian Americans have also been designated the "model" minority. According to the model-minority myth, Asian Americans are hard working, smart, and respectful of authority. Interestingly though, the portrayal of Asian American men is more likely to fit within the myth than the portrayal of Asian American women. Many Asian Americans reject the model-minority stereotype as inaccurate and divisive within the Asian community and across race. Sometimes Asian media characters are not stereotypically "bright." It is, however, rare to see the model-minority myth turned on its head, as it is with the Asian American female character "London," on the Disney Channel show *The Suite Life of Zack and Cody*. Mostly, though, Asian Americans are invisible in the mainstream media.[7]

The mass media casts Asian Americans as objects of both desirability and disdain. The desirability includes both sexual attractiveness and intelligence. On the other side, though, is the image of otherness—as nerds and as foreigners. Another link to the portrayal of Asian Americans as foreigners involves discussions about international adoptions—the increasing number of White families that adopt Asian babies.

Latinos

At 14 percent of the U.S. population, Latinos are the country's largest minority group. They still, however, have only a marginal presence in the major media. Their public presence comes in different forms, typically as entertainers (comedians and singers) and athletes (baseball). There are only a handful of well-known Latino actors and entertainers. This list includes America Ferrera, Eva Mendes, Salma Hayek, Eva Longoria, Penelope Cruz, Jennifer Lopez, Jimmy Smits, Benjamin Bratt, John Leguizamo, and George Lopez. Baseball players Alex Rodriguez and Sammy Sosa are among the most popular athletes. Latinos are more likely to appear as part of an ensemble cast, such as *Grey's Anatomy, Desperate Housewives,* and reality television shows. New Mexico governor and 2008 Democratic presidential candidate Bill Richardson also has name recognition.

On television, few programs have focused on a Latino family or feature a Latino lead character. In the first decade of the twenty-first century, the pickings were slim. *Ugly Betty,* based on a Spanish-television hit, centers on a young Latina woman (played by America Ferrera), a plain Jane in need of a makeover. Notably, most of the main characters on the show are not Latino. The *George Lopez Show* has a Latino lead actor, and comedian Carlos Mencia has a comedy show on cable television. In the prior decade, Michael DeLorenzo co-starred in *New York Undercover.* This was the first show in which the lead co-stars were Black and Latino. *Chico and the Man,* which ran from 1974 to 1978, was the first show featuring a Latino lead actor, Freddie Prinze.

Latinos, Like Asian Americans, are often portrayed as outsiders and foreigners. National and regional media discussions about Latinos often revolve around issues of immigration, specifically about illegal immigration and border patrol along the southwestern states. This includes discussion of proposed legislation designed to address border security—to keep out those who live south of the border. It also ties to debates about bilingualism—for example, whether the United States should be an "English-only" country and whether Latinos are unfairly burdening social services and the public school system.

With the persistent focus on relationships between Blacks and Whites, Latinos are frequently omitted from the "official" record. A contemporary example of this omission involves a PBS documentary on World War II, produced by Ken Burns. During previews it was observed that the film made scant reference to Latino veterans or their contributions to the war. Following a great deal of criticism and pressure, Burns ultimately agreed to feature narratives from Latino and Native American veterans, including on-camera testimony, personal archives, and combat history.

On the other side, Latinos as a group are often talked about but are not always direct participants in the conversation. This racial chatter happens in varied media arenas, including the Sunday-morning news-roundup shows and late-night talk shows. Latinos are also second in line—behind African Americans—as the face of the feared American criminal.

African Americans

Blacks represent a mixed bag of media images. Arguably it is both the best and the worst of times for Blacks in the mainstream media. Since the 1980s, African Americans have been a consistent and broad presence in the media, as athletes, actors, comedians, singers, lawyers, public intellectuals, talk-show hosts, journalists, professors, entrepreneurs, authors, doctors, and artists. Annual polls show that Americans consistently place African American celebrities on their lists of people they most admire, including Oprah Winfrey, Michael Jordon, Colin Powell, Bill Cosby, and Tiger Woods. It bears noting that Blacks also top the list of the most reviled celebrities, O. J. Simpson, Barry Bonds, and Michael Vick.

Today's reality is in stark contrast to earlier times, when it was rare to see Black people on television. Oprah Winfrey has commented on this fact, noting that when she was growing up in the 1950s and 1960s, a family member would announce, "Black people are on!" so that everyone could witness this unusual event.

At its inception, television operated as a segregated space. It was surprising to see people of color, and when they did appear (usually in movies), they were relegated to stock, stereotypical roles. For Blacks this meant the butler, mammy, chauffeur, or entertainer. There were some "firsts." In the 1950s, crooner Nat King Cole was the first Black person to have his own television show. *The Nat King Cole Show* premiered as a weekly fifteen-minute variety show. The broadcast, however, was short-lived. Advertisers shunned the show, fearful that southern audiences would boycott their products.

In response to the longstanding barriers to entry, Blacks developed their own organizations to showcase their talent. This was true for sports, where the Harlem Globetrotters, the Negro Leagues in baseball, the United Golf Association, and others were created to provide a home for Black athletes. It was also done regarding cinema. The work of pioneering Black film directors, such as Oscar Micheaux, Clarence Muse, and Melvin Van Peebles, offered more-nuanced portraits of Black life.[8] The Black press was instrumental in providing an alternative view of African American life. Today there are more than seventy-five Black newspapers. Black magazines such as *Ebony* and *Jet* have been in existence for more than fifty years.

During the 1960s, increasing numbers of Blacks appeared on television, primarily as entertainers or professional athletes on shows such as

The Ed Sullivan Show and Johnny Carson (*The Tonight Show*). In the following decade, there were series that featured Blacks in lead roles, including Diahann Carroll in *Julia* and Bill Cosby in *I Spy*. And there were a few Black shows, including *Sanford and Son, Soul Train, Good Times, What's Happening!!,* and *The Jeffersons*. Blacks, however, were more likely to be part of an ensemble cast—for example, *Room 222, Welcome Back Kotter, Hill Street Blues, Benson, Soap, The White Shadow,* and *WKRP*. Blacks were also increasingly featured in mainstream Hollywood movies, such as *Sounder, Lady Sings the Blues,* and *Mahogany*. Daytime soap operas also began to include African Americans. For instance, *All My Children* featured a years-long storyline involving young, Black star-crossed lovers (Angie and Jesse). Comedian Flip Wilson had a weekly variety show. As the sports of football, basketball, and baseball became more integrated, more Black professional athletes rose to national prominence. With the exception of Max Robinson (ABC News), however, few Blacks made it to a national news anchor desk.

The 1980s saw an exponential increase in the number of Blacks featured in the media, as sitcom stars, major recording artists, business owners, sports legends, new members of the middle class, authors of best-selling books, talk-show hosts, and Pulitzer Prize winners. During this period a range of television shows featured African Americans as lead characters, such as *The Cosby Show, Frank's Place, A Different World, The A-Team,* and *Miami Vice*.

In the 1980s and 1990s, rap music became an increasingly popular music choice for American youth. Straying from its origins, rap, which began as fun and boastful, became a political force, then shifted to become gangsta rap. The lyrics were bold, angry, and in-your-face. The rap music video, which by then was a staple of cable television, began featuring barely clad women, young men with guns, and lots of simulated sex. These images became a large part of the media's visual representation of African American youth. Many observers cried foul.

Today rap and hip-hop music continue to provide keen insights into how Blackness is shaped, presented, and consumed. Hip hop—the music, clothes, language, and affect—is now a major export. The music continues to face criticism for its emphasis on clothes, cars, crime, money, and women. Given the popularity of rap and its influence, many people have appealed to rap artists to present a different, more complex face of Black life. These calls were heard again in 2007, in the wake of shock-jock Don Imus's racially charged comments about the Rutgers women's basketball team (*see* chapter 2 discussion). For many people who listen to rap music, particularly non-Blacks, it is often viewed as offering the true picture of Black America.

Working Blacks. Tales of the Black working class—the group that constitutes a sizeable core of the Black community—are largely missing from contemporary media. We see the poor, the victimized, the drug afflicted and those who prey on them (e.g., *NYPD Blue, Law & Order,* and *The Wire*). We see Black professionals on shows such as *Law & Order, Kevin Hill,* and *Girlfriends.* Many series that feature larger casts of African Americans exist in media ghettos, such as the TV One network (e.g., *For Your Love, All of Us,* and *Eve*). Two shows that have tackled this slice of Black life are *Everybody Hates Chris* (based on comedian Chris Rock's childhood) and Tyler Perry's *House of Pain.* In earlier decades there were a few shows centered around a working-class family, including *Good Times* and *Roc.*

Though the media representations of African Americans have grown more diverse, Blacks are still the face of crime in America. For most of us, television's overpowering images of Black deviance—its regularity and frequency—are impossible to ignore. These negative images have been seared into our collective consciousness. It is no surprise that most Americans wrongly believe that Blacks are responsible for committing the majority of crime. No doubt, many of the suspects paraded across the nightly news are guilty criminals. The onslaught of criminal images of Black men, however, causes many of us to incorrectly conclude that most Black men are criminals. These images also make it hard for many people to believe that most crime is *intra*racial, involving an offender and victim who are the same race. Regardless of race, the person most people fear is a young, Black man. This is what I refer to as the myth of the *criminalblackman.*

Trends, Issues, and Concerns

This section will highlight some overlapping issues among racial groups and identify some particular areas of concern. Given that people of color constitute approximately one-third of the U.S. population, it is troubling that so few minorities are visible within the mainstream media. Among all minority racial groups, there are some overlapping issues.

Disappearing People. Some practices work to "disappear" people of color from the media. A particularly interesting example occurs when a television show is set in an area with a large minority population but does not include them (as main characters or as extras). The long-running series *Seinfeld* and *Sex in the City* were criticized for showing very little ethnic diversity in racially rich New York City. A much earlier series, *Magnum, P.I.*, faced similar criticism: the show, set in Honolulu, had relatively few Asian actors. It is both hopeful and lamentable that it is children's television that best reflects racial diversity (e.g., *Sesame Street* and *Barney*).

In Absentia. The fact that Native Americans and Asian Americans are largely absent from the media does not mean that they are completely invisible. When a group is not allowed to shape its own public image, it will then be shaped by other groups. For instance, it is not unusual to hear White comedians make unflattering "jokes" about Asian Americans —for example, comments about how they drive (poorly), how they speak (broken English), and where they work (nail salons and takeout diners).[9] Notwithstanding the fact that "one person's vulgarity is another person's lyric,"[10] these kinds of comments reinforce the notion that Asian Americans are foreigners, outsiders who are not really Americans.

This practice of allowing non-group-members to define a racial group also diminishes the group's history as longtime and hardworking citizens in this country. The point here is not whether comedians or satirists should be entitled to say what they want to. Rather, we should *notice* when a racial group does not have a self-defined media presence and thus observe the difference between a group that is engaged in shaping and molding its media image and one that is not. Groups that fall into the latter category are unable to say who they are and are forced to occupy racial boxes—good, bad, or otherwise—created by others.

I See Black People. TV One, a Black-owned channel, features an ad series, "I See Black People . . . Living, Loving, Laughing." This motto succinctly states what is missing from much of television: a nuanced portrait of African Americans. The problem is that the existing images are rigid and thus inaccurate. The same is true for other racial groups as well.

The pervasive image that Blacks are clowns and criminals persists. Why is this so, given that today, more than at any other time in our history, Blacks are featured more prominently on television and the media in general? It is in part because the new wave of Black images—as successful, as rich, as accomplished, as smart—has not washed away the tidal wave of images of Black deviance. The reason that Black success stories do not counterbalance images of Black criminality is because Black success is given a unique interpretation. In the minds of many people, particularly Whites, Blacks have "overcome," as the old Negro spiritual promises. Consequently, these people believe that Blacks have no legitimate basis for complaining about race. In many instances, though, Black superstars are not perceived in relation to their Blackness.

A scene from Spike Lee's 1989 movie *Do the Right Thing* illustrates this point. Two young men, Mookie, who is Black, and Pino, who is Italian, have a discussion about racism. Pino hates Black people and refers to them as "niggers." In an attempt to point out his racial double standard, Mookie reminds Pino that all his favorite celebrities are Black (Magic Johnson, Eddie Murphy, and Prince). Pino responds, "They're not really niggers. . . . They're not really Black, they're more than Black."[11] Lee continues to explore the theme of racial representation in his underrated movie *Bamboozled*. Here he shows the direct link between early twentieth-century images of Blacks and early twenty-first-century images. Although it may look like the Black image has radically changed, it has not changed as much as it appears. To some Whites, Blacks who achieve large-scale success and acclaim—like Oprah Winfrey, Barack Obama, Michael Jordan, Colin Powell, Condoleezza Rice, and Tiger Woods—transcend their Blackness and ultimately become colorless, while those Blacks who conform to the criminal stereotype are "Black." In this racial calculus, famous Blacks tell the story of racial progress. And it is Blacks in the margins, those who are poor, downtrodden, or deviant, who embody the masses.

Given this complex imagery, it is predictable that Blacks are viewed as emblematic of both success and deviance. The contradictory media representation of Blackness signals a double-edged resentment: the threat of Black crime and the threat of Black success. The result is cross-wired thinking about Blacks and Blackness. As is true for most Whites, most Blacks are neither supersuccessful nor superdeviant. Although the media does portray some neutral and in some cases positive images of Blacks, these images simply cannot compete with the overwhelmingly negative characterizations.

Today Blacks are ubiquitous staples of the mainstream media. A generation ago, we could not have envisioned that there would be so many Black faces staring back at us from commercials, soap operas, movies, variety shows, comedies, dramas, reality television, game shows, and broadcast news. All of this leads to the question of whether a more pronounced media presence is always a good thing. What is important to note about race and racial representation in the media, however, is not the volume of images but rather the substance of these portrayals. Arguably more is not always more. Sometimes more is less. When the images are stereotypical and retrograde—such as "cooning" (think *Amos 'n' Andy*)—less may be more. So, regardless of increasing representations of Blackness, the important question is whether the racial representations are an advance, a setback, or something else.

In the Mix. A new twist has been added to the question of how race is represented in the media. The use of, for lack of a better description, a racially ambiguous character or personality (e.g., a news-show journalist or sitcom character) has been added to the mix. This racial ambiguity is a physical description—that is, the person appears to be racially "mixed." The character is non-White, but it is not clear to which racial group he or she belongs. Typically no "clues" are given about the character's race. For instance, the character does not have racially identifiable speech patterns, or the character does not make reference to membership in any race-specific organizations. No doubt, the presence of such characters provides some much-needed "color"; it is just not clear what exactly to make of it. Perhaps this is the media's nod to the increasing numbers of mixed-raced individuals—six million according to the 2000 census. Perhaps it is a cynical attempt to check off "diversity," by adding an exotic flair to the cast. Or it may be something more benign. Regardless of intention, this practice does not address the concerns about race based group representation in the media.[12]

The use of an ensemble cast presents another aspect of the way race is represented. Several popular shows have had at least one lead character who is a person of color. *Desperate Housewives* has a Latina actress, Eva Longoria. In the action drama *24*, Dennis Haysbert, an African American, was cast as president of the United States. In *The King of Queens,* the main character, who is White (Kevin James), has a best friend who is African American (Victor Williams).

Grey's Anatomy, a hospital drama and ratings winner, provides an interesting case study of a multiracial cast. In its second season (2006–2007), approximately one-half of its doctors were racial minorities: three Black, one Latina, and one Asian American. Many of the standard racial tropes are turned upside down here. The Asian American woman doctor is neither easygoing nor quiet (played by Sandra Oh). The Black men are well-respected doctors; one is a noted surgeon, and the other one runs the hospital (Isaiah Washington and James Pickens Jr.). The Black woman doctor, the resident surgeon, is both respected and feared (Chandra Wilson), and the Latina doctor is top in her field (Sara Ramirez).

Without question, the show takes big steps toward more positive and more nuanced presentations of minorities. The show, however, does a neat trick with these characters. With one exception, each of these of-color characters is with or has been with a romantic partner of another race. The series is a showcase for interracial relationships. Although there are several White couples, there are no visible Black, Latino, or Asian couples. What is missing is that the of-color characters are not shown in nurturing same-race relationships. This is an odd presentation when you consider that most people are involved with people who are members of their same racial group. It appears that the characters of color, though more plentiful and polished than on most shows, are still being used as "color"—to showcase the relationships between White characters.

The whitewashing of minority characters is not uncommon. *Boston Legal* offers an example of this phenomenon. One storyline featured Clarence, a cross-dressing Black man (Gary Anthony Williams). He was alternately shy and sassy. His major love interest was another lawyer at the firm, a White woman.

Racial Ventriloquism. There is another twist on the portrayal of people of color within the media. It can be called "racial ventriloquism": when Whites portray actors of color. The entertainment industry has a long history of this practice. Blackface routines were a Vaudeville staple. Al Jolson's "mammy" routine is well-known. In film, Whites regularly portrayed members of other racial groups. In D. W. Griffiths's film *Birth of a Nation*, White actors wore grease paint to portray violent, murderous Blacks. White film stars, including Bob Hope and Bing Crosby, performed in Blackface. Whites have also performed in other colors. Whites regularly played Asians in films, such as in the Charlie Chan series. Silver-screen legends Katharine Hepburn and Shirley MacLaine portrayed Asian women. Also, Whites were regularly cast as American Indians in films. In the 1950s, Burt Lancaster played a Native American athlete in *Jim Thorpe —All American*. Another example is actress Elizabeth Taylor playing the lead in *Cleopatra*, the story of the Egyptian queen. In a memorable 1970s antilittering commercial, a White actor portrayed an Indian, dressed in full native dress and head gear, who shed a tear after witnessing the impact of litter on the environment. Another example is the 1970s series

Kung Fu, in which White actor David Carradine played the lead role of the martial artist. Madonna was cast in the title role of *Evita,* the story of Argentina's beloved Eva Peron. In 2007, White actress Angelina Jolie was criticized for portraying mixed-race Mariane Pearl in the movie *A Mighty Heart.*[13]

This whitewash has not been limited to stage and screen. Prior to the 1960s, many times Black recording artists were not featured on their own album covers. So-called race music was sanitized for White audiences with cover photographs of White women, landscapes, and other images deemed "acceptable" to White crossover listeners. The "cover" record represents another turn in the racial landscape of media representations. This occurred when a White recording artist—like Elvis Presley or Pat Boone —took a hit song previously recorded by a Black artist and rerecorded it. This "cover" practice was dramatized in the 2006 movie *Dreamgirls.*

Diverse Impressions. The overall theme that emerges from the mainstream media today is that it represents and embraces different races. Existing images are an improvement over those that were available a generation ago. Today we are all represented in the pot that is melting. We are now in a good place, and the hard work of racial integration in media is behind us. This view, however, encourages us to accept the status quo as the best we can achieve. There is still more, much more, that can be done. Let us consider a few of the racial representations highlighted by the 2006 Academy Awards.

The movie *Crash* does an unusually good job of exploring the intersections of race, gender, and class. It offers thoughtful, heart, flesh, and bones portrayals of people of color. The cast includes Latinos, Asians, Blacks, Whites, Persians, and some who are mixed race. The characters are distinct and memorable. At its core, the movie examines the unexpected ways that various lives become intermingled with one another. Relationships are forged through a series of criminal acts, including murder, political corruption, sexual assault, carjacking, obstruction of justice, attempted murder, and drug abuse. The movie both challenges us to acknowledge our racial stereotypes and in some ways reinforces them. *Crash,* however, strikes an odd note when we observe that it is primarily the characters of color who experience physical harm.

Though far from perfect, *Crash* challenges us to look beyond the façade of skin color. By doing so, it serves as a reminder that when we uncritically characterize people based on their skin color, we emphasize our differences rather than our similarities—and in the process become blind to their humanity. The movie makes the case that we should not use a person's race as an indicator of his or her personality, work ethic, capabilities, interests, or goodness.

The movie *Hustle and Flow* presents a much more common picture of race in America. The story centers on DJay, a struggling pimp played by Terrance Howard, who has dreams of becoming a rapper. There is nothing glamorous about his life. We watch as he works, bargains, and cajoles potential johns into sex with his prostitutes. His "pimp mobile" is a broken-down heap of steel, with no air conditioning. Though the film attempts to humanize and not glorify the life of a pimp, in the end he is still the hero of the story, the one we root for. DJay dreams of becoming a big-time rapper. His ticket to success is a song titled *It's Hard Out Here for a Pimp*. The song includes the lyrics,

> You know it's hard out here for a pimp
> When he's tryin' to get this money for the rent
> For the Cadillacs and gas money spent
> Because a whole lot of bitches talkin' shit[14]

The refrain is "Whomp that trick." When DJay's dream of having his rap song played on the radio finally happens—he hears it on the radio while he is serving time for assault—the audience is poised to feel good for him. It is a happy ending.

When it was released, *Hustle and Flow* was adorned with a halo of praise. Critics hailed the movie as authentic, refreshing, and redemptive. Ebert and Roeper gave it two thumbs up ("way up!"). The movie won the Sundance Festival's Audience Award and received a $9 million distribution contract. Howard appeared on the cover of various publications, including *Essence* and *Jet* magazines. Howard was nominated for an Academy Award for best actor for his portrayal of DJay. No doubt, Howard turns in a winning, credible performance. DJay's song "It's Hard Out Here for a Pimp" was nominated for an Academy Award for the best original song. It won. This was the first time an African American hip-hop group won in this category and the first time a hip-hop group was invited to perform at the Academy Awards ceremony.

It is perfectly reasonable, however, to wonder why this movie, its music, and Howard's role received such lavish attention and acclaim. By choosing *Crash* as the year's best picture and "It's Hard Out Here for a

Pimp" as best original song, the Academy of Motion Picture Arts and Sciences managed simultaneously to pat itself on the back and to thumb its nose at racial progress in the industry.

Whose Story Is It?

How race is projected through entertainment provides us with one piece of the puzzle. News stories are another important component in the assessment of how race is framed by the media. How news stories are covered, which ones are covered, and the extent to which they are covered tell us a lot about the issues that society considers important.

For instance, from the beginning, the media coverage of the 2006–2007 Duke lacrosse rape case suggested that the young men had been falsely accused. The case involved a young Black woman who alleged that she had been raped by three White members of the team. The woman, who had been hired to perform as a stripper at a team party, was never perceived as credible. Historically, allegations of rape by Black women have not been taken seriously. The cloak of media support that the young men received helped to galvanize their supporters and ultimately resulted in the criminal charges being dropped (for further discussion of this case, see chapter 6).

Another example is the news coverage of Hurricane Katrina. For several days after the 2005 storm hit, there were news reports about violence in its aftermath. It was reported that rapes and murders were rampant in New Orleans. There were stories that bands of lawless Black men were roaming the city, robbing tourists and anyone else who was unlucky enough to cross their paths. We were also told that the lawless were shooting at police helicopters. It was later determined that reports of crime had been wildly overstated. This led to the firing of the police chief. Though the truth was finally reported, as the saying goes, you cannot "unring" a bell. The visual images of Black criminals could not be withdrawn from the national psyche.

A third example involves the stories of missing women. In recent years there have been a number of high-profile cases involving women (or girls), some pregnant, who have gone missing. For the most part, however, the stories that have garnered sustained national attention have involved White woman—for example, Stacy Peterson, Lori Hacking, Natalee Holloway, Jessie Davis, Jennifer Wilbanks, and Laci Peterson. Some observers have referred to this emphasis as the media's "Missing White Woman Syndrome." Without question these cases should have received media attention. However, there are a number of other cases, involving missing women of color, that did not receive the same kind of media interest or attention. These include the cases of Stepha Henry, Tamika Huston, Reyna Alvarado-Carerra, LaToyia Figureoa, and Dymashal Cullins. This disparity indicates that race, gender, and physical features factor into whether a missing persons' story is "news."

Conclusion

The media is awash in a cornucopia of racial images. TV in particular is no longer a White facebook. With the civil rights movement, the global marketing forces of "inclusion" and diversity, and the infinite number of television and cable stations, we regularly see people of various hues, nationalities, and ethnicities on the small screen. This chapter presents an alternative view of what these new, more diverse images mean. Although there are more people of color visible in various mediums, it is important to consider what these new images show us and whether they offer new insights, challenge old stereotypes, or only appear to be something new.

2

The Skin Game

Depending on whom you ask, we either talk too little or not enough about race in this country. It seems we are often on the precipice of discussing race but have to be pushed to the edge before we engage in any assessments of progress. This "edge" usually comes in the form of new stories wherein issues of race rise to the top, such as O.J. Simpson, hanging nooses, or public uses of the N-word. Those who think there is too much talk about race and racism point to how far we have come regarding race relations. They remind us that Blacks dominate in three of the major-league sports, sit on the U.S. Supreme Court, and are corporate CEOs and that Oprah, Bill Cosby, Will Smith, and Tiger Woods are beloved international icons. On the other side of the debate are those who point out that racism is a historical fact with contemporary manifestations and consequences. They tell us that racism comes in many shapes and sizes—personal and direct, subtle and indirect, and "big box" (structural), which may be direct, indirect, personal, or subtle.

This chapter looks at some of the ways that race matters in the United States. The discussion considers how incidents involving race and images of race affect the racial dimensions of the criminal justice system. The first section examines two kinds of racial assaults, microaggressions and macroaggressions, and how these racial assaults frame race and reflect racial beliefs. The section also considers the impact of "Black-sounding" names on our discourse about race. The second section highlights the link between the deviance attached to Blackness and racial disproportionality in the justice system. How we conceptualize and treat race has myriad manifestations within various institutions, including the police, courts, and corrections systems.

Racial Insult, Racial Assault

Each year, it seems, there are incidents involving high-profile Whites who make disparaging public remarks about Blacks or about Blackness itself. Let us consider a short list:

- Michael Richards, a comedian who is best known for playing the character Kramer on *Seinfeld,* engaged in an infamous N-word rant. Richards, while appearing at a comedy club, went on a tirade against some Black hecklers, shouting among other things, "Fifty years ago we'd have you upside down with a fucking fork up your ass" and "Throw his ass out. He's a nigger. He's a nigger! He's a nigger!"[1]
- Bill O'Reilly, a Fox News host, in a conversation with a Black journalist about his visit to Sylvia's restaurant—a Harlem institution—commented, "I couldn't get over the fact that there was no difference between Sylvia's restaurant and any other restaurant in New York City. I mean, it was exactly the same, even though it's run by blacks, primarily black patronship." O'Reilly, who had been invited to the restaurant by the Reverend Al Sharpton went on to say, "There wasn't one person [there] screaming 'MF-er, I want more iced tea.' . . . It was like going to an Italian restaurant in an all-White suburb. . . . people were sitting there . . . ordering and having fun. And there wasn't any kind of craziness at all."[2]
- Don Imus, known as a "shock jock," said of the Rutgers women's basketball team, "That's [*sic*] some nappy-headed hos." Imus's comments about the majority-Black team followed his co-host's reference to team members as "hard-core hos." His co-host went on to state that the Rutgers team "look[s] exactly like the Toronto Raptors" (a men's basketball team). These comments were made on Imus's MSNBC television show.[3]
- James D. Watson, a world-renowned scientist, told the *London Times*, "All our social policies are based on the fact that their [Blacks'] intelligence is the same as ours—whereas all the testing says not really." Watson won the Nobel Prize in 1962 for deciphering the double-helix of DNA.[4]

Each of these comments was made for public consumption; these words were not overheard or passed along to the press by a third party. They were public offerings. Richards was hired to perform three nights at The Laugh Factory, a comedy club in Los Angeles; O'Reilly made his comments during his radio show and during a radio interview that he did with Black journalist Juan Williams. Imus's comments were made on his MSNBC *Imus in the Morning* simulcast. Watson offered his sentiments about Blacks during an interview with the *London Times*, an internationally known and well-respected newspaper. Pseudoscientific remarks about the alleged link between race and intelligence—such as those uttered by Watson—lay the foundation for making off-the-cuff racial remarks, such as those made by Imus and O'Reilly.

When comments such as these are made, a series of routine responses by the mainstream press follows. These responses include claims that the person making the remark is not racist; that the person's comments have been taken "out of context"; that there are more important issues of race on which to focus than one person's racial gaffe; that once the person has apologized (e.g., Richards, Imus, and Watson), they should be forgiven; that although the person made some "politically incorrect" statements, he has been publicly shamed by the media attention, and any further punishment would be overkill—for example, the person should not lose his job; and finally, that the incident presents an opportunity to "begin a conversation about race."

All this hand wringing, which is often mistaken for an actual conversation about race, misses a larger and more important point. These seemingly off-handed and unintended racial slights invoke, yet again, the image of Black skin as a representation of deviance—or Blackness as usual. The outcome of a particular incident involving racist speech—whether there is widespread condemnation of the comments or whether the person apologizes—is of little consequence. What matters more is that there is a continuous drum beat of verbal racial assaults targeted at African Americans. These incidents are a persistent part of the racial landscape. Further, they are part of a larger group of race-related offenses commonly experienced by Blacks.

Microaggressions and Macroaggressions

Microaggressions have been described as "subtle, stunning, often non-verbal exchanges"[5] that amount to "put downs" of Blacks by Whites. Examples include a White person who refuses to hold an elevator open for a

Black person, a White person who will not make direct eye contact with a Black person while speaking to him, a White person who enters a business office and assumes that the person she sees is in a low-status position, and a cab driver who refuses to take a Black fare.

While Bill Clinton was president, he made some particularly thoughtful comments about this type of racial assault:

> Let's be honest with ourselves: racism in America is not confined to acts of physical violence. Everyday African Americans and other minorities are forced to endure quiet acts of racism—bigoted remarks, housing and job discrimination. Even many people who think they are not being racist still hold the negative stereotypes and sometimes act on them. These acts may not harm the body, but when a mother and her child go to the grocery store and are followed around by a suspicious clerk, it does violence to their souls. We must stand against such quiet hatred just as surely as we condemn acts of physical violence.[6]

Nooses, Nooses, Nooses. In 2007 the "Jena Six" case made national news. The case involved racial tensions at a predominantly White high school in Jena, Louisiana. The student body, which was 85 percent White and 15 percent Black, had longstanding racial traditions in place. For instance, at school assemblies White students sat on one side of the auditorium, while Blacks sat on the other. The school also allowed students to hold separate dances, one for Blacks and another for Whites. Another race-based practice involved a tree. The school had a "White" tree, an oak tree under which only White students sat. A Black student asked a school administrator for permission to sit there and was told that he could. A day later, three nooses were found hanging from the tree. Referring to the incident as a "prank," the school principal declined to take any action against the White students who left the nooses. Racial sentiments were now officially stirred up, and racial tension increased among the students. A series of events followed, culminating in a group of Black students beating up a White student. Following the assault, one of the young men, Mychal Bell, was charged with attempted murder. Bell was held in jail for months.

Once the Jena story was widely circulated, there were national calls to release Bell, who at the time of the brawl was a minor. Questions were raised about the fairness of the school's decision not to punish the young White men, the state attorney's decision not to file any charges against them, and the state attorney's decision to charge Bell with attempted murder. More than twenty thousand people attended a protest rally in Jena. Following the September 2007 march, police arrested two White men who had two nooses hanging from the bed of their truck.

Within one month of the march, a score of nooses were left in various venues across the country. At the University of Maryland at College Park, a noose was placed on a tree outside the Nyumburu Cultural Center. The Black culture building, built in 1996, sits at the center of the bustling campus. At Columbia University, a Black professor of psychology, who teaches classes on race, found a noose left on the doorknob of her office. Additionally, a Black ironworker in Pittsburgh discovered a noose that was left at his third-story workstation, and a Black school superintendent in Guilford County, North Carolina, discovered a noose hanging from a high school flagpole. Since 2001, the Equal Employment Opportunity Commission has filed more than two dozen racial harassment cases involving nooses.[7]

Macroaggressions. Macroaggressions are microaggressions writ large. Macroaggressions are group offenses: attacks, insults, or pejorative statements made against Blacks as a group. They also include nonverbal communication. A macroaggression may be directed at a specific person, but it becomes a group offense once it is made public, repeated, and heard around the world. The incidents involving Don Imus, Bill O'Reilly, Michael Richards, James Watson, and the noose incidents are examples of macroaggressions.

Intraracial Aggressions: Isiah Thomas and Gangsta Rap. In some instances Blacks use language that insults, undermines, and marginalizes other Blacks. These can be thought of as *intra*racial macroaggressions. These too are harmful, as they legitimize the racial disrespect and loathing that are at the core of interracial macroaggressions. They offer a kind of license for anti-Black sentiment and expression. Comments by New York Knicks general manager and coach Isiah Thomas offers a noteworthy case. During a trial involving allegations that he sexually harassed a Black female employee, Thomas testified that in his opinion a Black man calling a Black woman a "bitch" carries a different, lesser weight than if she were called a "bitch" by a White man. Of course, this is an empirical question, and many Black women say that "bitch" is "bitch," regardless of the speaker. Thomas's double standard implies that it is acceptable for Black men to speak disparagingly to and about Black women. If it is acceptable for Thomas and other Black men—who most intimately know Black women—to talk badly about them, then it is acceptable for others to follow suit and disrespect Black women.

Both microaggressions and macroaggressions are often dismissed as marginal or occasional offenses that the targets should shrug off and move on to more important issues. However, these racial offenses matter and should not be dismissed. How we respond to these types of incidents sets the tone for how race matters. If we offer a collective shrug when Don Imus utters a racial offense, what can we expect next? If doing nothing is an acceptable response to name calling by a well-placed, well-paid, and longtime interviewer of movers and shakers, then what message does *that* send? If dangling nooses do not cause racial alarm bells to go off, then what should? This brings to mind a parent's advice to a child who has been assaulted by a schoolyard bully: you have to fight back, regardless of whether you win or lose. It is the willingness to fight that matters. Actual victory may be in the future. Regarding racial assaults, inaction encourages more outrageousness that may be dismissed as "joking" and "nothing serious" and as having been "taken out of context."

There is another important concern: the effect of macroaggressions on young people. Our media images and cultural language implicate Blacks as deviant. These negative representations are a signpost declaring who Black Americans are and what Blackness means. If African Americans eating in a restaurant and not cursing is worthy of public comment and Black female student athletes can be characterized and dismissed as nothing more than unattractive street women, what chance does the average person of color have at fair, unbiased treatment in education, in employment, and within the justice system?

Who You Calling Sheniqua?

One of the ways that a linkage is made between Blacks and deviance is cultural talk about how different Blacks are from Whites. For example, a number of comedians, such as Chris Rock, Dave Chappelle, Cedric the Entertainer, D. L. Hughley, and Carlos Mencia, have used routines expressing the distinctive and opposing ways that Blacks and Whites live in and see the world. Compared to Whites, Blacks speak loudly, have a bad attitude, wear bright-colored clothing, love sports, have crazy, unpronounceable names, show up late for appointments, wear flamboyant hairstyles, are quick to anger, love to dance, are sexually experienced, do not value hard work, speak in Ebonics, and carry weapons. These images of difference and deviance are reinforced by various media, from situation comedies to music videos (see chapter 1).

First or given names are one way that Blacks are tagged as different. In recent years "Black names" have taken on an added dimension. A study done in 2003 found that job applicants who have "Black-sounding" names are much less likely to be called for an interview than those who have "White-sounding" names. Professors Mariane Bertrand and Sendhil Mullainathan reviewed birth-certificate data for babies born in Massachusetts between 1974 and 1979, examining frequency rates for names. They identified as uniquely African American and uniquely White those names that were typically given only to Black children or White children. The researchers identified White names including Allison, Carrie, Emily, Brad, Brendan, and Geoffrey, and they identified Black names including Lakisha, Ebony, Tamika, Leroy, Tyrone, and Jermaine. The researchers checked to see whether social class affected the decision to interview, to determine whether race was being used as a proxy for socioeconomic status. Overall, the researchers found that the probability that applicants would be called for an interview increased when their resumes included zip codes that were in wealthier areas. However, Blacks who listed zip codes in wealthier areas did not fare any better at getting interviews than Whites who listed zip codes in less-wealthy areas. This suggests that names—Black names —were being used to indicate something beyond simply determining an applicant's class status.

Law professors Angela Onwuachi-Willig and Mario Barnes argue that the law falls silent and fails to protect employees adequately from name-based racial discrimination.[8] They observe that race itself is socially constructed and that Title VII of the Civil Rights Act, for instance, does not adequately address the many ways that employers use racial indicators, such as names, to discriminate against employees. Whether the racial bias is conscious or unconscious, the law should sanction it. Regarding race, Onwuachi-Willig and Barnes find that although one's name may be viewed as a signal of other characteristics, such as socioeconomic status, it is the perceived race attached to a name that drives the assessment. They state,

> Names . . . become difference-markers or tools to distinguish between the acceptable and unacceptable Blacks. The tool could be a proxy for race and socio-economic status, social compatibility, or political agenda.

Race, however, is always present in the consideration. What one's name tells the world about how one performs, his or her race controls the ultimate decision.[9]

Onwuachi-Willig and Barnes conclude that the courts should not seek to treat name-based discrimination as somehow different and less harmful than racial discrimination. In their discussion they point out that Whites and other non-Blacks who have Black-sounding names may also face discrimination based on the practice of using names as a proxy for race.

Some researchers conclude that both race and class determine the impact that one's name will have on one's life experiences. According to professors Steven Levitt and Stephen Dubner, the authors of *Freakonomics*, employers who would discriminate against someone named "DeShawn" may use the name "to signal a disadvantaged background. . . . an employer [may] believe that workers from such backgrounds are undependable."[10] They conclude, "Maybe DeShawn should just change his name."[11] This "resolution," however, denies the complex ways that racism operates. Having a White-sounding name does not miraculously inoculate one from racial bias. It simply shifts the site for potential race discrimination. The person with Black skin and a White-sounding name still has to drive a car and show up at the job interview, the realtor's office, the department store, the business mixer, or the restaurant.

Some commentators, most notably comedian Bill Cosby, appear to agree with Levitt and Dubner's line of thought. Black parents have been taken to task for giving their children obviously Black and, therefore, obviously "bad" names. These parents, it seems, have sealed their children's downward fate by failing to name them appropriately. Cosby, in remarks made during the NAACP's fiftieth-anniversary celebration of *Brown v. Board of Education*, made wide-ranging and detailed comments about what he believes is wrong with Black America. He was critical of the clothing, speech patterns, lifestyles, and names of lower-class Blacks. About Black-sounding names, Cosby remarked, "With names like Shaniqua, Taliqua, and Muhammad and all that crap, and all of 'em are in jail."[12] Although there may be a disproportionate number of Blacks with "Black-sounding" names in prison—an empirical question—this does not mean that changing their names would have changed that result. Racial disparity in incarceration has been a reality in the U.S. penal system for more than a century.

Other Race Signals. Black-sounding voices, like Black-sounding names, are also used as a way to determine race. "Linguistic profiling" is the term used to describe the practice of discriminating against someone who sounds Black, Latino/a, or like another person of color. Differential treatment based on one's voice or accent may arise in different contexts. Numerous studies have found that people with Black-sounding voices are more likely to be discriminated against when calling and inquiring about housing and employment.[13] Courts have also considered whether to allow witnesses to testify that a voice they heard sounded Black.[14] A number of commentators have argued that this linguistic profiling is a form of racial profiling, because it reinforces stereotypes about race and it is unreliable as a form of witness identification.

As the preceding discussion makes clear, signs of Blackness do not bode well—in employment, education, politics, or business. It appears to be commonly understood that Black skin operates as a kind of stain, subjecting the holder to slurs, a lethal assemblage of assumptions, and general suspicion as to motives and capabilities. The bottom line is that race talk affects and reflects and influences what we believe to be true regarding race.

So, how does this fact tie to race, crime, and the justice system? The images and representations of Blackness matter because the images of race, particularly images of Blackness, instruct us that African Americans are "other" people who somehow warrant differential treatment. Subtle and overt messages about racial differences buttress beliefs that there is something about Blackness that is deviant, and this supports some people's beliefs that these differences are explained by genetics. It is the focus on and belief in racial differences that keep us on a track to accept a two-lane justice system, one in which race matters most. These beliefs frame contemporary thinking about how Blacks deserve to be treated in the criminal justice system—and, ultimately, about what constitutes justice. The next section highlights some of the ways that the justice system is affected by stereotypically negative representations of Black skin.

Connecting the Dots

[M]ore than one half of the group had become outcasts. They were confined to former inner-city areas that had been divorced from their political boundaries. High walls surrounded these areas, and armed guards controlled entrance and exit around the clock.[15]

This quotation, from professor Derrick Bell's well-known and provocative chronicle "The Space Traders," is a hypothetical description of what Black America has become. Bell's science-fiction tale, written almost two decades ago, today seems to have been strikingly prescient. How did we get here? The scenario he forecasts is one in which Blacks are isolated, despised, and sequestered, a racial sector that is watched and observed but neither cared for nor cared about.

This chapter has detailed how Blackness is represented and responded to in mainstream society. Blackness, it seems, is both the cause and effect of deviance. How else can we explain the omnipresent finger pointing at Blacks, reminding them which types of jobs are available, where they can live, how they can look, how they should talk, what their names should be, and whether and where they can go to school? All this racial pigeonholing has a direct bearing on the criminal justice system. It affects which offenses society labels most serious (thereby determining how and where the police will go about doing their jobs) and how stiff the penalties will be. The end result is a highly punitive and racially skewed criminal justice system, a skin game in which race is the game and Black is the card no one wants to hold.

Consider the following:

Arrest Rates. In 2006, 70 percent of the people arrested were White, and 30 percent were Black. Approximately 1 percent were American Indian, and 1 percent were Asian or Pacific Islander.

Control Rates. There are approximately seven million people in the U.S. justice system. Whites make up 48 percent; Blacks, 36 percent; Latinos, 15 percent; and American Indians and Asian Americans, less than 1 percent. Blacks constitute 46 percent of the prison population; Whites, 36 percent; Latinos, 15 percent; and American Indians and Asian Americans together make up less than 3 percent.

Crack Cocaine. Though more than two-thirds of the people who use crack cocaine are White or Hispanic, 85 percent of federal crack defendants are African American (9 percent are Hispanic, and 5 percent are White). The federal crack law imposed a mandatory sentence for the sale of crack cocaine that was one hundred times more severe than the sentence for the sale of powder cocaine. Under the law, the sale of 5 grams of crack resulted in a mandatory-minimum sentence of five years. Under the same law, one would have to be convicted of selling 500 grams of powder cocaine to receive a five-year sentence. In 2007, the U.S. Sentencing Commission slightly reduced the disparity in penalties.[16] In a pair of decisions centered on the federal sentencing guidelines, in 2007 the U.S. Supreme Court held that the guidelines are advisory, not mandatory.[17]

Probation and Parole. Of the seven million people under correctional supervision in 2006, approximately five million were on probation or parole. Whites made up 55 percent of the probation population; Blacks, 30 percent; Hispanics, 13 percent; and 1 percent each for American Indians and Asians and Pacific Islanders. Of the people on parole, 41 percent were White, 40 percent were Black, and 18 percent were Hispanic.[18]

Prison and Jail. In 2005, there were close to 1.5 million state and federal prisoners. Blacks made up more than 39 percent of the state and federal prison population. This compares with 34 percent for Whites and 20 percent for Hispanics. In 2006, of the approximately 750,000 people in jail, 41 percent were White, 38 percent were Black, and more than 15 percent were Hispanic.[19]

Lifetime Chances of Going to Prison. In 2001, 3.4 percent of Whites were expected to go to prison, compared with 18.6 percent for Blacks and 10 percent for Hispanics. The numbers for men are even more startling. The figures indicate that 6 percent of White men will serve time at least once. The percentage for Black males is more than five times higher (32.2 percent), and the percentage for Hispanic males is almost three times higher (17.2 percent).

TABLE 2.1
*Lifetime Likelihood of Going to Prison,
by Race and Gender, 2001*

	Overall	Male	Female
Black	18.6%	32.2%	5.6%
White	3.4%	5.9%	0.9%
Hispanic	10.0%	17.2%	2.2%

Source: U.S. Department of Justice, "Prevalence of Imprisonment in the U.S. Population, 1974–2001" (2003), p. 8, table 9.

Juveniles. Minority youths make up almost two-thirds of all youths who have been committed to or are being held at detention facilities. Minority youths, however, constitute only 34 percent of the total adolescent population in the United States.

Felony Disenfranchisement. Of the 5.3 million people ineligible to vote due to a felony conviction, 25 percent are African American (1.4 million), and 13 percent of all Black males are subject to felony disenfranchisement. Studies predict that for the next generation of Black men, three in ten will be disenfranchised at some point in their lifetime.

These statistics tell us that race matters in the criminal justice system. Specifically, Blackness matters. As discussed in chapter 4, racial discrimination and racial disparity can coexist. So, the fact that Blacks disproportionately commit street-crime offenses does not mean that any and all amounts of racial disproportionality in the court system are justified. There appears to be a tacit willingness to allow the incarceration numbers to mount without regard to either racial impact or long-term social benefit. Our failure to collectively address racial disparity, regardless of what we say, suggests that we believe that the purported link between Blackness and deviance is real—that there is something about Black skin that represents deviance and criminality.

This reduction of Black skin to a criminal marker is both represented and influenced by how we treat Blackness in social life. We not only "see" race in skin color; we also "hear" race in people's names and in how they speak. These racial sensors are used in everyday life—employment, education, and housing—to define and determine who belongs where. These same sensors also have a long-lasting and damaging effect on the justice system. The legal system, rather than an enlightened beacon that gives, among other things, the poor and tired a hearing before the bar of justice, represents the end of the road in terms of race. To paraphrase Shakespeare, there is something rotten in our criminal justice system.

3

History's Strange Fruit

Debate continues as to whether the U.S. legal system is just and fair and, if so, for whom and under which circumstances. There is little debate, however, as to the justice system's racist origins. An evaluation of the workings of the contemporary criminal justice system is incomplete without a consideration of its historical practices and their underlying rationales. A historically rooted analysis allows us to do two things. First, it allows us to assess the degree of racial progress we have made and, more to the point, to determine whether and to what degree past race-based practices still exist within our current system. Second, it allows us to identify the minimal components necessary for a racially equitable system of punishment. The history of African Americans and the law provides the framework for this discussion. This examination includes some consideration of how other groups of color—specifically, Latinos, American Indians, and Asians—have fared within the American legal system.

Slave Codes, Black Codes, Black Laws, and Jim Crow

From 1619 to 1865, slave codes embodied the criminal law and procedure that was applied against enslaved Africans.[1] Virginia was the first state to enact slave-code legislation. Though codes varied by state, they were uniform in their goal to regulate slave life from cradle to grave. The codes not only enumerated the applicable law but prescribed the social boundaries for slaves. In addition to restricting Black slave life, the codes established parameters for the business of slavery, including who could be sold as slaves, the hours slaves could be made to work, who was responsible when slaves were injured, the punishment for stealing slaves, and the reward for capturing escaped slaves.

The harshest criminal penalties were reserved for actions that threatened the institution of slavery, such as slave rebellions. Slaves who attempted to escape could face death. Harriet Tubman, a slave who escaped to freedom, returned to help scores of other slaves travel to free soil. The success of her "underground railroad" made her the object of slave catchers and bounty hunters who were promised a large reward for her return—dead or alive.

White fear of slave uprisings was so widespread that it was debated at the Constitutional Convention and ultimately included within the U.S. Constitution. Under the Fugitive Slave Act, the militia can be called to stop invasions and to suppress "insurrections." Whites who acted to undermine slavery—those who helped slaves learn to read, organize escapes, and arrange abolition meetings—faced severe penalties under the code.

Bloodlines. Whites were placed atop the racial hierarchy as a pure race category. Anyone who had even a trace amount of Black blood was precluded from claiming Whiteness. The obsession with racial purity—monitoring the boundaries of Whiteness—is exemplified by laws that measured Blackness and Whiteness by degrees of Black blood. According to the one-drop rule, a Black person was someone with any known African Black ancestry.[2] Thus, someone who was biologically more White than Black (e.g., a quadroon or octoroon) was classified as Black. This rule worked to the benefit of White slaveowners, making the child of a slave master and slave a slave. The codes not only created a caste system under which Whites and Blacks were accorded separate status; it also created an in-between tier for "others," such as mulattoes. Thus, a slave's punishment could be determined by his "degree of Blackness." For example, some slave codes excused or reduced a mulatto's punishment if he had a White mother. Though slave codes rarely made explicit reference to Native Americans, they too were enslaved and subjected to the inhumane rule of the slave codes.

Although race was the most important factor in determining punishment under the slave codes, gender and socioeconomic status of the offenders and victims played a role. These factors also determined whether justice would be meted out in White courts or slave courts.

Punishments. Table 3.1 provides examples from the Virginia slave codes. As indicated, slaves faced death for numerous criminal offenses. Harsh sanctions, such as brutal public executions, were imposed to keep slaves in their place. Under Maryland law, for example, a slave convicted of murder was to be hanged, beheaded, and then drawn and quartered. Following

TABLE 3.1
Criminal Penalties, by Race, in Virginia

Crime	White Offender	Black Slave Offender
Murder (White victim) petit treason[a]	Maximum penalty, death	Death
Murder (Black victim)	Rarely prosecuted hard labor, or death	If prosecuted, whipping,
Rape (White victim) if minor victim	10–20 years, whipping, or death	Death or castration[b]
Rape (Black victim)	No crime	No crime, exile, or death[c]
Assault (White victim)	1–10 years (if done with intent to kill)	Whipping, exile, mutilation, or death

Source: A. Leon Higginbotham Jr. and Anne Jacobs, "'The Law Only as Enemy': The Legitimization of Racial Powerlessness through the Colonial and Ante-Bellum Criminal Laws of Virginia," *North Carolina Law Review* 70 (1992): 969.
[a] Murder of a slaveowner.
[b] Same penalty for attempted rape.
[c] If rape was of a *free* Black woman, penalty could be death.

this, the slave's head and body parts were to be publicly displayed. Deterrence is one possible rationale for such a punishment, but the harshness of it suggests that there was something much larger at stake: the preservation of White economic dominance.

Criminal Penalties by Race in Virginia

Enslaved Africans faced other barbaric sanctions, including iron branding. A letter might be burned onto the cheek or forehead to represent the crime committed by the slave (e.g., "R" for runaway). Another form of punishment consisted of placing slaves in the galleys or requiring them to wear heavy collars (e.g., five pounds) around their necks. Yet another punishment sent slaves to the pillory for offenses such as hog stealing. Their ears were nailed down and later cut off.

Whippings were common. Also, referred to as lashes, whippings were administered to the bare back with a leather strap. As brutally depicted in the miniseries *Roots* and the movie *Sankofa* and as hauntingly described in Toni Morrison's *Beloved*, some slaves were whipped so severely that their backs were disfigured beyond recognition. A number of slave code violations mandated thirty-nine lashes (e.g., using abusive language, preaching without permission).[3] Although some slaveowners believed that administering more than thirty-nine lashes at one time violated Christian tenets, untold numbers of slaves were subjected to whippings of more than one hundred lashes.[4]

Slaves lived with the constant fear that at any time they could be accused of and punished for offenses they did not commit. They also lived with the knowledge that if they were the victims of assault, there was no opportunity for redress—no slavery ombudsperson. The slave codes of most states allowed Whites to beat, slap, and whip slaves with impunity. An 1834 Virginia case held that it was not a crime for a White person to assault a slave.[5]

In some instances, however, Whites did face punishment for extreme acts of brutality against slaves. They were punished not because they violated a slave's rights but because they had interfered with the property rights of a slaveowner. For example, under a nineteenth-century South Carolina law, a White man found guilty of killing a slave could be fined. The fine was paid to the slaveowner, not the kin of the murdered slave.[6]

Sex Crimes

Interracial sex assaults offer the best example of how racial double standards worked under the slave codes. A Black male slave who forced sex with a White woman faced the most severe penalty, and a White man who forced sex with an enslaved Black woman faced the least severe penalty. As table 3.1 indicates, a Black man could be hanged for having sexual contact with a White woman. There were more Black men executed for raping a White woman than there were Black men executed for killing a White person.[7] White fear of Black male sexuality is the only possible explanation for why the rape of a White woman by a Black man was the only crime for which castration could be imposed under Virginia law. The fear of Black male sexuality coexisted with the widespread belief in Black inferiority.

The prohibition against interracial liaisons was based on the view that Whiteness and personhood were inextricably linked. Enslaved Black men could never attain manhood. Therefore, Black men had no business with White women. Laws prohibiting interracial intimacy were the first line of defense against race mixing. It was assumed that a White woman would not consent to sex with a Black man. Laws outlawing interracial marriage served as a second line of defense.

Raping a Black woman was not a crime under most slave codes. This was a crude reflection of the reality that slave women were sexual and economic property.[8] If a slave master wanted to force sex on his human chattel, this was perfectly legal. The number of mulatto children born to slave women was tangible evidence of this practice.

Some codes, though, did punish White men for having sex with Black slaves. In *In re Sweat*, a 1640 Virginia case, the court determined that a White man had impregnated a Black slave who was owned by another White man. For this race-mixing crime, the White man was sentenced to do "public penance" at a church. This was a slap on the wrist compared with the punishment that the slave woman received. The slave woman was tied to a whipping post and beaten.[9]

In addition to the ever-present threat of being raped by White men, Black female slaves had a further burden to bear. It was also not a crime for one slave to rape another slave. The formal legal system might be invoked, however, if an assault caused an injury to the slave that hampered her ability to work, because this amounted to economic interference. Eighteenth-century Virginia law reports few cases involving a Black male slave charged with raping a Black female slave. In the one case that did result in a criminal conviction, the male slave was removed from the county.[10]

Several rationales have been offered to explain why most slave codes neither acknowledged nor sanctioned the rape of Black women. One reason is that slave women were viewed as naturally promiscuous, making forced sex a legal impossibility.[11] Another reason is that the rape of a slave woman did not usually threaten the maintenance of slavery. In fact, if the rape resulted in offspring, this meant one more child was available for slave labor. Finally, there was little awareness or concern about the physical and emotional trauma caused by rape. All these rationales allowed slaveholders to remain psychologically detached from the harms of slavery and physically bonded to the permanence of the institution. Faulting Black women slaves for being victims of sexual assault allowed Whites to assuage the moral offense, harm, and shame of their actions. This reasoning represents an early and classic example of blaming the victim.

In addition to prohibitions against interracial sex between Black men and White women, the slave codes punished Blackness in many different ways, making certain activities criminal only when committed by someone Black. For instance, a slave who "lifted his hand against" a White Christian or used "provoking or menacing language" against a White person faced a punishment of thirty-nine lashes. It was also an offense for seven or more Black men to congregate, unless accompanied by a White person. Under many slave codes, a free Black person who married a slave became a slave. Some states made an exception if the free person was a mulatto who had a White mother.[12]

At their core, the codes denied slaves political, social, and economic equality. Slaves, themselves property, were barred from owning anything. They could have pets, with the permission of the slave master, who was the lawful owner of any animals. Slaves could be mortgaged and sold. They were also prohibited from entering into contracts, including marriage, without the consent of their owners. Not surprisingly, slaves were barred from holding elected office. This is another example of how the law was used to criminalize Blackness. Only convicted White criminals were barred from holding elective office. Blacks who had never been convicted of a crime were treated like Whites who had been.

Enslaved Africans were not the only race singled out for punishment under the codes. As noted earlier, Whites who acted to thwart the slavery system could face serious sanctions. In Mississippi, for instance, a White person who taught a slave to read or helped a slave obtain freedom risked being fined, imprisoned, or possibly executed.[13] Some states barred White abolitionists from jury service, some sentenced White women to prison for marrying Black men, and others fined White women who had children by Black men. Notably, a White man who fathered a child by a Black woman was not guilty of any crime.

Slave Patrols and Justice. Slave patrols or "patterollers" operated to keep a tight rein on slave activity. Whites greatly feared slave insurrection, and the slave patrols were established to monitor and quell suspicious slave conduct. Slave patrols, enumerated by the slave codes, were the first uniquely American form of policing. Slave patrollers, who worked in conjunction with the militia, were permitted to stop and search slaves and their living quarters. They were also permitted to beat slaves who did not have proper written permission to be away from their plantation. Patrollers stormed slave cabins to search for runaways, weapons, and any evidence of literacy, such as books, writing implements, and paper.

Patrollers frequently beat slaves, whipping the men and beating and sexually assaulting the women.[14] Many states explicitly protected assaults by slave patrols. For instance, in North Carolina the patrollers were not liable for punishing slaves unless their actions showed malice toward the slaveowner.[15]

Whites were encouraged and enlisted to serve in the slave patrols. In some states, including South Carolina and Georgia, Whites were required to serve as patrollers. In Alabama, all slaveowners under the age of sixty, and all other Whites under the age of forty-five, had to participate in the slave patrols. By the mid-1850s, the patrols existed in every Southern colony.[16] The work of the slave patrols, which was considered low status, often fell to non-slave-holding Whites. As interest and compliance with serving on patrols declined, money was offered as an incentive.

Not only did the codes create separate crimes and punishments for Blacks, but "justice" was also administered in separate, special tribunals. These tribunals were designed to uphold the rights of White slavehold- ers. These separate forums had different procedural practices from courts for White defendants. In these courts, slave defendants did not have the right to a jury trial, could be convicted with a verdict that was less than unanimous, were presumed guilty, and did not have the right to appeal a conviction. Slaves could not serve as jurors or witnesses against Whites. This meant that even in those instances when a slave was overworked, underfed, and brutalized, he had no legal recourse— his "word" was no good in court against a slave master. Under an 1818 Georgia law, no slave was allowed to be a party to any suit against a White man.[17]

Racism in the administration of justice was not confined to the court system. In some cases, Blacks charged with a crime were subjected to "plantation justice." The codes gave slaveowners private enforcement au- thority, allowing them to act as both judge and jury. Plantation justice was consistent with the classification of slaves as property. It permitted a slaveowner to impose sanctions, including lashings, castration (by knife), dismemberment (e.g., ears, fingers) and hangings. Slave laws sanctioned other forms of extrajudicial punishment, such as slaveowners' hiring bounty hunters to capture runaway slaves. Although most slave masters wanted their human chattel returned alive, some others were satisfied with evidence that the slave was dead.

This discussion fails to convey the harsh reality created, enshrined, and enforced by the slave codes. To say that slaves were viewed as less than human is a gross understatement. Under the law, animals fared better than slaves. Slaves ranked below dogs, cats, and other breathing, feeling animals. Horses and cows were legally protected against senseless cruelty.

In their totality, the slave codes reveal the vast difference in how Whites and everyone else fared under the law. Virginia legislation, for example, permitted slaves to receive the death penalty for numerous offenses. First-degree murder, however, was the only offense for which Whites could be sentenced to death. What was considered a crime, which court would hear which cases, which sanctions were imposed, and the applicable constitutional protections were all determined by race.

Black Laws and Black Codes

Black laws existed during the same period as the slave codes. These laws governed the movements and actions of Blacks in non-slave-holding states and territories. In 1804, one year after achieving statehood, Ohio enacted Black laws. These free-state laws established bond fees for state entry, outlined rules for Blacks who sought work as craftsmen, and imposed local taxes for public services (services that Blacks could not access, e.g., schools). Ohio required that Blacks entering the state post a $500 bond and produce court papers attesting to their free status.

On the heels of the passage of the 1863 Emancipation Proclamation, the conclusion of the Civil War, and the adoption of the Thirteenth Amendment, which abolished slavery, Black codes were enacted. In 1865, Ohio passed the first Black codes, laws that governed the movements of the formerly enslaved population. Newly freed Black women and men were given the right to marry and enter into contracts.[18] In some ways the Black codes operated as both shield and sword. At the same time that new rights were granted, laws were enacted that undercut these protections. For example, vagrancy laws allowed Blacks to be arrested for the "crime" of being unemployed. Mississippi's statute was representative:

> [A]ll freedmen, free negroes and mulattoes . . . over the age of eighteen years, found on the second Monday in January, 1866, or thereafter with no lawful employment or business, or found unlawfully assembling themselves together . . . shall be deemed vagrants, and on conviction thereof, shall be fined . . . not exceeding fifty dollars . . . and imprisoned . . . not exceeding ten days.[19]

In an attempt to protect White labor, licensing requirements were imposed to bar Blacks from all but the most menial jobs. Court approval and a fee were necessary to obtain a license to become a mechanic, artisan, or shopkeeper. Blacks who were fortunate enough to obtain a license could lose it if there were complaints about their work. Laws criminalizing gun possession, voting, desertion, and assembly after sunset were also used to restrict Black mobility and employment.

In their totality, the Black codes created and supported a system of involuntary servitude, expressly prohibited by the newly adopted Thirteenth Amendment. Laws were routinely applied in a discriminatory manner. Race discrimination worked in many ways. Blacks faced harsher criminal penalties than Whites. For instance, thousands of Blacks were executed for offenses that Whites were given prison time for committing. Further, White crimes committed against Blacks were largely ignored. For instance, the Texas codes made it a crime for a White person to murder a Black person. Yet, in Texas, between 1865 and 1866, there were acquittals in five hundred cases in which someone White was charged with killing someone Black.[20]

The enforcement arm of the law was not limited to the courts or legal officials. The fact that former slaves now had rights served to mobilize White vigilantes, including the Ku Klux Klan (KKK). The KKK and its sympathizers were responsible for murdering thousands of Blacks. In the 1874 case of *United States v. Cruikshank*, two Black men were ambushed and killed by more than three hundred Klansmen. After the attack, ninety-seven Whites were indicted on murder and conspiracy charges, and only nine went to trial. In all nine cases, the White defendants were acquitted of murder. Only three were found guilty of conspiracy to murder.[21]

Lynching, the hallmark of the Klan, introduced a new form of oppression against Blacks. This unique form of extralegal Southern "justice" resulted in death for thousands of Black children, women, and men.

The Lynching Ritual. Carried out as an extreme form of vigilante justice, lynchings rose to prominence after the Civil War. Though lynch victims were often selected at random, lynchings themselves involved a series of well-established ritualized sequences: selection of the victim, selection of the killers, selection of the location (based on the anticipated size of the crowd), and selection of the method of death (e.g., hanging, shooting, burning, or a combination of these). If the lynch victim was to be hanged, lynchers had to select a tree. Lynching implements—rope, wood, guns, kerosene, tar, and feathers—were also gathered.

Most victims of lynching were Black. However, members of other racial and ethnic groups were also lynch victims, including Asians, Mexicans, and Italians. In fact, around the turn of the twentieth century, the U.S.

State Department paid approximately half a million dollars in reparations to China, Italy, and Mexico on behalf of lynch victims.[22]

Lynchings had the look and feel of a sporting event, a one-sided rigged one, in which the outcome was predetermined. Entire families, including women and small children, attended lynchings. Schools and businesses were closed. Spectators arrived with food, drink, and spirits. It was not uncommon for White mobs, which sometimes included police officers, to gather to witness or participate in the murder.[23]

In some instances, newspapers featured lynching announcements. These advertisements provided the date, time, and location of upcoming lynchings. Referring to a particularly violent 1917 lynching, W. E. B. Du Bois wrote,

> A Negro was publicly burned alive in Tennessee under circumstances un-usually atrocious. The mobbing and burning were publicly advertised in the press beforehand. Three thousand automobiles brought the audience, including mothers carrying children. Ten gallons of gasoline were poured over the wretch and he was burned alive, while hundreds fought for bits of his body, clothing, and the rope.[24]

Lynch victims, both men and women, were usually required to strip na-ked. Black men were usually castrated, and sometimes their bodies were used as target practice. The murderous assault ceremoniously concluded with Whites fighting over the remains of the Black victim. Teeth and other body parts were collected as souvenirs.[25]

What could trigger such a morbid and vile practice by Whites? Beyond a rumor that someone Black had committed a serious crime (murder, rape, robbery, or barn burning), there was an endless list of offenses. As detailed in Ida B. Wells-Barnett's work, offenses included the following:

- Being "saucy" (verbally disrespectful) to someone White
- Making lewd advances toward a White woman (e.g., whistling)
- Being related to someone suspected of committing a crime
- Being in the wrong place at the wrong time
- Insulting someone White (e.g., buying a new car)
- Engaging in boastful talk
- Expressing race prejudice
- Defending self from physical assault[26]

As this list makes clear, very little was required to instigate a lynching. The only requirement was that someone White took offense to someone's alleged actions. The stated rationale for lynching was to safeguard White womanhood from the Black brute. Official records, however, show that it operated differently in practice. Allegations of sexual assault against White women accounted for fewer than one-third of all lynchings. Though the lynching ritual was devised and widely supported as a call to protect White women and thus the White family, this was simply a cover. The goal was to send an unequivocal threat and promise to Blacks—to stay in their place, or else. Lynching was widely used as an extralegal tool to punish Blackness and derail Black progress.

According to official U.S. records, 4,745 people were lynched between 1882 and 1964.[27] Blacks made up approximately 75 percent of the total (3,449). Lynching historians cite a much higher figure than the government's. Ida B. Wells-Barnett estimated that between 1882 and 1899 alone, there were 2,553 Black people lynched. Wells-Barnett, an antilynching crusader, painstakingly collected newspaper accounts of lynchings across the United States. In 1892, she documented 241 lynchings; 161 were Black victims. This represents the highest recorded number of Blacks lynched in a single year. Wells-Barnett estimated that there were close to ten thousand lynch-murders from the end of the Civil War through the early 1900s. According to government figures kept through the 1960s, overall, Blacks accounted for 75 percent of lynch victims.

Table 3.2 lists some lynching cases that took place in 1930. In several cases, White mobs forcibly removed Blacks from legal custody—the courthouse or a jail cell—so that they could be lynched. In many instances Blacks were murdered before they had been formally charged with any crime.

Photographs taken by lynching onlookers sometimes became postcards. The book *Without Sanctuary: Lynching Photography in America* features several examples. One photo shows a gruesome 1916 lynching in Robinson, Texas. The charred remains of a Black man who had been hanged are barely recognizable as a human body. Nearly as startling as the lynching itself is the fact that the photograph was used as a "scenic" postcard. The back of the postcard reads, "This is the barbecue we had last night . . . your son, Joe."[28] Lynching postcards were commonplace.

In many of the photographs there are scores of White men, in shirts, ties, and wearing hats—dress typically reserved for important social events. The book's photos reveal the sizeable crowds that were frequently present at lynchings. Lynch-mob murders were held in various places, including in town squares, over bridges, by the side of the road, and on courthouse lawns.[29]

TABLE 3.2
Selected Black Lynchings, 1930

Alleged Crime	Method of Lynching	Circumstances
1. Rape/murder	Burned to death	No formal arrest
2. Murder	Shot to death	No formal arrest
3. Rape	Shot to death	Removed from jail
4. Rape	Burned to death	Jail where Black man was held was burned down. His burned body was removed and left in Negro section of town.
5. Murder	Shot to death	Body was tied to a car and dragged through town. Later, body was burned in front of a Negro church.
6. Rape	Shot and stabbed to death	Lynch mob broke into jail and removed victim.
7. Rape	Shot to death	No formal arrest
8. Rape	Shot to death	No formal arrest
9. Murder	Shot to death	Victim had been arrested but was left unguarded.
10. No crime	Beaten to death	—
11. Rape/assault	Hanged	Removed from jail
12. Resisting arrest	Shot to death	—
13. Rape	Shot to death	Removed from jail
14. Murder	Shot to death	Killed in jail
15. Robbery	Hanged	Taken from police officers
16. Attempted rape	Shot to death	Taken from police officers
17. No crime	Shot to death	Victim (Black man) had been the star witness in a case against two White men charged with raping a Negro woman. He was shot to death in his home.
18. Murder	Hanged	Removed from jail
19. Rape	Shot to death	No formal arrest

Source: Arthur Raper, *The Tragedy of Lynching* (University of North Carolina Press, 1933), 469–471. Raper notes that there were twenty-one lynchings in 1930, but he only lists twenty. The nineteen with Black victims are listed in this table.

Lynchings have been characterized as a twisted kind of "performance." This characterization is rooted in the fact that some were held in public theaters—the price of admission guaranteed a seat and a chance to shoot at the victim.[30] Another aspect of the performance involved lynching ballads, which were sometimes distributed at the "show."[31] This bizarre mix of features suggests that the lynching ritual, itself an execution, was also a cross between a sporting event, circus show, and stage drama.

The drumroll of lynchings did not begin or end without a protest. There were numerous antilynching crusades. Most notably, the impetus for the founding of the National Association for the Advancement of Colored People (NAACP) was to combat mob violence. The organization, which was established in 1910, formed an antilynching committee, worked for decades to the gather information on lynching assaults, and lobbied for the passage of federal law that would outlaw lynching. Between 1890 and 1960, almost two hundred antilynching bills were introduced in Congress. Congress was repeatedly asked to intervene and adopt federal law that would acknowledge lynching as a crime. None of these bills was passed. In 2005, approximately forty years after the last official record of a U.S. lynching, the U.S. Senate issued a strong apology for its failure to enact legislation that would have protected Blacks from lynchings. This apology is the first time that Congress has apologized to African Americans. The nonbinding Senate resolution included the following statements:

- Lynching succeeded slavery as the ultimate expression of racism in the United States following Reconstruction.
- Lynching was a crime that occurred throughout the United States, with documented incidents in all but four states.
- Ninety-nine percent of all perpetrators of lynching escaped from punishment by state or local officials.
- Nearly two hundred antilynching bills were introduced in Congress during the first half of the twentieth century.
- Between 1890 and 1952 seven U.S. presidents petitioned Congress to end lynching.[32]

Though nowhere on the scale of the postbellum period, lynchings still occur today.[33]

Jim Crow Segregation Statutes

The slave codes, Black laws, and the Black codes represent versions of state-sanctioned double standards. "Jim Crow," which came into common usage in the early 1900s, refers to laws that mandated separate public facilities for Blacks and Whites. Segregationist practices, however, came long before the term "Jim Crow." For example, the Louisiana law challenged in *Plessy v. Ferguson* (upholding racial segregation in railway cars) was enacted in 1890. One constant remained as the slave codes became the Black codes and the Black codes became segregation statutes: Blackness itself was a crime.

Jim Crow also relegated other groups to second-class status. Other non-Whites, for instance, were not allowed to marry or live with Whites.

For example, an 1880 California law prohibited marriage between a White person and a "Negro, mulatto, or Mongolian."[34] Also, laws were enacted to deny testamentary capacity. For instance, in *People v. Brady* the California Supreme Court upheld a law that prohibited Chinese witnesses from testifying against Whites.[35]

At one time, Jim Crow signs littered the American landscape. There were all manner of signs: some printed on placards, some engraved on steel plates, and others printed by hand. There were signs posted on the highway, signs posted on wooden poles in front of stores, signs on doors inside buildings, and signs above water fountains. There were no spaces exempt from Jim Crow's rule. Jim Crow was more than a directive determining access to particular locations. It was a pervasive threat backed by the violent force of vigilante mob rule. Jim Crow had a broad reach. It also targeted Native Americans, Asians, and Mexicans. A look at photographs taken during the Jim Crow era reveals nothing close to "separate but equal" but, rather, separate and despised. Jim Crow rules were neither polite nor genteel. By today's standards, the language is jarring:

- "No niggers allowed" (store sign)
- "Drinking Fountain" (with arrows pointing in different directions for "White" and "Colored")
- "White Women, Senoras Blancas" (restroom door at a train station)
- "We cater to White only. Niggers, Mexicans and Puerto Ricans not allowed" (road sign)
- "White Baggage Room" (train station)
- "No colored allowed" (building sign)
- "This part of the bus for the colored race" (sign on back of city bus)
- "No dogs, no Negroes, no Mexicans" (business sign)
- "Negroes and freight" (railway sign)[36]

Jim Crow's reach was so expansive that it regulated beyond the public sphere. Not only did Jim Crow laws determine which public facilities Blacks could use; they also determined who could serve Blacks in those facilities. For instance, there were laws prohibiting White female nurses from treating Black male patients, a clear indication of the taboo against interracial sex. There were also laws prohibiting Black teachers from teaching White students and White teachers from teaching Black students.

Segregation-era laws encompassed a broad range of social actions.

Blacks could be punished for walking down the street if they did not move out of the way quickly enough to accommodate White passersby, for talking to friends on a street corner, for speaking to someone White, and for making direct eye contact with someone White. Jim Crow's rules of racial etiquette, many of them unwritten, required that Black men refer to White men as "Mister" or "Sir." At the same time, however, Whites would commonly refer to Black men as "boys." The rules governing racial manners also required Blacks to step aside and bow their heads in the presence of Whites. These practices were humiliating for Blacks, as my grandfather, Charlie Russell Sr., could attest. Born in 1912 and raised in northeast Louisiana, he told stories of how as a grown man he had to step off the curb to accommodate an approaching grade-school-aged White boy. Likewise, my grandmother, Katie King Russell, born in 1914 in northeast Louisiana, could purchase clothes from White-owned businesses but could not try them on. Once purchased, however, they were final sales; the items could not be returned.

All the while, White fear of race mixing remained steadfast. The murder of Emmett Till illustrates this fear. Till, a Black teenager from Chicago, visited Mississippi in the summer of 1955. He made the fatal mistake of speaking to a White woman. He was killed by several White men, including the woman's husband. After the killing, a gin fan was tied to Till's neck to weigh down his body. His bloated, mutilated body was found floating days later in Mississippi's Tallahatchie River. A jury of twelve White men acquitted the men responsible for Till's lynching. In an interview published in *Look* magazine the following year, J. W. Milam and Roy Bryant confessed to murdering Till and provided details of the killing. In 2005, the U.S. Department of Justice reopened the case. It was closed in 2006—no new charges were filed.

Jim Crow's race-based system of social, economic, and political deference supported the widespread White belief that no matter how much racial equality the Constitution promised, Whites would never view Blacks as their social equals. Jim Crow regulations extended to the following:

beaches	hospital wards	prisons and jails	school textbooks
cemeteries	hotels	public transportation	swimming pools
chain gangs	lunch counters	(waiting rooms and	theaters
church bibles	orphanages	ticket windows)	water fountains
courthouses	parks	restrooms	
golf courses	phone booths	schools	

Ostensibly designed to outlaw racial interaction in public places, the long arm of Jim Crow reached private areas as well. Anti-miscegenation and anti-cohabitation laws made it unlawful for Blacks and Whites to marry or live together. The 1967 case of *Loving v. Virginia* involved a marriage between a Black woman and White man. After marrying in Washington, D.C., the couple returned home to Virginia. A grand jury charged them with violating Virginia's anti-miscegenation law: "Intermarriage prohibited . . . It shall hereafter be unlawful for any white person in this state to marry any save a white person, or person with no other admixture of blood than white and American Indian."[37] The U.S. Supreme Court held that the Virginia law deprived the couple of liberty without due process, in violation of the Fourteenth Amendment's due process clause.

Although *Brown v. Board of Education* was decided in 1954, it did not eradicate racial segregation in public education. Attempts at desegregation frequently inspired a prosegregation response. In 1957, Montgomery, Alabama, passed the following ordinance: "It shall be unlawful for white and colored persons to play together . . . in any game of cards, dice, dominoes, checkers, pool, billiards, softball, basketball, football, golf, track and at swimming pools or in any athletic contest."[38] This ordinance is notable for its degree of specificity regarding the social interactions of Whites with non-Whites. This legislative mandate to separate sports by race mirrored the rampant segregation that existed in organized sports. During this period, professional sports were almost entirely segregated by race. By necessity, Black sports leagues were created. The Negro Leagues for baseball, the American Basketball Association, and the United Golfers Association are some examples.

A look at the laws and practices in effect during Jim Crow is eye-opening. A review of the law, however, does little to indicate the toll that these laws took on Black life. Not only did Jim Crow regulate Black movement; it confined aspirations and tamped down life opportunities for Black Americans. Jim Crow simply reflected the majority belief that the proper place for Blacks was one tier below Whites. The mainstream sentiment was that Blacks were separated from Whites for their own good and because they were dumb, dirty, and deviant. With the backing of the government (federal and state) and private businesses, Jim Crow predetermined where a Black child could be born, where she could go to school, which neighborhood she could live in, which job or career she could pursue, whether she was eligible for health insurance, which restaurants she could frequent, which motels she could stay at, and whether she could secure a car loan or home mortgage.

In an additional widespread and deeply rooted segregation practice, Blacks, Latinos, American Indians, and Asians have been intentionally and systematically barred from thousands of towns and cities across the country. These "White-only" towns, known as "sundown towns," have two distinct characteristics. They are all-White and have race-based policies in effect that bar Blacks from living in the town and prohibit them from remaining there after nightfall. In his book *Sundown Towns*, professor James Loewen details these towns. He estimates that from 1890 to 1940 there were approximately fifteen thousand sundown towns in the United States. Another two thousand to ten thousand were created between 1900 and 1968. Today there are approximately one thousand sundown towns.[39] Enforcement of sundown laws has often led to violence, injury, and death to "trespassers."

The legal death knell has sounded for Jim Crow. The civil rights movement of the 1950s and 1960s led to the passage of civil rights legislation including the 1964 Civil Rights Act and the 1965 Voting Rights Act. Unfortunately other manifestations of racial bias and violence persist. We are still left to address the question of what are the components of a racially equitable criminal justice system.

Fairness Principles. Can anything be learned from the slave codes, Black codes, Black laws, and Jim Crow? These systems of punishment are object lessons in how not to structure a racially fair criminal justice system. Antebellum and postbellum criminal law stood as the antithesis to a racially just system. Today, almost four hundred years later, several basic principles appear to be minimally required for an equitable system of justice:

1. Criminal penalties apply to everyone equally, regardless of the race of the *offender*.
2. Criminal penalties apply to everyone equally, regardless of the race of the *victim*.
3. The race of the offender is not relevant in determining whether his or her actions constitute a crime. The offender's actions would have been considered criminal even if he or she were another race.
4. The race of the victim is not relevant in determining whether the offender's action constitutes a crime.

5. The offender's racial pedigree (e.g., "degree of Blackness") is not used to determine punishment.
6. There are checks and balances that mitigate against racial bias within the legal system.

These fairness principles, though not exhaustive, provide a useful test for measuring the racial equity of a criminal justice system. The principles can be thought of as minimum requirements, since it is hard to imagine a nondiscriminatory legal system that does not adhere to each one. The following chapters analyze various aspects of race and criminal justice, including the criminal law, how it is applied, and how race and crime are framed in public discourse. The fairness principles provide a reference point for evaluating whether today's U.S. criminal justice system operates in a racially fair manner.

4

Discrimination or Disparity?

Study after study shows that Blacks and Whites hold contrary viewpoints about the fairness of the criminal justice system. Blacks are more likely to believe that the justice system works against them, and Whites are more likely to believe that the justice system works for them. Two common expressions capture these opposing viewpoints: "The system works" (Whites) and "Justice means 'just us'" (Blacks). Like Blacks, Latinos believe that they are more likely to experience racial profiling. Interestingly, where Blacks and Hispanics see racial bias, Whites see "rational discrimination." Higher numbers of Blacks and Hispanics than Whites say that they have been unfairly treated by the police. In the wake of the September 11 attacks, Muslims have reported being increasingly subject to racial targeting by law enforcement officials. They have received heightened scrutiny and attention—in their homes, in their cars, and at the airport—as "potential terrorist threats." These experiences influence race-based perceptions of how well the police do their job.[1]

Research on racial discrimination tends to support the view that isolated pockets of racial discrimination exist (e.g., drug-related offenses, capital punishment). The prevailing view, however, is that racial discrimination is not a serious problem. This "no discrimination" conclusion is largely based on research that focuses on select stages of the justice system, such as arrest, charge, sentencing, and conviction. Unfortunately the potential for racial bias exists at many points along the criminal justice system's continuum. An expanded analysis would include, for instance, a consideration of prearrest actions, courtroom language, and postconviction decisions. By focusing on the bright lines of discrimination, criminal justice research tends to overlook these critical points. Until these other unmeasured stages are included within mainstream analyses, no conclusion can be drawn that the justice system is free of racial bias.

This chapter provides an overview of the current research on racial discrimination, outlines the criticisms of this research, and demonstrates why the most important informal stage—prearrest contacts with police —should be subject to official measurement. The findings challenge the mainstream view that racial discrimination exists only at certain points along the criminal justice system continuum. Without expanding our assessment of racial bias, we miss and therefore cannot accurately determine its prevalence. The other points need to be measured and included within the calculation of how race affects justice.

Hysterical Blindness

Depending on your vantage point, the existence of racial discrimination in the justice system might be considered a historical relic, an entrenched present-day reality, something that happens to the poor, a random and rare event, something that happens to the guilty, or a nagging side-effect of an otherwise well-working system. These varied takes on the presence of racially fair treatment make it difficult to "see" racial discrimination and, thus, hard to hear an SOS call to fix it. Further, consensus on what to do is hard to achieve because so many different standards are being used to evaluate whether racial justice exists. All told, these soup-to-nuts perspectives create a kind of hysterical blindness about the workings and viability of the justice system.

There are many causes for the wildly varying viewpoints on the racial equity of the justice system. Criminal justice researchers have some responsibility for this state of affairs. In the post-civil-rights era, mainstream research has largely concluded that racial discrimination in the justice system is, with few exceptions, neither intentional nor widespread. What follows is a four-part critique of this research, which makes a strong argument for reconsidering a "no discrimination" thesis.

Single versus Multistage Research

Many studies that purport to examine the existence of racial discrimination evaluate a single phase of the justice system. These studies are fairly characterized as being marred by tunnel vision. Research that analyzes race discrimination at a single stage of the criminal justice system cannot detect racial discrimination that exists in other parts of the system. For example, a study of how race influences sentencing in State A may find no racial disparity. This finding, however, does not mean that State A does not have a racially discriminatory criminal justice system. Racial discrimination may not exist at sentencing but may permeate other stages (e.g., prosecutorial charging, plea bargaining).

Further, a study involving several criminal courts that finds that no racial discrimination exists may mask discrimination that exists in a few of the courts. For instance, an aggregate analysis of the sentencing decisions of ten courts might indicate that there is very little racial discrimination. A look at these ten courts individually, however, might reveal the existence of sizeable discrimination in two of them. Aggregate studies, therefore, may minimize the existence of race discrimination in sentencing. At best, single-stage studies provide important, though limited, information about the role race plays in the criminal justice system; they cannot reliably answer the broad question of whether racial discrimination exists in the American criminal justice system.

Multistage research poses the same basic problem as single-stage research. Although multistage research covers more ground than single-stage studies, the fact that discrimination is not evident at two or three stages (e.g., bail and sentencing) does not mean that it is absent from other stages. Additionally, single and multistage studies cannot be generalized across states. In other words, a finding that there is no racial discrimination at the prosecutorial charging and sentencing phases in five states does not prove that there is no racial discrimination in the court systems of the remaining forty-five states. State variations, including differences in criminal code statutes, prosecutorial charging practices, jury-pool eligibility, and judicial selection, mean that the empirical findings for one jurisdiction do not necessarily apply to another. Many researchers have failed to acknowledge the limitations of single- and multistage research, and this has led to an unreliable assessment of the degree and amount of racial discrimination in the criminal justice system.

Defining "Disproportionality." Another criticism of the discrimination research is that it does not provide an accurate definition of "disproportionality." The term has been used to refer to whether a group is involved in the criminal justice system at a rate that exceeds its rate in the general population.[2] Using this formula for disproportionality, Blacks, who comprise about 13 percent of the U.S. population, are grossly overrepresented in arrest and incarceration figures. Blacks account for almost 30 percent of all arrests and approximately one-half of the correctional population.

TABLE 4.1
*Indicators of Social Marginality, Proportional
Representation by Race, 2006*

	White	Black
Arrests	69.8%	27.8%
Incarceration	35.2%	41.0%
Nonmarriage births	23.0%	68.4%
Female head of household	64.8%	29.2%
Unemployment*	4.4%	10.0%
Below poverty line	10.8%	24.7%

Sources: National Urban League, *The State of Black America* (2006);
FBI, Uniform Crime Reports, 2005, Bureau of Justice Statistics
(2006).
  * Reflects within-race percentages of the unemployed.

Conversely, Whites are said to be underrepresented in arrest and incarceration figures because their rates are below 75 percent, their percentage in the U.S. population.

Some researchers reject this conventional formula for disproportionality, preferring a more complex analysis. They ask the question, *why* should a group's percentage in the population determine disproportionality? Specifically, some criminal justice researchers state that we should expect arrest rates to mirror more closely indicators of social marginality. Accordingly, the conventional measure of disproportionality is useful only if we assume that all racial groups are on equal social footing.

Table 4.1 provides data on select social indicators for Blacks and Whites. When compared with Whites, Blacks have much higher percentages of out-of-wedlock births, infant mortality, illiteracy, unemployment, female-headed households, and poverty. On almost every measure of social disadvantage, the Black rate exceeds the White rate. Notably, Black figures for out-of-wedlock births, female-headed households, unemployment, and poverty are more than twice the White rates. Given these data, is it surprising that Black arrest and conviction rates follow a similar pattern? Almost fifty years ago, noted criminologists Marvin Wolfgang and Bernard Cohen reached a similar conclusion:

[I]f a careful detached scholar knew nothing about crime rates but was aware of the social, economic and political disparities between whites and Negroes in the United States . . . what would be the most plausible hypothesis our scholar could make about the crime rate of Negroes? Even this small amount of relevant knowledge would justify the expectation that Negroes would be found to have a higher crime rate than Whites.[3]

Indicators of social marginality, such as high rates of unemployment and crime, are interdependent, and we would reasonably expect them to be positively correlated: as unemployment rates rise, so do arrest rates.

The current definition of disproportionality is not so much misleading as it is incomplete. Perhaps it is best thought of as one of the many indices of social status, rather than as a definitive measure for crime rates. For instance, understanding why Blacks offend at rates that exceed their percentage in the population requires a consideration of other factors that may have a direct or less obvious effect on crime. The empirical reality is that race, poverty, employment, crime, and education are interacting variables. Whether a group offends at a high or low rate generally indicates how it will fare with other social indices.

Researchers have also considered other baselines for racial profiling. Some have suggested various measures, including the racial group's percentage of the driving population, percentage of those with automobiles, percentage of the population (in a particular area), and percentage of licensed drivers. Although there is no clear consensus among researchers as to the best measure, at least the question is being asked.[4]

Disproportionality and Discrimination. Another important issue is how racial discrimination and racial disparity are analyzed, comparatively, in the research. They are typically discussed as if they are competing, antithetical phenomena, when in fact, they coexist. Those who are left-of-center tend to focus on racial discrimination, and those who are right-of-center tend to focus on the disproportionately high rate of Black offending. For example, liberals are more likely to focus on the law (e.g., selective enforcement, disparate impact), and conservatives are more likely to focus on the criminals (e.g., crime rates and the increasing number of repeat offenders). Despite these political distinctions, research shows evidence of racial discrimination against Blacks in the criminal justice system *and* evidence that Blacks disproportionately offend. The precise relationship between disparity and discrimination is unclear: the two may be correlated, be causally related, or operate independently of each other.

It may be that the high rate of Black offending has caused many researchers to deemphasize, to the point of ignoring, racial discrimination in the criminal justice system. It is almost as if disproportionate Black offending is viewed as a justification for race discrimination or as an acceptable social fact. The problem of racism in the justice system is too important to play second fiddle to other criminal justice system realities, including disproportionate offending rates. Researchers on either side of the disparity-versus-discrimination debate have been hesitant to acknowledge that both racial discrimination and racial disproportion exist *and* that both are problems that must be addressed.

Even some researchers who embrace a "no discrimination" thesis concede that the high rate of Black incarceration is not completely explained by disproportionate rates of offending. For instance, in a seminal article, professor Alfred Blumstein readily acknowledges that 20 to 25 percent of the incarceration rate for Blacks is *not* explained by disproportionate offending. He surmises, however, that a 20 to 25 percent gap is no great cause for alarm, because eliminating this gap would not change the incarceration picture dramatically. By Blumstein's calculation, the 20 to 25 percent of unexplained disparity between arrest and incarceration figures represents about ten thousand Black prisoners.[5] Although ten thousand prisoners is a statistical drop in the bucket of the overall prison population (less than 1 percent), socially it is no small number. Ten thousand Blacks, who may have been treated more harshly by the criminal justice system *because* of their race, is proof of an enormous social problem. If ten thousand Blacks have been subjected to discrimination, this means that some were unjustly convicted and unjustly sentenced to lengthy prison terms.

Further, the impact of the race discrimination would extend beyond those Blacks who were direct victims of discrimination. This would include the economic and social impact on their families (e.g., children, spouses, and parents) and their communities (e.g., social services). By what logic could we excuse or, worse, ignore this unexplained 20 to 25 percent gap? Blumstein states that the high rate of Black incarceration is "not so much due to racial discrimination."[6] How could he know this to be true? Can the issue of discrimination be dismissed so easily? It is likely that Blumstein did not intend to downplay the impact of racial discrimination. His analysis, however, serves to illustrate a serious weakness of aggregate analysis.

Some researchers studying the disproportionately high rate of Black arrests have questioned whether it is caused by crime rates or whether other factors are at work. A few have suggested that the workings of the legal system may enhance Black disproportionality. For instance, national studies show that a higher percentage of Whites than Blacks state that they have used drugs during their lifetime. The 2005 National Survey on Drug Use and Health reports that approximately 9 percent of Whites admitted to using illicit drugs (in the previous month). For Blacks the percentage for illicit drug use in a large metropolitan area was 10 percent; for Asians it was 3 percent; and for Hispanics, 7.2 percent. The group with the highest figure, 11.2 percent, was American Indians. Although the percentage for Whites is relatively low (given their numbers in the overall population), in actual numbers, there are many more Whites who use drugs than American Indians or Blacks.[7]

A look at the racial impact of the cocaine laws provides even further evidence of racial disparity. Studies indicate that two-thirds of all crack-cocaine users are White or Hispanic. Blacks, however, are most likely to be crack-cocaine defendants. In 2005, 82 percent of all crack-cocaine defendants were Black, 8.2 percent were White, and 8 percent were Hispanic. This racial disparity continues in sentencing. Not only do Blacks have a 20 percent greater chance of receiving a prison sentence than Whites; they also are more likely to serve a longer sentence than Whites.[8] These racial disparities illustrate one of the problems with current measures of racial discrimination in the criminal justice system.

The U.S. Supreme Court's decision in *United States v. Armstrong* highlights how certain kinds of race discrimination can elude traditional checks and balances.[9] In the 1996 case, the Los Angeles federal public defender's office argued that the U.S. Attorney's office was selectively prosecuting Black defendants under the federal crack-cocaine statute. The public defender's office, noting that the penalty for a crack conviction is much harsher under federal law than under California law, argued that Black offenders were being targeted for federal court. Under the mandatory federal crack law, a conviction for the sale of crack cocaine was punished one hundred times more severely than the conviction for the sale of powder cocaine (5 grams of crack resulted in a five-year prison term, whereas it took 500 grams of powder to result in a five-year prison term). In 1991, all twenty-four of the Los Angeles federal crack cases handled by the public defender's office involved Black defendants. The public defender's office requested records from the prosecutor's office reporting how many Whites and Blacks had been prosecuted in state court. The U.S. Attorney's office was also asked to state its criteria for deciding whether to prosecute a case in federal court. The public defender sought to establish that White crack offenders were being prosecuted in state court because the penalties were less harsh.

The Court held that the defense would have to offer some minimal proof of racial discrimination *before* the prosecution could be legally required to turn over its case records. Not surprisingly, without the records from the prosecutor's office, the public defender's office was unable to meet this legal burden. The *Armstrong* decision does not mean that the U.S. Attorney's office is not selectively prosecuting Blacks in federal court. Rather, it means that the prosecutor can withhold evidence of it.

The Court's decision is just one example of a legal roadblock that makes it difficult to measure race discrimination in the criminal justice system. The legal reasoning indicates that forms of discrimination that are difficult to measure may escape penalty. *Armstrong* symbolizes the legal barriers to identifying race discrimination in the criminal justice system, but empirical barriers also exist.

This brings us to the fourth criticism of the racial disparity research: that researchers have failed to expand their examination of racial discrimination to include nontraditional measures. Researchers, in their attempt to measure race discrimination, usually confine their analyses to the formal stages of the criminal justice system. Formal stages are those that are subject to criminal justice record keeping, such as arrest, bail, sentencing, and parole.

Petit Apartheid. Criminologist Daniel Georges-Abeyie observes that mainstream measures of racial bias begin with arrest. He notes, however, that there are numerous opportunities for racial bias to occur prior to arrest. One example is the point at which a police officer decides whether to make a traffic stop. Georges-Abeyie argues that unmeasured stages, such as prearrest actions by law enforcement, have causal consequences. They signal a gateway for entry into the justice system. He uses the term "petit apartheid" to describe race-affected practices that are not included within mainstream analyses of racial bias.[10]

Beyond prearrest, petit apartheid encompasses trial court processes, including decisions made during bench conferences, during jury deliberations, and in judges' chambers. This would include a look at the use of race in courtroom language, for instance, an examination of how the terms "black" and "white" are used in closing arguments by prosecutors —for example, as implicit and explicit references to guilt and innocence.[11] An analysis of petit apartheid opens the door to the "backstages" of the criminal justice system.[12] This sheds light on previously closed processes and allows us to see *how* race matters in criminal law.

Postconviction racial bias is yet another large area of bias that until recently was barely discussed in the mainstream research. The Innocence Project, founded in 1992, assists prisoners who seek to prove their innocence through DNA testing. Through the work of The Innocence Project, more than two hundred people have been exonerated after DNA tests revealed their innocence. Of these, fifteen had served time on death row, 60 percent were African American, 28 percent were White, and less than 10 percent were Latino.[13] The bottom line of Georges-Abeyie's analysis is that an analysis of the informal phases of the criminal justice system would reveal a stark pattern in which people of color consistently and unfairly receive harsher treatment from legal officials (e.g., police and judges) than Whites receive.[14]

A thorough assessment of race effects within the justice system requires that we focus on the bookends of the justice system—that is, racial profiling and postconviction—as well as those stages that have been ignored in earlier research. Only then can we purport to have a more accurate picture of our court system's racial viability. The next section examines how police treat Black men prior to arrest. The discussion shows how this informal stage should be measured and the social, economic, and criminal justice consequences of failing to measure it.

Black Men and the Police

As a group, Black men have an endless supply of stories of police harassment. These include being mistaken for a criminal, being treated like a criminal, being publicly humiliated, and in some instances, being called derogatory names. Often their encounters with the police arise from being stopped in their cars. They are subject to vehicle stops for a variety of reasons, some legal, some not:

- Driving a luxury automobile
- Driving an old car
- Driving in a car with other Black men
- Driving in a car with a White woman
- Driving early in the morning
- Driving late at night
- Driving a rented automobile
- Driving too fast
- Driving too slow
- Driving in a low-income neighborhood known for its drug traffic
- Driving in a White neighborhood
- Driving in an area where there have been recent burglaries

- Fitting the profile of a drug courier
- Violating the vehicle code (e.g., failure to signal, excessive speed, exposed tail light)

It seems that no matter what Black men do in their cars, they are targets for criminal suspicion. It is so commonplace for Black men to be pulled over in their vehicles that this practice has acquired its own acronym: DWB (Driving While Black).

Police harassment comes in many forms. One example is the number of times Black men are stopped, questioned, and assaulted by police as they go about their daily lives. Racial harassment is often a fact of life for Blacks. "Living While Black" has taken many forms, some mere inconveniences, some troubling, and others deadly. There are numerous cases involving Blacks who have faced police force while they were walking, standing in a vestibule, shopping, running, or sitting in an idling vehicle.

There are, however, clear distinctions between police harassment and police brutality. Police brutality typically refers to the unlawful use of excessive force. Harassment covers a range of police actions, some lawful, some unlawful (e.g., conducting a stop on less-than-legal cause). For many Black men, consistently negative encounters with the police have caused the line between harassment and brutality to become blurred. For Black men, who are more likely to be stopped by the police than anyone else, each stop has the potential for police brutality. The frequency of contact between Black men and the police has led a generation of Black men to teach their sons "The Lesson": instructions on how to handle a police stop without getting hurt.[15] Studies attest to many black men's general fear of and loathing for the police.[16] Professor Jerome McCristal Culp Jr. has called this "the rules of engagement of black malehood." According to Culp, these rules, taught to Black males over five years old, instruct that "at all times we [Black men] make no quick moves, remove any possibility of danger and never give offense to official power."[17] Professor David Troutt offers "the law of mothers" to describe how Black women warn and worry about their Black sons' encounters with police.[18]

Many Black men have developed protective mechanisms either to avoid vehicle stops by police or to minimize the potential for harm during these stops. The primary shield they use is an altered public persona. This includes a range of adaptive behaviors, like sitting erect while driving, traveling at the precise posted speed limit, avoiding certain neighborhoods, not wearing certain head gear (e.g., a baseball cap), and avoiding flashy cars. Vanity tags denoting professional status are another preemptive strike, though they are available to only a select few (e.g., "M.D." or "ESQ"). Of course, vanity tags can work as both a magnet and a deterrent for a police stop. Black men are used to structuring their encounters with police during car stops: placing both hands on the steering wheel, responding to an officer's questions with "sir" or "ma'am," and quite creatively, keeping the car radio tuned to a "non-Black" music station (e.g., classical or country). Black men are wise to take measures like these because studies consistently show that a suspect's demeanor affects whether he will be arrested.[19]

Groups' differing experiences with law enforcement and perceptions of those experiences may explain why impressions of the legitimacy and trustworthiness of police treatment vary by race. This is particularly true regarding public views of racial profiling. Studies indicate that one's perceptions about racial bias by police are affected by personal experience and by one's race. For instance, Blacks are more likely to believe that they receive harsher treatment at the hands of police, are more likely to be critical of police, and are more likely to believe that profiling is widespread.[20]

In addition to the experiences of the larger Black citizenry, Black police officers present an interesting twist on the issue of police abuse. They too have stories of abuse and harassment at the hands of other police officers (of all races). Out of uniform they are Black, not blue. The long list of cases involving Black undercover officers who have been mistaken for criminals by White officers illustrates this point.

Black distrust of the justice system is not new. It is historically rooted in the role that police played in enforcing the slave codes, Black codes, Jim Crow segregation, and the ultimate form of vigilante justice, lynching. In his treatise on race in America, Gunnar Myrdal reported that between 1920 and 1932, White police officers were responsible for more than half of all the murders of Black citizens.[21] Historical accounts also show that White policemen were often present at lynchings. Today, police brutality barely resembles its past forms. Many Blacks alive today, however, still remember the widespread, persistent, and inhumane abuse that Blacks suffered at the hands of police.

Further, it has been only within the past half century that Blacks have been allowed to police White communities on a wide scale. Into the 1960s, Black officers were viewed as second class and assigned to patrol only Black communities. "Separate but equal" meant that Black officers could not arrest White suspects. Police racial segregation was practiced in most large cities, including Miami and Houston. A large percentage of the people alive today were alive during a time when Black officers were *de facto* barred from policing White communities. For most Blacks, police oppression is far from a distant memory. A consideration of this history helps to explain why Black skepticism and disdain for police is a continuing phenomenon.

The Police at Work

The number of famous Black men who report that they have been unfairly stopped and harassed by law enforcement offers one measure of the prevalence of police abuse. These men, allegedly immune from such discriminatory treatment, offer a high-beam spotlight on police practices. A wide range of Black male celebrities have had encounters with the police, including athletes (Marcus Allen, Dee Brown, Tony Dungy, Joe Morgan, Edwin Moses, Brian Taylor, Al Joyner, and Jamaal Wilkes); educators (Cornel West, Michael Eric Dyson, William Julius Wilson, and Roger Wilkins); businessmen (Earl Graves Jr.); attorneys (Johnnie Cochran and Christopher Darden); actors (Don Cheadle, LeVar Burton, Blair Underwood, Reginald Dorsey, Will Smith, Tico Wells, and Wesley Snipes); journalists (Michael Wilbon); authors (Walter Mosley); and musicians (Wynton Marsalis). Legendary trumpeter Miles Davis had a unique method for handling police harassment. To avoid being stopped and questioned by police, Davis would call and notify the Beverly Hills police department *before* leaving his home.

Mae Jemison, the first Black female astronaut, had a remarkable run-in with police in her hometown, Nassau Bay, Texas. The officer informed Jemison that she had made an illegal turn. After the officer discovered that Jemison had an outstanding traffic ticket, Jemison was arrested and handcuffed, and her head was pushed face-down onto the pavement. She was also forced to remove her shoes and walk barefoot from the patrol car into the police station. After her release, Jemison filed a police-brutality complaint against the White officer. He was cleared following an internal department investigation. The fact that at the time of the incident Jemison wore a close-cropped afro has caused some people to speculate that she was initially stopped because the officer mistook her for a Black man.

In too many cases, however, the encounters between Black men and the police have gone far beyond a minor inconvenience. In 2006, twenty-three-year-old Sean Bell was gunned down by police outside a Brooklyn nightclub. Bell was at the club with friends celebrating his wedding, which was to take place later that day. Undercover officers shot at Bell and his passengers fifty times, as he pulled his car out of a parking spot. The police said that they thought he or one of his friends had been involved in an altercation at the club. Three officers were acquitted of criminal charges related to Bell's death.

In 2006, based on an informant's tip of drug activity, undercover police outside Atlanta approached the home of Kathryn Johnston, an eighty-eight-year-old grandmother. When they arrived to execute the search warrant, the police announced themselves, then broke down Johnston's front door. Johnston, who was alone in her home, responded by shooting her gun. Police returned fire, and Johnston was killed.

In 1999, Amadou Diallo was shot by undercover New York officers as he stood in the vestibule of his apartment building. Police believed that he was the rape suspect for whom they were searching. When Diallo, a Guinean immigrant, was ordered to halt, he held up his wallet. The police mistook this for a gun and shot at him forty-one times. The four officers charged with murder were acquitted.[22]

These are just a few of the more well-known cases involving innocent people who were involved in deadly encounters with the police. Notably, each of these cases involved undercover law enforcement officers. Although the value of undercover law enforcement is well known, it is worth considering what a reasonable citizen's response is to an approach by what appears to be a stranger or group of strangers, at night in a high-crime area. For instance, what might have run through Sean Bell's mind when he saw an unknown man approach his car with a gun: carjacker, thief, troublemaker, drunk, police officer?

In recent decades, there have been numerous other national cases of police brutality. The list includes Arthur Colbert, Patrick Dorismond, Joseph Gould, Malice Green, Don Jackson, Donavan Jackson, Rodney King, Abner Louima, Arthur McDuffie, Desmond Robinson, Brian Rooney, and Ron Settles.[23] Notably, two of these cases, those of Don Jackson and Desmond Robinson, involved Black off-duty police officers who were assaulted by another officer.

Jackson's case is particularly compelling because he went undercover to expose the racism of the Long Beach, California, police department. Jackson invited a television news crew to videotape his drive through a high-crime area. He and another man traveled through the area at the posted speed. They were pulled over by two White officers and told that their car had been weaving in traffic. Jackson politely questioned the basis of the stop but did nothing to escalate the encounter. After Jackson stepped out of the vehicle, one of the police officers bashed his head and arm through a plate-glass window. Jackson was ultimately charged with resisting arrest. The videotape of the incident called into question the statements made by the officers in their case report. Both officers were charged with use of excessive force and filing a false police report.

Is each of these an exceptional case? After all, most police officers, regardless of race, carry out their professional duties without resorting to racial harassment, abuse, or brutality. Some people suggest that most officers do not violate the law and that, therefore, police abuse is not a serious problem. The fallacy of this claim is made clear by applying it to another context. In most years, a fraction of the total population is arrested for criminal activity. We do not ignore the small fraction of law violators. By the same logic, we should not ignore the small fraction of police who abuse and mistreat citizens. Just as it is worthwhile to study offenders, it is worthwhile to study law enforcement officials who discriminate against Black citizens.

Legalized Racial Profiling?

The "out-of-place" doctrine gives police a legal support for stopping and questioning Blacks at a disproportionate rate. It allows police to use a person's race as a factor in making a stop when someone is in an area where another race predominates. A number of courts have upheld the doctrine as a useful police practice to stem crime. The doctrine arguably encourages police to view Black men as *de facto* guilty, without regard to legal indicators of criminal activity (e.g., reckless driving, speeding, making a drug sale). It permits Blacks to be stopped at a disproportionate rate since there are far more White neighborhoods than Black neighborhoods. This practice also supports and perhaps encourages racial segregation—people should stay with "their own kind." We can only speculate as to the toll— spiritual, psychological, and physical—exacted on a group whose freedom of movement is consistently challenged.

In 1996, the U.S. Supreme Court addressed the issue of pretextual vehicle stops. In *Whren v. United States,* the Court was asked to decide whether it is constitutional for the police to use a minor traffic violation to stop a driver whom they suspect of criminal activity.[24] Michael Whren and another Black man, James Brown, were stopped in a "high drug area" in Washington, D.C. The undercover officers became suspicious of drug activity after observing Brown pause at a stop sign for more than thirty seconds, fail to use his turn signal, and take off at a high speed. One of the officers saw Brown looking in the direction of passenger Whren's lap. At this point, the officers had probable cause to believe that there had been a violation of the vehicle code. After they pulled the car over, drugs were found, and the two men were arrested.

In a unanimous decision, the Court held that as long as a traffic stop is based on probable cause, the stop is valid. The individual officer's motive for the stop is irrelevant. In this case a traffic law had been violated, thus establishing probable cause. Obviously Brown violated the traffic code. However, because the police do not stop most people who engage in the same conduct, the question arises whether Brown was stopped because he was Black. The direct and indirect experiences that Blacks have with the police affect their perception that the criminal justice system is skewed against them. Court decisions such as *Whren* bolster this viewpoint. A complete assessment of the role that race plays in police stops requires the scrutiny of the actions of Black men *and* the actions of the police— and an assessment of reasonable response by motorists when they are un- knowingly approached by undercover officers.

Many people would argue that it is unfair to blame the police for be- ing suspicious of Black men. After all, Black men are disproportionately engaged in crime. It is reasonable, then, that the police disproportionately suspect them of criminal activity. Black men do commit street crimes at high rates, rates far exceeding their percentage in the U.S. population (6 percent). The important question, however, is, Are Black men stopped and questioned by the police at a rate that greatly exceeds their rate of street crime? If so, the high number of police stops cannot be legally justified.

The available research suggests that Black men are stopped and ques- tioned at a rate much higher than the level of their involvement in crime. The few studies on this issue indicate that Black men are significantly more likely to be stopped than anyone else, at a rate far above their rate of arrest. One way to determine the disparity is to compare the rate of police stops for Black men with the rate of Black men who are involved in criminal activity. For example, assuming that one-third of all young Black men are involved in crime, we would predict that about one-third of them would be subject to police stops.

Estimates are that anywhere from *one-third to one-half* of all Black men believe they have been unfairly stopped by the police.[25] Statistically, Black men comprise less than 7 percent of the population. Young Black men, between the ages of fifteen and forty, account for approximately 3 percent of the population. What accounts for this group's high encounter rate with police? Black men should be subject to police stops to a degree that more closely approximates their rate of offending.

The Big Picture

Police-Public Contact Survey. Since 1999, the Bureau of Justice Statistics has gathered annual data on contacts between the police and citizens. According to the 2005 study, White, Black, and Hispanic drivers were stopped by the police at similar rates (between 8 and 9 percent). However, Blacks (9.5 percent) and Hispanics (9 percent) were searched by the police at a rate three times that of Whites (3.6 percent). Overall, the figures show that 20 percent of Whites had contact with the police, compared with 16.5 percent of Blacks and 16 percent of Hispanics. Thus, Whites are underrepresented in contacts with police, while the contact rates for Blacks and Hispanics approximates their percentage in the overall population. What happens after the stop is noteworthy. Black drivers are twice as likely to be arrested as Whites (4.5 percent versus 2.1 percent). For Hispanics the figure is 3.1 percent. Hispanics are more likely to be ticketed than are Blacks or Whites, and Whites are more likely to be issued a verbal or written warning than are Blacks or Hispanics.[26]

Traffic Stops Statistics Study Act and Other Data. Each year since 1997, Congressman John Conyers has introduced the Traffic Stops Statistics Study Act.[27] The bill would direct the attorney general to gather statistics on all routine traffic stops made by law enforcement officials, including data on the number of traffic stops, identifying characteristics of the persons who were stopped (e.g., gender, race, age), reason for the stop, whether contraband was found, and whether an arrest was made. Data gathered under this bill would not reveal police or citizen identities, and statistics would be gathered directly from law enforcement officials (see appendix A).

Studies of racial profiling extend far beyond police stops. In 2000, the General Accounting Office (now called the Government Accountability

Office) released a report that reviewed the practices of the U.S. Customs Service. The study was conducted in response to numerous claims that customs officials were harassing Black female travelers. The study found that 95 percent of the passengers who were stopped were subjected to a frisk search, of whom 4 percent were strip-searched and 1 percent were subjected to x-ray screening. Black women were the group most likely to be profiled as drug couriers and searched; they were searched at a rate higher than the rate for Black men. Being stopped for "traveling while Black" was even more pronounced for Black women who were U.S. citizens. They were nine times more likely than White women to be x-rayed following a frisk search. Notably, these high search rates for Black women are not explained by the find rates: Black women were less than half as likely to be found carrying contraband as White women.[28]

Lawsuits. Since the 1990s, a number of law enforcement agencies have been charged with racial profiling. *Wilkins v. Maryland* was a watershed racial profiling case. It was perhaps the earliest and best-known of the cases in the latest era of racial profiling litigation. In 1992, Maryland State police pulled over a vehicle on Interstate 68 in Cumberland, Maryland. Police said they stopped the vehicle because it matched a drug-courier profile (a law enforcement list of characteristics of someone believed to be likely engaged in transporting drugs within or across state lines). One passenger was Robert Wilkins, who at the time was a Washington, D.C., lawyer. Wilkins told the officer that he and his family were returning from a funeral in Chicago and that he had to make an early morning court appearance in D.C. The officer ordered everyone out of the car. Wilkins politely yet sternly objected. He questioned the basis for probable cause. Without answering, the officer informed the family that they would be detained until they exited the vehicle. Eventually they got out of the car, and a narcotics dog searched their vehicle. No drugs were found. Forty-five minutes after they had been pulled over and after a $105 speeding ticket had been issued to the driver, the family was released.

The American Civil Liberties Union, which represented the Wilkins family, discovered evidence of a race-based policy in effect for the Maryland troopers. The policy was enacted to stem the entry of drugs into western Maryland. A confidential police memorandum referenced the increasing drug problem in the area and offered the following description of drug importers: "The dealers and couriers are predominantly black males and black females."[29] The implicit message was that the troopers would get the biggest bang for their buck by targeting Black drivers. The memo did not mention other racial groups. The signal to the police officers was clear: because Blacks are responsible for much of the area's drug influx, they can be justifiably stopped, questioned, and searched. The race-based directive was problematic because it encouraged the police to suspect all Black drivers. Because "predominantly" is a vague term, each officer was allowed to have wide-ranging suspicion of Black motorists, depending on his subjective interpretation of the term. "Predominantly" could mean that Blacks were responsible for anywhere between 51 and 99 percent of the drug imports. No evidence was offered to show that Black motorists are more likely to violate traffic laws or are substantially more likely to transport drugs through the interstate. The Wilkins case was settled for just under one hundred thousand dollars.

As part of the settlement, the Maryland State Police were instructed to maintain computer records of all motorist stops over a three-year period. In 1995, Maryland troopers conducted 533 searches along the Interstate 95 corridor (a fifty-mile stretch of highway extending from Baltimore to the Delaware border). Of the searches conducted by Maryland troopers, 77 percent (409) involved vehicles driven by Black motorists, 18 percent involved White drivers, and 1 percent involved Hispanic drivers (table 4.2). Drugs were found on 33 percent of the Black motorists who were stopped and 22 percent of the White motorists.

Table 4.3 provides a breakdown of Maryland trooper searches by the Special Traffic Interdiction Force (STIF) unit. This enforcement team was formed to intercept interstate drug transport. In 1995, STIF troopers, all White, conducted a total of 202 searches, 76 percent of which (153) involved Black motorists. For five of the six STIF troopers, they were most likely to stop a car driven by Black motorists and conduct a search. STIF unit members searched Black motorists at rates ranging from 40 percent of all stops (Officer 5) to 100 percent of all stops (Officer 6) (table 4.3).[30] STIF troopers found drugs in 34 percent of the searches involving Black

TABLE 4.2
Maryland State Police Data, I-95 Stops, 1995

I-95 Stops	Black	White	Hispanic	Other	Total
Number	409	97	20	7	533
Contraband found	33%	22%	10%	42%	—

Source: ACLU of Maryland.

TABLE 4.3
Maryland State Police, Individual Trooper Stops,
Special Target Interdiction Force, I-95 Stops, 1995

	Total Stops	% Black	% White	% Hispanic
Officer 1	38	84	13	0
Officer 2	55	87	11	2
Officer 3	44	64	23	4
Officer 4	30	93	7	0
Officer 5	30	40	47	10
Officer 6	5	100	0	0

motorists and 13.5 percent of those involving White motorists. No drugs were found in their searches involving Hispanic motorists.

It is unclear why the Maryland State Police stopped Black motorists so frequently. As noted, no studies indicate that there are more Black motorists driving on the interstate, and there is no evidence that Blacks are responsible for more than one-half of interstate crimes or interstate trafficking. One study done at the time showed that along I-95 Blacks account for approximately 17 percent of the motorists and 17.5 percent of traffic-law violators. Notably, even after the settlement in the Wilkins case, with knowledge that their stops were being monitored, STIF troopers continued to stop and search Black motorists at a disproportionately high rate (more than 70 percent).

As a direct result of racial profiling lawsuits, a number of jurisdictions collect and report data on police-citizen interactions. In the wake of Amadou Diallo's death, the New York Police Department (NYPD) was required to compile a quarterly report of police stops. According to the 2006 stop-and-frisk report, 86 percent of the people who were stopped by police were Black (52 percent) or Latino (33.6 percent). Notably, only 10 percent of these stops resulted in arrests or issuance of a summons. Whites accounted for 12 percent of the stops, and Asian Americans and American Indians accounted for less than 1 percent each.

Racial profiling lawsuits provided limited insight into the prevalence of profiling. Justice Department figures on the number of lawsuits it brings against police departments represent only a fraction of the total number of police abuse and brutality incidents. The lack of national statistics has forced researchers to rely on a range of other indicators, including newspaper reports of police abuse, the number of judgments entered against police departments (civil and criminal), the number of police departments under investigation for corruption, and the number of brutality complaints filed against police departments.

Conclusion: A Costly Enterprise

Numerous costs are associated with race-related police abuse. Blacks individually and as a community are psychologically harmed. Each case of police abuse or police harassment involves an individual officer and an individual citizen, but the cases do not exist in isolation. For example, one Black man's painful encounter with the police is negatively reinforced when he learns that other Black men have had similar experiences with the police. The impact of police harassment is cumulative. Each negative experience creates another building block in the Black folklore about police.

It is unreasonable to expect that the net of the criminal justice system will capture only the guilty. We would expect that *some* Blacks who are not involved in crime would be mistakenly suspected of criminal activity. It is not reasonable, however, to expect that close to half of all Black men believe they have been wrongly suspected of criminal activity when less than one-third are involved in criminal activity. To more fully explore this issue, research on racial disparity must be expanded to include analyses of prearrest police contacts.

Police practices that allow law enforcement officials to act on negative Black stereotypes will continue to expand the gap between Black and White experiences and perceptions of police. For Blacks, race-based policies raise questions about the legitimacy of the police and further alienate them from the criminal justice system. Robert Wilkins, the successful plaintiff in the Maryland State Police case observed, "[There] is no compensation for the type of humiliation and degradation you feel when for no other reason than the color of your skin . . . you're charged and placed in a category of drug trafficker."[31]

Citizens who do not face the daily threat of being detained largely because of their race are unable to appreciate just how burdensome these stops can be: they become a heavy weight. To someone who is pulled over by the police once a month for no apparent reason other than his race, the stops take on an onerous feel. Race-based policies pit law enforcement against minorities and create an unbreakable cycle. Racial stereotypes may motivate police to arrest Blacks more frequently, but the fact that

Black men are disproportionately engaged in crime is not a justification for racial discrimination. High rates of Black arrests generate statistically disparate arrest patterns, which in turn form the basis for further police selectivity by race. What many Whites view as the police "doing their job" is viewed by many Blacks as harassment.

Beyond causing harm to Black men, race-based police stops also harm the larger society. There is the societal cost of perpetuating inaccurate stereotypes, which produces exaggerated levels of fear and more-pronounced levels of scapegoating—such as racial hoaxes (detailed in chapter 5). Although Blacks are responsible for a disproportionate share of crime, they are not responsible for the majority of crime.

Police harassment of Black men operates as a denial of their civil rights. Jerome McCristal Culp explains:

> [T]he police and citizens have to figure out ways to allow me to have rights as a black male too. Every time there is a conflict between the rights of the majority and my rights as a stereotypical black male, my rights cannot always be subordinate, or else I have no rights at all.[32]

Treating Whites as if their constitutional rights are worth more has negative long-term consequences. Law enforcement is legitimately concerned with crime by Blacks. The strategies it employs, however, should not end up causing greater racial damage, such as increased crime.

Racial targeting and abuse by police is costly. U.S. taxpayers have paid tens of millions of dollars in police-brutality lawsuits. Many of the nation's cities are in need of greater police services. The huge sums of money paid out in legal damages should instead be available to protect and serve the people. Police abuse, harassment, and brutality exact a tremendous social and financial toll on society.

Many Blacks believe that their antipolice sentiments are justified by the racially discriminatory practices of the police. Particularly for young Black men, the police represent public enemy number one. Dismissing the problem of excessive targeting of Black men hampers our efforts to reduce crime and reinforces the perception that "the police don't like Black people."[33] For example, the perception that Black men are unfairly targeted by the police may make some Black jurors less likely to believe police testimony. It may also make some Blacks less likely to report crime and others less likely to cooperate with police investigations. Perhaps the issue of police abuse is downplayed because national data are not available. Also, the issue of disproportionality has blurred many people's ability to see the problem of racial discrimination. The reality of racial targeting can be dismissed, rejected, or trivialized. However, the problem is a real one and imposes enormous costs, both social and financial, on the effective working of the criminal justice system.

5

Are We *Still* Talking about O. J.?

POSTACQUITTAL CONVERSATION

White woman: How can you say you agree with the verdict when you believe
O. J. killed them? Anyway, the case wasn't about race.
Black woman: There was reasonable doubt. Race matters.
White woman: The jury's verdict makes a mockery of the justice system.
Black woman: Why are you so upset about this case? You weren't this upset
after the officers who beat Rodney King were acquitted.
White woman: Those cases are totally different. Isn't domestic violence im-
portant to you?
Black woman: Of course I care about domestic violence. Are you saying that
if I agree with the verdict that I'm for domestic violence?
White woman: I give up!

This exchange is based on an actual conversation between the author and
a White female friend. The dialogue offers a glimpse of the racial tensions
that surfaced during the O. J. Simpson case. Though many years have
passed since Simpson was found not guilty of murdering his ex-wife, Nicole Simpson, and her friend, Ronald Goldman, the case still resonates
and remains unsettling to many people. Polls taken in 2007 indicate that
more Whites believe Simpson committed the murders (74 percent) than
did at the time of the criminal trial (72 percent). Notably twice as many
Blacks (60 percent) indicate that they believe Simpson is guilty than did
during the criminal trial (30 percent).[1] However, Blacks continue to believe that the there are two justice systems, one for Whites and another
for Blacks. This shift in opinion may be the result of other incidents involving Simpson, including a much-publicized Las Vegas arrest for armed
robbery of his sports memorabilia and his plan to publish a book titled
If I Did It, a hypothetical account of how he might have committed the
murders of his wife and her friend.

The Simpson case had all the requisite elements for a classic courtroom drama: race, interracial sex, class, celebrity, violence, a handsome, rich, and athletic defendant, attractive victims, unpredictable witnesses, odd-ball jurors, and larger-than-life attorneys—all with a Hollywood back-drop. Simply put, the case pushed all our social hot buttons.

The O. J. Simpson case is one for the history books. It was a months-long spectacle, one that millions of people watched unfold in their living rooms. It was high racial drama. This chapter offers a sociological capsule of the case—what happened, what it means, what it says about our society, and why the case still matters today. This chapter poses new questions about the Simpson case, focusing primarily on the criminal case and its aftermath. The discussion of "Black protectionism" looks at the Black community's "strong love" for Simpson and other similarly situated defendants. The chapter concludes with an assessment of how the media's fixed gaze on the Black/White divide led to the exclusion of other racial groups.

A Look Back

The O. J. Simpson criminal case was a combination of time travel and science fiction. Unfortunately, as far as race relations go, the time travel was backward. The national narrative of the criminal case could not have been more fantasy-like than if it had been written by Edward Bellamy, Ray Bradbury, or Octavia Butler.

Public opinion appeared to vacillate between fascination and disgust during the eighteen-month saga. Throughout, the case was riveting, and even at its most disturbing it remained compelling. Everything about the Simpson case was writ large. It featured an ever-expanding cast of characters who were constantly reinvented.

For many people, the low-speed car chase was the first media visual of the case. After Simpson was identified as a murder suspect and had agreed on a date and time to surrender to police authorities, he fled. In a dramatic act of loyalty, his best friend, Al Cowlings, served as both the getaway driver and counselor to a suicidal O. J. The ensuing chase on the San Diego Freeway resembled a cavalcade for visiting dignitaries. Several police vehicles trailed Simpson and Cowlings, as scores of people lined up along the freeway. A few held up signs showing support for Simpson —one read "Go O. J. Go!"

Simpson's suicide note was read during the chase. The letter sounded like a cross between an acceptance speech and a high school yearbook signing. In it, Simpson thanked several people, including former football teammates and golfing buddies. He also thanked his first wife, Marguerite: "thanks for the early years. We had some fun."[2] The bizarre, handwritten note ended with Simpson placing a smiley face inside the O of his signature. Ironically, the chase, which signified the Heisman Trophy winner's downward spiral, happened at the same time that the two top-rated NBA teams fought for their sport's highest honor.

The criminal trial continued the spectacle. One notable highlight was White defense attorney F. Lee Bailey's repeated use of "nigger" during his cross-examination of Los Angeles police officer Mark Fuhrman. Witnesses and others affiliated with the case were cast and recast into new roles. One witness was said to have close ties to the Mafia. The court released a female juror when it learned that she was suicidal. Following this, the former juror posed nude for *Playboy*. By the end of the case, Fuhrman had practically become a poster child for the Ku Klux Klan, and Geraldo Rivera, known for putting sleaze TV on the map, had reincarnated himself into a serious legal analyst.

Everlasting O. J. The O. J. television drama created one of the most successful cottage industries ever. Dozens of books have been written about the case. Lawyers, jurors, ex-wives, ex-girlfriends, best friends, neighbors, victims' family members, police officers, journalists, and the defendant have written their own accounts. Several of these landed on the *New York Times* bestsellers list. Mark Fuhrman's book, *Murder in Brentwood*, reached the number-one spot. In a miraculously quick turnaround, Fuhrman, a convicted perjurer, managed, with the help of the press, to rehabilitate his image. Since the trial he has gone on to publish other bestsellers and is a Fox News analyst. Both of the lead prosecutors, Marcia Clark and Christopher Darden, wrote their own books. Personal affiliations were rewarded as well. Paula Barbieri, O. J.'s ex-girlfriend, published a tell-all book for a hefty sum.

By far the most unusual book to come out of the case was the one that was not published. More than a decade after the trial, Simpson and book publisher Judith Regan contracted to write a fictional narrative detailing how Simpson *would* have killed his ex-wife and her friend, if he had done it. The book, *If I Did It: Here's How It Happened*, was scheduled to be published in 2007. Once word got out about the unpublished book, it was instantly controversial and denounced as scandalous, morally offensive, and insensitive to the victims' families. The book was canceled, Regan was fired, and Simpson was ordered to repay the advance. In an odd turn of events, the family of Ronald Goldman requested and won the rights to the book. They had it repackaged and published.

The Simpson case became a television-marketing bonanza, which was used to both reinvigorate and launch careers. Both the criminal and civil trials created several cable-TV spin-offs including *Burden of Proof* (hosted by Greta Van Sustern and Roger Cossack), *The Charles Grodin Show, Gerry Spence,* and *Cochran & Company*. Rivera's show provided a daily analysis of the case. Not everyone was lucky enough to have his own television show. Others, such as Simpson's houseguest, Kato Kaelin, attempted to parlay their trial exposure into entertainment careers. Faye Resnick, Nicole Simpson's best friend, wrote a book about the case and, following the civil verdict, bared her body for *Playboy*.

Time, energy, and money spent discussing and dissecting the case were in evidence everywhere: the locker room, boardroom, street corner, talk radio, barbershop, bedroom, and grocery store. The criminal trial literally tapped each of our senses. Few could erase the sight of Denise Brown sobbing on the witness stand or O. J. sitting at the defense table staring blankly ahead. Most of us remember sounds from the trial, including the 911 call by a petrified Nicole Brown Simpson, the three "thumps" that Kato Kaelin heard the night of the murders, and the neighbor's recounting of the Simpson dog's "plaintive wail." Many people will remember almost feeling the black leather gloves that Simpson could not fit. Likewise, many will recall forensic chemist Greg Matheson's testimony, describing the smell of Ronald Goldman's blood-soaked clothing. Ultimately, the case left most of us with a sour taste in our mouths. The criminal case became a convenient springboard for airing our frustrations about race, class, gender, crime, courts, and the media. We may have learned more than we wanted to know about ourselves and the state of U.S. race relations. More than just arousing our curiosity, the Simpson case piqued our anxieties.

The Race Numbers Game. Before, during, and after the trial, an endless barrage of poll data indicated a wide gulf between Blacks and Whites. We were told that Blacks and Whites had mirror-opposite opinions about the case. Surveys consistently reported that 70 percent of Blacks believed Simpson was innocent, while 70 percent of Whites believed he was guilty. The opinion polls heightened tensions between Blacks and Whites because neither group was able to comprehend the other group's position. At some point, the bewilderment turned to anger. Whites were angry with Blacks for not recognizing that Simpson was obviously guilty. Blacks were angry at Whites for not understanding the race issues and not considering the possibility that Simpson might have been innocent and might have been set up. The result of this racial friction was a racial standoff between Blacks and Whites. Media reports on public opinion about the case only served to stoke the fire by failing to address several issues:

- One could agree with the verdict and believe that Simpson committed the murders.
- The voices on either side of the Black/White racial divide were not equal in number.
- In actual numbers, more Whites than Blacks thought Simpson was not guilty (see table 5.1).
- There were millions of Blacks and Whites who had similar views on the Simpson case (see table 5.1).
- A sizeable number of Blacks thought Simpson was guilty (see table 5.1).
- Economic status was rarely factored into media analyses of the role that race played in reactions to the case.

The media's crude depiction of the split between African Americans and Whites on the question of Simpson's guilt, implied that there was a group of Whites on one side with their opinions and an equal number of Blacks on the other side with opposing opinions. The media glossed over the fact that for every Black who thought Simpson was not guilty, there were six Whites who thought he was guilty. The power, and thus the volume, of the racial voices was not equal. Table 5.1 illustrates this point.

TABLE 5.1
Black/White Simpson Poll Data
(Extrapolating Poll Data into Actual Numbers)

	Believe Simpson Is Guilty	Believe Simpson Is Not Guilty
Black	10 million (30 percent of Blacks)	22 million (70 percent of Blacks)
White	139 million (70 percent of Whites)	60 million (30 percent of Whites)
Total	149 million	82 million

Note: These numbers are based on U.S. Census population estimates for 1996 (total U.S. population, 264 million, Whites 75 percent, Blacks about 12 percent).

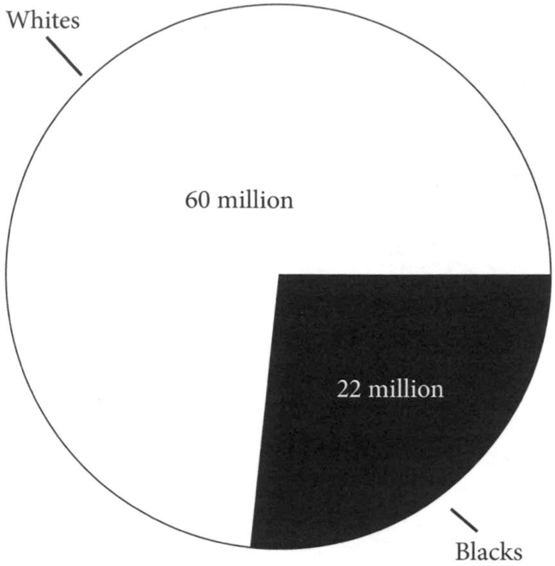

Fig. 5.1. Number of Whites and Blacks who believed
Simpson was not guilty

A conversion of poll figures to actual numbers indicates that there were
approximately 139 million Whites who believed Simpson was guilty, compared with approximately 22 million Blacks who believed he was innocent.
The dueling choirs of angry, exercised voices were not evenly matched. In
reality, the 70-30 split between Blacks and Whites indicates that, in actual
numbers, Blacks who believed in Simpson's innocence represented a small
fraction of public opinion (8 percent). The constant media focus on those
Blacks who thought Simpson was innocent aided in creating the image
that African Americans were a racial monolith—a slightly crazed and fa-
natical one.

In the midst of the hype associated with the racial fallout it was also
difficult to see that there were many Whites who believed that Simpson was innocent. In fact, they *outnumbered* the number of Blacks who
thought Simpson was innocent by a three-to-one margin. This indicates
that there were more Whites who agreed with the verdict than there were
Blacks who agreed with it. The postverdict split-television screen, which
showed Whites shocked and Blacks elated, could just as accurately have
been a split-screen with one side showing Whites who agreed with the

verdict and the other side showing Whites who disagreed with the verdict. As indicated in table 5.1, approximately sixty million Whites believed Simpson was not guilty, compared with twenty-two million Blacks.

The media's overemphasis on how differently Whites and Blacks viewed the criminal case also masked the fact that many Blacks believed Simpson was guilty. The surveys indicated that one-third of Blacks polled believed Simpson was guilty, representing approximately ten million Blacks (see table 5.1). It is understandable that the media focused on the majority Black viewpoint, but it is not acceptable that it practically ignored the perspectives of the other 30 percent. The opinions of the approximately ten million Blacks who thought Simpson had killed Nicole Brown Simpson and Ronald Goldman were effectively silenced. Although the media was frequently criticized for overreporting on the Simpson case, some aspects of the case received little attention. For example, we rarely heard from African Americans who thought Simpson was guilty.

Polls conducted after the criminal verdict did an abysmally poor job of drawing out racial viewpoints on the jury's decision. The media consensus was that most Blacks were pleased if not elated with the verdict. The untapped data might have revealed that many Blacks, though in accord with the verdict, thought that Simpson had committed the murders. The opinion polls appeared to confound factual guilt and legal guilt. Actually, one could believe that Simpson was guilty and believe that the prosecution did not prove its case. The superficial reporting about the racial implications of the verdict and its aftermath was not surprising, given how racial issues were handled throughout the criminal trial.

Black/White Simpson Poll Data

The media's insistence on using race to explain reactions to the verdict precluded an analysis of other important factors. Specifically, did class status affect one's viewpoints about the case? Some studies reported that people with high incomes were more likely to believe Simpson was guilty. Of people earning fifty thousand dollars or more per year, 65 percent believed that Simpson had committed the murders. Conversely, 41 percent of people making seventy-five hundred dollars or less per year believed he was not guilty.[3] Unfortunately, this poll did not report findings on the interaction between race and class—for example, whether high-income Blacks had a perspective on the case different from low-income Blacks. If there were national polls that examined the race-class relationship, they were not widely reported.

White Rage

The depth of the White community's outrage over the Simpson verdict was exemplified by its very public display of dissatisfaction with the verdict. It is hard to remember another time when Whites were so outdone-angry-disappointed with a court decision. The White response to the Supreme Court's decision in *Brown v. Board of Education,* which outlawed racial segregation in public education, comes to mind. The widespread outrage at the Simpson verdict was largely because millions of people were able to watch the trial unfold in their living rooms.

Whites have distanced themselves from the verdict by both turning it into a joke and by characterizing Black support of Simpson as irrational. Quips about Simpson's guilt and the jury's ignorance were regularly heard on late-night comedy shows including David Letterman, Jay Leno, Conan O'Brien, and Bill Maher. One of the more popular jokes that made the rounds after the acquittal was, "It's finally official, murder is legal in the state of California." Years later, jokes about the Simpson case persist.

White outrage also found a refuge on cable television. *Rivera Live* focused almost exclusively on the criminal trial. Geraldo Rivera, whose appetite for all things related to O. J. was unmatched, regularly shared his opinions about the case and his belief in Simpson's guilt. Referring to the racial gap in the polls, he stated, "*Even* educated African Americans I have known and loved for years are rooting for [Simpson]. People who are so objective and analytical on almost any other topic, including race, seem to me irrational on this one."[4] Rivera's comments crystallized much of the anti-Simpson sentiment. His surprise that "even" educated Blacks supported Simpson implies that only blind race loyalty could explain why an educated Black person could believe Simpson was innocent.

The Charles Grodin Show was another notable spectacle during the Simpson trial. Grodin, an actor, is best known for his work in movie comedies. For more than two years, a visibly restrained Grodin used his cable-TV platform to present minutes-long soliloquies on Simpson's guilt. A seated Grodin would stare directly into the camera and pontificate about O. J.'s culpability and philosophize about the death of innocence. Mainstream print journalism's response to the Simpson acquittal is captured by the July 1996 cover of the *Weekly Standard* magazine, which depicted a dark, sinister-looking caricature of O. J. The accompanying article, "Why He Still Haunts Us," begins, "Two years after murdering his ex-wife Nicole and Ronald Goldman . . ."[5] Another example of anti–O. J. expression is Vincent Bugliosi's boldly titled bestseller, *Outrage: Five Reasons Why O. J. Simpson Got Away with Murder.*

Before and after the verdict, the media continually mocked the idea that Simpson could be innocent, and it promoted the view that the jury's verdict in the criminal case was irrational. The outcome of the civil lawsuits, filed by the families of Ronald Goldman and Nicole Brown, provided another opportunity to express anti–O. J. sentiments. Sixteen months following the acquittal, a mostly White jury found Simpson civilly liable for the deaths of Nicole Simpson and Ronald Goldman. A $33.5 million judgment was entered against him ($8.5 million in compensatory damages and $25 million in punitive damages). Not surprisingly the "Black" (criminal) and "White" (civil) juries were compared with each other. For the most part, the criminal jury has been dismissed as biased and the civil jury heralded as objective. The routine bashing of the criminal verdict was partly because the public had more facts about the case than the jury.

The depth of White anger at Simpson, however, raises the issue of whether it is historically rooted. As discussed earlier (chapter 3), White fear and loathing of intimacy between Black men and White women is a historical fact. States adopted harsh penalties to deter and punish these sexual liaisons, including antimiscegenation laws and prohibitions against mixed-race cohabitation. Many people believe that the White hostility toward Simpson comes from longstanding fears of race mixing.

The mass anger and disgust at Simpson may not abate until he is either in prison or pushing a shopping cart and mumbling to himself. In the years since the acquittal, public sentiment appears unchanged. The majority of people still believe he is guilty. For many of them he symbolizes what is wrong with the justice system. In particular, the murder of Ronald Goldman has come to represent the fear that most Americans have of random acts of violence.

The 1991 beating of motorist Rodney King by Los Angeles police officers represented the deep-seated fear that many Blacks have: that "justice" will be dispensed at the mercy of racist, White police officers. Similarly the Simpson case crystallized White fears: fear of violent Black-on-White crime, fear of justice gone wild, and the overarching fear of the *criminalblackman.*

The public's reaction to the Simpson criminal case was unique in that the jurors were cast as both biased and ignorant. Some people suggested, only half jokingly, that IQ tests should be required for jurors serving on a criminal case. No similar suggestion was made following the acquittal in the first Rodney King/LAPD trial, in which a mostly White jury acquitted four White officers.

White fear may explain the wide-ranging reforms proposed in the wake of the criminal and civil verdicts, most aimed at diluting the power of criminal defense attorneys. Proposals included abolishing the unanimity requirement in criminal cases, limiting the number of defense attorneys, prohibiting jury sequestration, banning cameras from the courtroom, prohibiting jury consultants, and barring lawyers from using race-based appeals in closing arguments. Two weeks before the start of the civil case, the then California governor Pete Wilson signed legislation to allow personal diaries to be admitted as evidence in civil cases (this ensured that Nicole Simpson's diaries could be offered in the civil trial). On the heels of the civil verdict, California passed legislation to have child custody revoked in cases in which a parent has been found civilly liable for the wrongful death of the other parent.

Underlying the attacks on the O.J. jury was the belief that the nine Black jurors coerced or tricked the three non-Black jurors (two White and one Hispanic) to vote not guilty. After the criminal trial, one of the White female jurors stated that she would have voted for conviction had she been aware of some of the evidence not admitted into trial. She has never said, however, that she was forced to vote for acquittal. The implicit speculation is that the Black jurors (and the other jurors at their direction) engaged in "jury nullification," that they acquitted Simpson not based on the facts but because of his race.

Black Indignation

The anger and disillusionment that many Whites expressed after the acquittal was evenly matched by the anger and disillusionment that many Blacks experienced. Black indignation is partly explained by Black protectionism, discussed in the next section. Whites were angry because of the verdict—angry that a guilty man could go free. Whites became frustrated with a criminal justice system that failed in spite of compelling, overwhelming evidence. How could the jury acquit Simpson, with his lengthy record of domestic abuse and no airtight alibi? What about the DNA evidence? Conversely, many Blacks could not understand why Whites were so upset, and they became angry that so many Whites were so angry. After all, what about the tainted blood evidence, the absence of a murder weapon, and the improbability of one person carrying out the murders? Most important, what about Mark Fuhrman? On the infamous audiotapes, Fuhrman discussed beating, assaulting, and framing people, bragged about lying to police officials, and used slurs to describe minorities and women. He also boasted about his membership in a police group, Men Against Women.[6] Taking a broad view, why did Whites feel so passionately about this case and not other cases (particularly those involving Black victims)?

Following the acquittal, there appears to have been a media "blackout," which forced Simpson to cancel public appearances. In one instance he had planned to attend a card-trading show, and in another he had scheduled an interview with Katie Couric (on NBC). Both were canceled after there were numerous complaints and threats of boycott.

For many Blacks, White outrage at the Simpson verdict was inexplicable when contrasted with White reaction to an acquittal in another criminal case, the Rodney King/LAPD criminal trial. In the wake of the acquittal of the LAPD officers, journalist William Raspberry wrote an editorial titled "Where's the Outrage from White America?" Raspberry said, "I'm waiting for responsible white leaders to tell me that [the] incomprehensible verdict outrages them as much as it outrages us."[7] Clearly, a case involving two brutal murders is not the same as one involving a billy-club beating. Polls taken after the King verdict indicated that most Whites believed the police defendants were guilty of using excessive force. Why, then, were Whites so quiet, relatively speaking, about the acquittal involving the officers who beat King but so outspoken regarding the Simpson acquittal?

Transcendental O. J., Other "Colorless" Black Men, and Black Protectionism

Many Whites and some Blacks were puzzled by the widespread, steadfast support that Simpson received from much of the Black community. How is it that Simpson, who many said "is not really Black," came to represent Blackness? Many commentators observed that long before 1994 not only had Simpson divorced his Black first wife; he had divorced himself from the Black community. Black protectionism explains the "strong love" for O. J. evinced by so many African Americans.

The term "Black protectionism" is used to describe what happens when the credentials, past history, or behavior of a well-known, successful Black person is called into question.[8] In these instances, the Black community's reaction is protective, almost maternal. The Black community builds a fortress around its fallen hero and begins to offer explanations and defenses. Whenever colorless Blacks fall into national disgrace and scandal, they are picked up and brushed off by the Black community. Like a good wife, Black people "stand by their man."

A growing number of Blacks have achieved megasuccess. There is, however, a relatively small group of highly visible, rich Blacks. In recent decades several Blacks have risen to national prominence as politicians, superstar athletes and entertainers, and military heroes. The Black middle class has also grown. The relative newness of Black megasuccess and achievement may partially explain Black protectionism. The next section examines the historical roots of Black protectionism, the rationales for it, to whom it applies, and how it works.

O. J. and the Roots of Black Protectionism. Many African Americans who have achieved wide-scale, mainstream success have "crossed over": like Clarence Thomas, Oprah Winfrey, Tiger Woods, Barack Obama, and Bill Cosby, O. J. Simpson had been accepted into polite White society. Simpson no longer belonged solely to Black people: he had transcended his race. How exactly is crossover status achieved? The seminal crossover indicator is that someone Black is embraced by a large, visible sector of the White community. By itself, being popular with Whites and Blacks is not enough to complete the crossover transformation.

Crossing over requires that the Black person take an affirmative step toward "color-free" status, such as proclaiming that he is colorless or declining to attach significance to being Black. O. J.'s colorless aspirations are reflected in his following remarks:

> I was at a wedding, my [first] wife and a few friends were the only Negroes there, and I overheard a lady at the next table say, "Look, there's O. J. Simpson and some niggers." Isn't that weird? That sort of thing hurts me, even though it's what I strive for, to be a man first.[9]

Claims of colorlessness and other dismissals of the relevance of race have been made by other prominent personalities, including Michael Jackson, Whoopi Goldberg, and golfer Tiger Woods.[10]

When someone Black receives widespread acceptance by Whites, it typically raises eyebrows among Blacks. Past experience has cautioned many Blacks to be suspicious of those Blacks whom Whites prop up as spokespersons, heroes, or role models. Affecting this suspicion is the question whether the Black person is someone who identifies with his Blackness or is someone who wishes to get as far away from it as possible—this is part of the "authenticity" calculation. Denzel Washington, Samuel Jackson, Chris Rock, and Shaquille O'Neal, who are widely adored and respected across color lines, are still viewed as "authentic." The bottom line on authenticity is whether the Black person "remembers where he came from." Public comments are scrutinized—for example, about their being Black or about Blacks in general, their political affiliation, their charity work, and whether she or he is married to someone White.

Senator and Democratic presidential nominee Barack Obama offers an interesting example of the issue of racial authenticity. Obama, who identifies himself as Black, has a White American mother and an African father. Some African Americans questioned Obama's Blackness because he does not have an African American parent (a U.S.-born Black parent). Social critic Stanley Crouch commented, "While he has experienced some light version of typical racial stereotypes, he cannot claim those problems as his own."[11] Although many Blacks have embraced Obama as one of their own, he would be more widely embraced (as Simpson was) if he were viewed as the target of racism.

Interestingly, crossover racial status, or colorlessness, has a fail-safe mechanism. It permits a "transcendor" such as O.J. to return home to the Black community whenever he is disrespected, accused of wrongdoing, or indicted by "the (White) system." The system can be any branch of government, corporate America, or the media. Numerous actions trigger the fail-safe response, including charging a famous Black person with a criminal offense (e.g., Michael Vick, O.J., Kobe Bryant, and Michael Jackson), unofficial allegations of criminal or unethical behavior (e.g., Barry Bonds), or perceived disrespectful treatment by the media (e.g., Clarence Thomas).

At this point, a logical question is, Why would the Black community rally behind someone who has taken great strides to remove himself from it or done little to affirm his place within it? It goes without saying that the Black community would support "colorful" Blacks, those who embrace their Blackness or those who are not running away from it. The sources of Black protectionism, which operates like a homing pigeon, are part historical and part current. Blacks are mindful that many of the people they have upheld as leaders, including Martin Luther King Jr., Malcolm X, Harriet Tubman, Jesse Jackson, Al Sharpton, Louis Farrakhan, and Fannie Lou Hamer, have been dismissed, ignored, or denigrated by Whites. For example, Jesse Jackson, who since the early days of The Rainbow/Operation PUSH organization, has been admired and respected by a sizeable percentage of the Black community, was not taken seriously by mainstream Whites until he garnered seven million votes in the 1988 presidential primaries.

As noted earlier, the relatively small number of Black success stories may help to explain the force of Black protectionism. From a population of more than thirty-three million, there exist few bona fide Black superstars. These few Black celebrities, whether they embrace their Blackness or not, are jealously guarded by the Black community. Discussing Black reaction to O. J. Simpson, professor Michael Eric Dyson notes,

> It can be viewed as the refusal of blacks to play the race authenticity game, which, in this instance, amounts to the belief that only "real" blacks deserve support when racial difficulties arise. But black responses to OJ can also be read less charitably. They can be seen as the automatic embrace of a fallen figure simply because he is black.[12]

Black protectionism arose during slavery, when, in the interest of group survival, Blacks had to present a united front to White slaveowners. A Black slave's minor infraction could result in a major penalty. One of the harsher penalties a slave master could impose was to sell the slave, which would destroy the family unit. A low-level offense could result in a whipping, torture, or execution. Denial of wrongdoing became a form of group protection against an irrational, racist system of formal and informal laws. A slave's admission to someone White that another slave had done something unlawful (e.g., learning to read) could forever seal the other slave's fate. The brutality of slavery created strong bonds between Blacks. Any slave who broke racial ranks and informed the slave master was viewed as selling out the race. Professor Harry Edwards supports a historical interpretation of Black support for Simpson:

[Black support of Simpson] has not been so much an act of undying loyalty as an act of self-defense, a collective, almost intuitive appreciation of the historical fact that the black community is inescapably bound to its members—for better and worse—impacted by their actions and outcomes irrespective of their disposition toward the black community. Black people's inordinate empathy with O. J. Simpson is, then, mostly an artifact of cultural memory.[13]

Beyond its antebellum roots, Black protectionism has a contemporary function. It creates a new, nondeviant way for Blacks to view themselves. Professor Regina Austin states that oppressed people reject mainstream definitions of themselves and "create their own concepts of justice, morality and legality."[14] In this way, Black protectionism can be said to operate as a shield, to defend against stereotypical views of Black deviance and criminality. At other times, Black protectionism is worn like a badge of honor. For example, during the criminal trial, many Blacks appeared to relish being "pro–O. J.," fully aware that this stance went against the status quo. Black protectionism is dynamic: the more Whites are perceived as closing in on a "target," the greater the community protection becomes.

The Deductive Logic of Black Protectionism. By design, Black protectionism guards Blacks against White assault. It operates regardless of whether the direct beneficiary of Black protectionism (e.g., Simpson) requests or wants the support. Black protectionism is a form of community redemption, though not redemption in the traditional sense because it does not require that the person apologize or atone. The target person's actions are only marginally relevant to Black protectionism. The key factor is how the Black community views the response from the White community—specifically, whether the targeted Black person is being mistreated and unfairly maligned by Whites, not whether he is a Johnny-come-lately to race.

Black protectionism is ostensibly a form of group self-interest. A superficial analysis might dismiss Black protectionism as a knee-jerk reaction at best or Black paranoia at worst. A look at how it works, however, suggests that it cannot be discounted so easily. When charges of misconduct are leveled against a well-known Black person, many Blacks ask themselves a series of questions about the circumstances. If, for example, it is determined that either the Black person did not commit the offense or that he may have committed the offense but was targeted because of race, Black protectionism goes into effect. Black protectionism is most easily

TABLE 5.2
Trigger Questions for Blacks and Whites

Blacks	Whites
1. Did he commit the offense?	1. Did he commit the offense?
2. Even if he did commit the offense, was he set up?	
3. Would he risk everything he has (e.g., wealth, fame, material possessions) to commit this offense?	
4. Is he the only person who has committed this offense?	
5. Are White people who are accused of committing this offense given the same scrutiny and treatment?	
6. Is this accusation part of a government conspiracy to destroy the Black race?	

triggered in cases involving well-off Blacks, because many Blacks would wonder why someone who has achieved the American dream would throw it all away. In the final analysis, the alleged actions of the Black person under scrutiny are measured against the actions of the state (e.g., police officers and prosecutors). If it is concluded that the government's actions are more culpable than the alleged wrongdoing, Blacks rally behind their fallen member. Former Washington, D.C., mayor Marion Barry is an example of this. Blacks do not condone crack smoking; however, many Blacks viewed the government's tactics (using a former girlfriend as bait to lure Barry to a hotel room) as unfair entrapment. On balance, many Blacks concluded that government entrapment was a worse offense than the mayor of the nation's capital smoking crack cocaine.

For many Whites, the analysis is much simpler: they begin and end with the question, Did he commit the offense? For Whites, the consideration of other factors, such as whether the government's behavior was over the line or whether race played a role, does not affect the answer to this question. As a result of how differently Whites and Blacks analyze the same set of facts, it is easy to understand how Whites conclude that Blacks are blinded by race loyalty. It is also easy to understand how Blacks conclude that Whites "just don't get it."

Clarence Thomas and Black Protectionism. The 1991 Clarence Thomas confirmation hearings offer a textbook example of Black protectionism. Justice Thomas sealed his colorless fate by preaching against affirmative action, denigrating his sister, arguing that Blacks are overly reliant on state aid, marrying a White woman, and dismissing law professor Anita Hill as a potential love interest because she was "too dark."

Once Hill's claims about Thomas became public and it appeared that

Whites were lining up against him, however, Thomas "became" Black again. Many Blacks believed he was being treated unfairly. Thomas stoked the existing fire by claiming that his treatment by the all-White, all-male Senate judiciary committee was akin to a lynching. He described the Senate Judiciary Committee hearings as a "high-tech lynching for uppity Blacks who . . . deign to think for themselves."[15] At that point, Thomas openly reclaimed his Blackness. In effect, his lynching metaphor was a trumpet call for Black support—or what journalist Clarence Page calls "Rally-Round-the-Brother Syndrome." For some people, the visual image of a Black man desperately trying to defend himself before a powerful group of White men conjured up images of an actual lynching. Many Blacks suspected that a conspiracy was afoot. According to one theory, Anita Hill was being used by radical feminists to bring another Black man down. Another theory was that the Senate Judiciary Committee did not want to fill the "Black seat" on the Court.

Like Thomas, Simpson had to be backed into a corner before he publicly addressed the issue of race. Throughout the trial and for months following the verdict, the Black community's embrace of Simpson was one-sided. Simpson did not comment, thank, or even acknowledge the overwhelming support he received from the Black community. Nor did he publicly address the racial implications and racial fallout from the verdict. His silence on the issue of race was remarkable in light of the fact that everyone else was so consumed by it.

Months after the acquittal, once Simpson realized he was no longer welcome in his former elite White inner circle, he slowly began to speak publicly about race. He gave his first television interview to Black Entertainment Television (BET), after protests led him to withdraw from a scheduled NBC interview. During the interview, Simpson insisted that most Whites agreed with the verdict. Ed Gordon of BET asked Simpson whether he should move out of Brentwood because of neighborhood protests. Simpson's startling reply was, "Where am I supposed to go? Africa?"[16] During the interview, Simpson appeared painfully unaware of the depth of White outrage against him.

Blacklash. Black protectionism has another interesting twist. While some colorless Blacks are allowed to reenter the community, others find that the cloak of Black protectionism is not a permanent one. They may later be exiled or ignored by Blacks. This appears to have happened with Clarence Thomas. Though most Blacks supported him during the confirmation hearings, the tide has since turned. Many who felt his treatment by the Senate Judiciary Committee was unfairly harsh and racist believed that he should be given a seat on the U.S. Supreme Court. After almost two decades on the Court, however, Thomas is now viewed by many Blacks as insensitive to issues important to the Black community (e.g., affirmative action, criminal procedure, and voting rights). It is one thing to be perceived as neutral about Black issues, but it is quite another thing to be perceived as hostile, and Thomas appears to have crossed the line.

Are Black Women Protected? Another important question raised by Black protectionism is whether its cloak extends to Black women. The answer appears to be no. First, women have far fewer avenues for attaining national stature than men do. For instance, many Black superstars are athletes, and women, by and large, do not have access to the world of pro sports. Even those sports that have been slow to open up to Blacks, such as golf and tennis, are more likely to open up to Black men first. The same is true for the motion-picture industry. There are few blockbuster movie roles for Blacks, and most of these roles go to Black men. Second, well-known women are much less likely to become involved in public scandals. Given these facts, there exist fewer opportunities to invoke Black protectionism for Black women. It is difficult to imagine the Black community rallying behind a high-profile, colorless Black woman if she were accused of committing a serious crime. It is unlikely that the Black community would be as steadfast in its allegiance to a Black woman as it was toward Clarence Thomas, Mike Tyson, O. J. Simpson, R. Kelly, Kobe Bryant, or Michael Jackson.

Several incidents involving Black women might have invoked Black protectionism. The first involved the nomination of law professor Lani Guinier to serve as the assistant attorney general for civil rights. President Bill Clinton withdrew her name after sizeable conservative opposition mounted against her. Though many Blacks were troubled by Clinton's actions, compared with the Clarence Thomas case, there was a low volume of Black protest.

The same is true for former surgeon general Dr. Joycelyn Elders. After making some controversial comments about sex education, she was summarily dismissed from her post. Again, though many Blacks were troubled by Clinton's actions, there was no groundswell of protest in support of Elders. If Black protectionism applies to Black women, it should have been invoked for Guinier and Elders. Both women have demonstrated a lifelong commitment to improving the conditions of their communities. If Black protectionism was not available for these women, it appears unlikely that it would be available for "colorless" Black women.

The Future of Black Protectionism. Black protectionism may partially explain the deep divergence between Black and White opinion on the Simpson case. Blacks understandably bring a different set of historical concerns to any racial issue than Whites do. In one of his seminal essays, sociologist W. E. B. Du Bois wrote about the "double-consciousness" that Blacks must have. He described it as "this sense of always looking at one's self through the eyes of others."[17] Blacks are ever mindful of their history of oppression in this country and are acutely aware of the negative image that Whites have of them. Many Blacks have heard stories, passed down through generations, about the savagery of slavery and Jim Crow. Blacks are also aware that Whites as a group are not as interested in this history and how it affects race relations today. For many Blacks, their treatment as legally mandated second-class citizens, which is scarcely two generations old, is more than a historical footnote.

In contrast, Whites as a group rejected claims that America's history of racial discrimination bore any significance to the Simpson case. The relevance of this history may have been ignored not out of maliciousness but out of ignorance. This may explain why the White response to Mark Fuhrman was shock, while the Black response was "I told you so." In the end, Blacks and Whites use entirely different criteria to analyze racial incidents. If Blacks and Whites are going to bridge any more of the racial gap, Whites will have to understand not only Black protectionism but also why it persists and the functions it serves.

The Dichotomy of Race

The American fascination with the tension between Blacks and Whites was never more apparent than during the Simpson criminal case. This interest was so intense that it overshadowed all other racial dynamics. During the trial, the racial pulse of the country was measured in Black and White.

One of the more problematic aspects of the criminal case, so far as media attention is concerned, is how Blacks and Whites were forced into separate statistical boxes. From the early days of the trial, the polls indicated that Blacks overwhelmingly believed Simpson was innocent and

Whites overwhelmingly believed he was guilty. Pollsters, aided and abetted by the media, told us only what Blacks and Whites thought, overlooking people of all other races. Not surprisingly, the media's racial pigeonholing forced individual Blacks and Whites to become spokespersons for their entire race. Few newspaper or television polls taken during the trial looked beyond race to consider gender, socioeconomic status, region, education, or age.

"Black" was treated as a monolithic racial category that includes Blacks from anywhere in the world (e.g., Black Americans, Black Africans, Black Europeans, and Black Caribbeans) and living anywhere in the United States. It is possible that each of these groups, based on its racial experiences in this country and its history, had a different opinion of the Simpson case because of these different historical experiences. Likewise, Whites were treated as a singular group. White opinions about the Simpson case might have varied by ethnicity, geography, or class. Notably, the media provided only crude data on Blacks and Whites. The media boxes into which Blacks and Whites were forced did little to illuminate how and why race matters regarding perceptions, experiences, and attitudes toward the justice system.

The statistical boxes we did not see were equally unsettling. Race was dichotomized to mean "Black" and "White." Few, if any, major news stories or polls reported the viewpoints of Asians, Latinos, or Native Americans. The media's racial blind spot is no minor oversight, considering that at the time of the Simpson case, approximately 15 percent of the U.S. population was neither Black nor White. Hispanics made up approximately 11 percent; Asians, 3.5 percent; and Native Americans, less than 1 percent. A century from now, when historians study public opinion in the Simpson case, one of the more perplexing questions may be why there was so little accounting of Asian, Native American, and Hispanic viewpoints.

If the polls had included a wider cross section of the populace, we would have had a more colorful and more accurate picture of American racial dynamics. For instance, the different group experience that Blacks have had with law enforcement could have explained why Blacks are more suspicious of the criminal justice system, particularly the police. Latinos, who also have strained relations with law enforcement, share similar views. This information should have been sought out and deemed newsworthy. Rather than adopting the media's widespread conclusion that the reaction to the Simpson case was a "Black thing" or a "White thing," perhaps the best conclusion is that it was an "experiential thing."

Conversely, survey data might have shown that Hispanics were more closely aligned with Whites in their perceptions of the Simpson trial. It is also possible that Hispanics held viewpoints on the Simpson case dissimilar to both Whites and Blacks. One of the problems with making race a two-column category is that it causes us mistakenly to believe that there are only two viewpoints. In addition to being ignored in poll data, Asian, Latino, and Native American media spokespersons were also in short supply during the Simpson trial. Though there are relatively few non-Black journalists of color (less than 5 percent), there were many who could have offered alternative insights into the case.

In the late 1990s, Los Angeles was one of the most diverse cities in the country. It was approximately 40 percent Hispanic and 10 percent Asian. Los Angeles County continues to have the largest Hispanic population outside Latin America. A few Latino voices managed to break through the Black/White conversation. Speaking about the absence of "other" perspectives on the Simpson case, journalist Richard Rodriguez commented,

> As someone who thinks of himself as neither white nor black, I used to hear such talk as a kind of family quarrel. It went over my head. Today, I sense a weird nostalgia to such talk and a vanity. It is as though many whites and blacks cannot imagine an America peopled by anyone, except each other.[18]

The virtual absence of Asian commentary on the Simpson case is notable given that the judges in both the criminal and civil cases were Japanese American: Lance Ito and Hiroshi Fujisaki. The viewpoints of Asians, who have had a unique experience with the U.S. criminal justice system, one different from Blacks, Whites, and Hispanics, should have been part of the racial dialogue generated by the case.[19]

Black and White journalists did not adequately incorporate the perspectives of other racial groups. After the acquittal, a Chinese American college student noted, "I feel like an invisible conduit. Both my Black and White friends feel like they can come up to me and express their rage and joy about the verdict. . . . But sometimes I just feel caught in the middle —that my perspective doesn't count."[20] One Latino commented, "Blacks and Whites had too much invested in the case to be objective about it. . . . 'They should have let us Latinos decide it. We're an impartial jury.' "[21]

Diversity of opinions matters precisely because of the racial fallout from trials similar to the Simpson case. The post-verdict eruption was necessarily Black versus White, because it was the only picture the media represented. Not surprisingly, the fact that there was a Hispanic person on the Simpson jury got lost in public fervor over the "Black" verdict. That there were two Whites on the jury was also minimized. The majority of the conversation about the verdict has been about the decision of the "mostly Black jury," "Black jury," or "predominantly Black jury."

One reason for the divergence of opinion between Blacks and Whites is the longstanding tension between the groups. Many Blacks believe that they have not been adequately compensated for slavery. Conversely, many Whites strongly assert that racism is a historical relic. The friction is so longstanding and deep-seated that it is difficult for members of either group to think globally with regard to other races. The fact that Blacks have always been the largest minority group in the country may also explain the media's tunnel vision on race.

Media attempts to represent the views of a larger cross section of the population would not have solved the racial schism in the Simpson case. Still, the media's failure to offer a more nuanced picture of the racial issues raised by the case was a missed opportunity. Rather than throwing fuel onto an already explosive issue, a lot more could have been done during the trial to report not only how race affected opinion about the case but also how other factors played a role. Additionally, the media might have spent more time analyzing the overlap in opinion across races, and not just the Black/White racial gap. Finally, more attention should have been devoted to explanations for the racial divide.

Conclusion

If nothing else, the Simpson case reminded us that race not only matters but figures centrally in our views of justice. It reinforced the fact that Blacks and Whites have very different realities. For Blacks, this reality includes Black protectionism. For Whites, this reality includes White denial. The case also instructed us that we know very little about how Asians, Hispanics, Native Americans, and other groups view their racial circumstances and the criminal justice system.

The greatest threat of the Simpson case is that we will reduce it to a spectacle without learning from it. The case continues to offer us an opportunity to learn and reconsider what we know to be true regarding America's racial realities. Thus far, in this post–O. J. era, however, we each continue to dig in our racial heels a little deeper and point our fingers outward, continuing to talk past one another. Though the Simpson acquittal was a racial watershed, we have not yet figured out how to use it as a marker of change, rather than simply as a marker of a time past.

6

Racial Hoaxes

I am an invisible man. . . . I am a man of substance, of flesh and
bone, fiber and liquids—and I might even be said to possess a
mind. I am invisible, understand simply because people refuse
to see me. . . . When they approach me they see only my sur-
roundings, themselves, or figments of their imagination—indeed,
everything and anything except me.
                              —Ralph Ellison, *Invisible Man* (1947)

The racial hoax is a classic example of "playing the race card."
It is a cynical manipulation of our deepest fears about race and violence.
Racial hoaxes are not new and are deeply woven into our sociological and
historical landscape, past and present. For centuries Black men were offered up as scapegoats for the crimes of Whites, real and fabricated. At
the turn of the twentieth century it was not uncommon for Black men to
face false allegations of rape. The fear of the Black brute sexually violating
the White female was the purported rationale behind the lynch laws. The
punishment for these crimes—beatings, prison, being run out of town,
and lynchings—all served to uphold White rule.

Today hoaxes are less common, but no less incendiary. They are the
subject of satire and art exhibits and serve as plot twists for books (e.g.,
Richard Price's *Freedomland*), movies (e.g., Ben Affleck's *Gone Baby
Gone*), and television shows (e.g., Fox's *New York Undercover*). The continuing harms of the racial hoax are difficult to measure but are neverthe-
less real. They tell us where we are as a country with regard to race, our
racial values, and the process through which we link crime and race. For
some people, hoaxes invite a kind of racial malaise. At the same time that
they signal that racism persists, they also suggest that it is peripheral and
that hoaxes are only committed by people on the social fringes.

There has been very little academic attention devoted to racial hoaxes. This chapter evaluates hoaxes, especially the differences between hoaxes with Black perpetrators and those with White perpetrators. It also looks at the harm done by hoaxes, including the effect on race relations, and the appropriate sanctions for these false allegations.

In Black and White

In 1994, Susan Smith, a White mother in South Carolina, told police that she had been the victim of a carjacking. She described her assailant as an armed, young Black male, twenty to thirty years old. According to Smith, the man drove off with her two sons, ages three years and fourteen months. In the days that followed, Smith appeared on national TV and pled for the lives of her boys: "Your momma loves you. . . . Be strong."[1] The press and the public bought the story whole. Based on Smith's description of the assailant, the police drafted and widely disseminated a sketch of a young Black man. The FBI was brought in, and there was an extensive air and ground manhunt for the assailant. Police received calls suggesting the whereabouts of the boys, from all over the country.

Nine days later we learned that Smith had fabricated the entire story. There was no Black carjacker. She had created the fictional bogeyman to shift attention away from herself. Smith had murdered her two boys. She had placed them in their car seats, driven to a lake, exited the vehicle, released the car's emergency brake, and allowed the car to plunge into the water.

Though Smith's claims strained credulity, skeptical media commentary was hard to come by. The public appeared to swallow her tale whole, an updated version of the Black savage terrorizing an innocent White family. Upon calm reflection, the question should have been asked, When was the last time you saw a young Black man with two small White children in tow? Unbeknownst to the public, early on the local police were suspicious of Smith's allegations. Her narrative and timeline were filled with inconsistencies.

In 1989, Charles Stuart told police that he and his wife, Carol, on their way home from a Lamaze birthing class, were shot and robbed by a Black man wearing a jogging suit. Carol Stuart and her unborn child died following the attack. Police invaded Mission Hill, a predominantly Black neighborhood in Boston, in search of Carol Stuart's killer. After viewing a police line-up, Charles Stuart picked a Black man named Willie Bennett as the person who "most resembled" the attacker.[2] Based on inconsistencies in Stuart's story and incriminating information obtained from his brother, Matthew Stuart, the police soon shifted their investigation to Charles Stuart. Shortly thereafter, Charles Stuart committed suicide. Police later determined that Stuart had planned the murderous hoax as a scheme to cash in on his wife's insurance policy.

The actions of racial hoax perpetrators have made prophetic the words of Ralph Ellison quoted at the beginning of this chapter. In 1947, when Ellison wrote about the invisibility of the Black experience, he could not have envisioned that the negative image of Blackness would become so pervasive that *imaginary* Black people would be regularly invented as criminals. The Smith and Stuart cases are not aberrations.

Defining Terms

A racial hoax takes place either

(a) when someone fabricates a crime and blames it on another person because of his race or
(b) when an actual crime has been committed and the perpetrator falsely blames someone because of his race.

Hoax perpetrators are most frequently charged with filing a false police report. In many instances, however, they are not charged with any wrongdoing. The prevalence of racial hoaxes suggests that false report statutes do not operate as effective deterrents. Some states have considered going further and enacting legislation to criminalize racial hoaxes, as did New Jersey after several high-profile hoaxes there. Because hoaxes impose social, psychological, economic, and legal costs on society, the actions of Susan Smith and others should be recognized for what they are, serious criminal offenses, regardless of whether they are used to cover up actual or fictional crimes.

Although a racial hoax can be perpetrated by a person of any race, against a person of any race, the primary focus of this chapter is on those cases involving Whites and Blacks. There are hoaxes perpetrated against members of other racial groups, but there are few reports of these cases (e.g., the "runaway bride" discussed later in this chapter). The large majority of hoaxes, however, involve perpetrators and victims who are the same race. These rarely make news. The interracial hoaxes involving Blacks and Whites are the most likely to be reported and the most likely to receive media attention. They also exact a high social and economic toll.

Anyone, of any race, who perpetrates a hoax with a Black villain should face criminal punishment. A hoax in which a Black person is singled out as the criminal deserves a special legal sanction because racial hoaxes that target Blacks create a distinct, more acute social problem than hoaxes that target people of other races. African Americans in general and African American young men in particular are already saddled with a negative image. In fact, crime and young Black men have become synonymous in the American mind. As discussed in chapter 1, these images have combined to create the *criminalblackman*. Given the pervasiveness of this stereotype, it is not surprising that so many people have manipulated this negative image to avoid criminal responsibility. Comedian Paul Mooney half jokingly comments on this phenomenon in his routine "1-900-Blame-A-Nigger":

> Didn't some white man in Boston shoot his pregnant wife and then shot hisself, crying, "Oh niggers did it." Always trying to blame some niggers. That's why I'm gonna start a new ad, "1-900 Blame-A-Nigger." So when white folks get in trouble, just call my agency. "[Hello] Blame-A-Nigger, I just pushed my mother down the stairs. I don't want to go to jail. Send a nigger over here."[3]

Racial hoaxes are devised, perpetrated, and successful precisely because they tap into widely held fears. The harm of the racial hoax is not limited to reinforcing deviant, centuries-old images of Blacks. Hoaxes also create these images for new generations of young people. The racial hoax should be recognized as a separate criminal offense, subject to a mandatory prison term, regardless of whether it is used to cover up an actual or fabricated crime.

Trends and Patterns

Table 6.1 provides case data for ninety-two hoaxes perpetrated between 1987 and 2006 (see appendix B for case summaries). As indicated in the table, the majority of hoaxes involved Whites who falsely accused Blacks of committing a crime (63 percent).[4] Table 6.2 provides a breakdown of racial hoaxes involving Blacks and Whites. Most of these hoaxes were located through a search of LexisNexis, an automated database that stores news articles. For each case table 6.1 includes information on the race of the hoax perpetrator, the race of the victim, the crime the perpetrator sought to cover up by the hoax, the amount of time before the hoax was uncovered, whether a false report charge was filed against the perpetrator, and whether any innocent people were stopped or questioned by the police. For some cases not all the information was available.

Notably, the cases included in table 6.1 represent only a fraction of all racial hoax cases. Most hoaxes are not classified or reported as such. For example, cases in which a newspaper reported on a hoax but did not state the race of the perpetrator or victim could not be included. More important, the overwhelming majority of criminal cases are investigated and closed by the police without ever making the news.

TABLE 6.1

Racial Hoaxes: Summary Data of Ninety-Two Cases, 1987–2006

Name of Perpetrator	Year	Perpetrator: Race/Sex, Victim: Race/Sex	Alleged Crime[a]	Duration of Hoax[b]	False Report Charge[c]	Police Stop[d]
ADAMS, Bradley	1995	P:W/M, V:B/M	Murder	Months	No	No
ALLMAN, Stevie	1997	P:W/F, V:B/M	Arson	Months	—	Yes
ANDERSON, Jesse	1992	P:W/M, V:B/M	Murder	1 Week	No	Yes
ANDERSON, Tisha, and LEE, William	1995	P:B/F, P:W/M, V:W/M	Hate crime (vandalism)	1 Month	Yes	No
ASBELL, Samuel	1990	P:W/M, V:B/M	Attempted murder	1 Week	Yes	Yes
AVENT, Anthony	1994	P:B/M, V:W/M	Assault	1 Week	No	No
BAISLEY, Adam	1996	P:W/M, V:B/M	Assault	1 Week	No	No
BIRT, Tracy	1996	P:B/M, V:W/M	Hate crime (vandalism)	—	Yes	—
BOLDUC, Daniel	1995	P:W/M, V:B/M	Vandalism	1 Week	Yes	No
BRAWLEY, Tawana	1987	P:B/F, V:W/M	Rape, Hate crime (assault)	Months	No	Yes
BYRDSONG, DeWayne	1995	P:B/M, V:W/M	Hate crime (vandalism)	Months	Yes	—
CAMPBELL, Toby	1995	P:W/M, V:B/M	Robbery	1 Week	Yes	Yes
CHERRY, Donald	1996	P:W/M, V:B/M	Murder	1 Week	Yes	Yes
CLARK, Emily	2004	P:W/F, V:B/M	Robbery	1 Week	Yes	—
CLEMENTE, Garrick	1995	P:B/M, V:W/M	Hate crime (vandalism)	Months	No	No
COLLINS, Sabrina	1990	P:B/F, V:W/M	Hate crime (threats)	Months	No	No
CRANE, Henry	1995	P:W/M, V:B/M	Carjack	1 Week	Yes	Yes
DACRI, Tanya	1989	P:W/F, V:B/M	Kidnap	1 Week	Yes	—
DiBARTOLO, Thomas	1996	P:W/M, V:B/M	Murder	—	No	Yes
DROGAN, Thomas, and PAPALEO, Louis	1993	P:W/M (2), V:B/M	Assault	1 Week	Yes	Yes

TABLE 6.1 (*continued*)

Name of Perpetrator	Year	Perpetrator: Race/Sex, Victim: Race/Sex	Alleged Crime[a]	Duration of Hoax[b]	False Report Charge[c]	Police Stop[d]
DUKE LACROSSE*	2006	P:B/FV:W/M	Rape	Months	No	Yes
DUNN, Kerri	2006	P:W/F, V:W/M	Hate crime (vandalism)	Months	Yes	Yes
FRAKES, Dawn	1995	P:W/F, V:B/M	Assault	Months	Yes	No
GATELEY, Tina, and KARAFFA, William	1993	P:W/M&F, V:B/M	Attempted robbery, Assault	1 Month	Yes	No
GAYLE, Matthew	1995	P:W/M, V:B/M	Murder	Months	No	—
GIBSON, Tonya, BUSH, Tynnush, HENLEY, Clayton, GIBSON, William, and SYNDER, Gary	1996	P:W/F, 4 W/M, V:B/M	Attempted murder, Burglary	1 Week	No	Yes
GILLIS, Kendra	1994	P:W/F, V:B/M	Assault	1 Week	No	No
GREEN, Joshua, PRATT, Daniel, and CROWLEY, Michael	1994	P:3W/M, V:B/M	Robbery	1 Week	Yes	No
HARDIN, Alicia	2005	P:B/W, V:W/M	Hate crime (threats)	2 Weeks	No	No
HARRIS, Persey, VIGIL, Ann, and HARRIS, Caryn	1996	P:B/M, 2B/F, V:W/M	Hate crime (assault)	—	Yes	Yes
HARRIS, Robert	1996	P:W/M, V:B/M	Murder	1 Week	No	No
HEBERT, Jeffrey	1995	P:W/M, V:B/M	Murder	1 Week	No	Yes
HUENEKE, Brenda	1995	P:W/F, V:B/M	Robbery	—	Yes	—
IRVINE, Frank	1994	P:W/M, V:B/M	Assault	—	Yes	—
JACKSON, Angela	1996	P:B/M, V:W/M	Hate crime (threats)	Months	No	Yes
JAMES, Sonia	1996	P:B/F, V:W/M	Hate crime (vandalism)	Months	Yes	—
JOHNSTON, Kathleen	1994	P:W/F, V:B/M	Assault, Robbery	Months	No	No
KASHANI, Miriam	1990	P:W/F, V:B/M	Rape	1 Week	No	No
LAMBIRTH, Mark	1995	P:W/M, V:AI/M	Kidnap	—	No	No
LEWIS, Mark	1994	P:W/M, V:B/M	Assault	—	No	No
LIMOS, Marcy	2003	P:W/F, V:B/M	Rape	1 Week	Yes	—
LUPUS, Josephine	1994	P:W/F, V:B/M	Robbery	1 Week	Yes	No
MAGRONE, Lucille	1990	P:W/F, V:B/M	Assault	Months	Yes	Yes
MARTINEZ, Ramon, MENDEZ, Luis, and DEGROS, Joseph	1995	P:H/M (3), V:B/M	Assault	1 Week	Yes	No
MAXWELL, Janet	1993	P:W/F, V:B/M	Kidnap, Rape	Months	Yes	No
MAYO, Daniel, and LAFOREST, Philip	1997	P:W/M (2), V:B/M	Hate crime (vandalism)	1 Week	Yes	—
McCOOL, Cecil	1995	P:W/M, V:B/M	Police misconduct	1 Month	No	Yes
McGUIRE, Kelli	1997	P:W/F, V:B/M	Rape, Kidnap	—	—	—
METCALFE, Milton	1993	P:B/M, V:B/M	Hate crime (assault)	1 Week	No	No

(*continued*)

TABLE 6.1 (*continued*)

Name of Perpetrator	Year	Perpetrator: Race/Sex, Victim: Race/Sex	Alleged Crime[a]	Duration of Hoax[b]	False Report Charge[c]	Police Stop[d]
MILAM, Richard	1994	P:W/M, V:B/M	Murder, Robbery	1 Week	No	No
MILLER, Phillip	1994	P:W/M, V:B/M	Robbery	1 Week	Yes	No
MITCHELL, DeAntrious	1996	P:B/M, V:W/M	Assault	2 Weeks	Yes	Yes
NICOLAS, Richard	1996	P:B/M, V:W/M	Murder	1 Week	No	No
O'BRIEN, Edward	1995	P:W/M, V:B or H/M	Murder	1 Week	No	No
PATTERSON, Brian	1996	P:W/M, V:B/M	Murder	1 Week	Yes	No
PITTMAN, Dennis	1996	P:W/M, V:B/M	Carjack, Kidnap	1 Week	No	No
POSNER, Maryrose	1994	P:W/F, V:B/M	Robbery	1 Week	Yes	—
PRINCE, Christopher*	1994	P:W/F, V:B/M	Attempted rape, Burglary	1 Year	No	Yes
REED, Loretta	1997	P:W/F, V:B/M	Carjack	—	Yes	—
RIVERA, Reggie*	1993	P:B/M, V:W/M	Rape	1 Year	No	No
ROBB, Katharine	2001	P:W/F, V:B/M	Rape	1 Week	Yes	Yes
ROUTIER, Darlie	1996	P:W/F, V:W/M	Murder	1 Month	No	No
RUSSELL, Judy	1988	P:W/F, V:MidEast/M	Assault	1 Month	Yes	No
SARABAKHSH, Zhaleh	1995	P:MidEast/F, V:W/M	Attempted murder	1 Week	Yes	No
SATTERLY, Ed	2004	P:W/M, V:B/M	Attempted murder	1 Week	Yes	—
SAULS, Jay	1997	P:W/M, V:B/M	Assault	2 Weeks	Yes	Yes
SCRUGGS, Shawnda	1996	P:B/W, V:W/M	Hate crime (vandalism)	—	—	—
SEALEY, Jaelyn	2000	P:B/F, V:W/M	Hate crime (vandalism)	Weeks	Yes	—
SHAVER, Dorne	2000	P:B/M, V:W/M	Assault	—	Yes	—
SHAW, Michael	1995	P:W/M, V:B/M	Kidnap	1 Week	Yes	Yes
SKIPPER, Carlton	1997	P:B/M, V:B/M	Assault, Robbery	—	—	—
SMITH, Susan	1994	P:W/F, V:B/M	Carjack, Kidnap	2 Weeks	No	Yes
SOLIMAN, Mounir	1994	P:MidEast/M, V:B/M	Robbery	1 Week	Yes	No
STUART, Charles	1989	P:W/M, V:B/M	Murder	Months	No[e]	Yes
TANCZOS, Lisa	1995	P:W/F, V:B/M	Assault	Months	Yes	Yes
TICKNOR, Harry	1997	P:W/M, V:B/M	Robbery	—	Yes	—
TULIA, TEXAS	1999	P:W/M, V:B/M & F (40)	Drug sales	Months	Yes	Yes
VEACH, Paul	1995	P:W/M, V:B/M	Kidnap, Robbery	1 Week	Yes	No
VEITCH, Neva, and CRAIG, David	1987	P:W/M&F, V:B/M	Murder, Kidnap, Attempted rape	2 Years	No	—
WAGNER, Candice	1995	P:W/F, V:B/M	Kidnap, Rape	Months	Yes	No
WIGHT, Lisa	1996	P:W/F, V:B/M	Attempted rape	1 Month	No	Yes

TABLE 6.1 (*continued*)

Name of Perpetrator	Year	Perpetrator: Race/Sex, Victim: Race/Sex	Alleged Crime[a]	Duration of Hoax[b]	False Report Charge[c]	Police Stop[d]
WILBANKS, Jennifer	2005	P:W/F, V:Hispanic/M, W/F	Sexual assault, Kidnap	1 Week	Yes	Yes
YENTES, Michele	1989	P:W/F, V:B/M	Rape	Months	Yes	No
YOUSHEI, Soloman	1995	P:MidEast/M, V:B/M	Robbery	1 Week	No	No
UNNAMED, Florida 1	1994	P:W/F, V:W/M	Kidnap, Rape	1 Week	—	No
UNNAMED, Florida 2	1996	P:W/F, V:B/M	Rape, Assault	1 Week	No	No
UNNAMED, Kentucky	2004	P:W/F, V:B/M	Kidnap	1 Week	Yes	Yes
UNNAMED, Louisiana	1994	P:W/F, V:B/M	Rape	1 Week	No	Yes
UNNAMED, Maine	1994	P:W/F, V:B/M	Assault	1 Week	No	Yes
UNNAMED, New Jersey	1994	P:W/F, V:B/M	Assault	—	—	No
UNNAMED, Virginia	1995	P:W/M, V:B/M	Assault, Carjack	1 Week	No	No
UNNAMED, Wisconsin	1996	P:W/F, V:B/M	Rape	1 Week	No	No

[a] Alleged crime: Crime alleged by hoax perpetrator.
[b] Duration: Indicates length of time before police discovered the hoax.
[c] False report charge: Whether hoax perpetrator was charged with filing a false report or a related offense.
[d] Police stop: Whether an innocent person was arrested, detained, or questioned about the hoax.
[e] Stuart committed suicide before formal criminal charges were brought against him.
[*] Name of the hoax victim rather than perpetrator.

TABLE 6.2
Racial Hoaxes Involving Blacks and Whites

Race	Number of Cases
White perpetrator/Black victim	62
Black perpetrator/White victim	18
White perpetrator/White victim	3
Black perpetrator/Black victim	2
Other hoaxes[a]	7
Total	92

[a] This category includes cases involving a perpetrator or victim of another race, for example, Native American or Hispanic, or cases in which the race of either the perpetrator or victim is unknown. Notably, in four of these cases, the hoax perpetrator said he had been victimized by a Black man (Ramon Martinez et al., Phillip Miller, Mounir Soliman, and Solomon Youshei).

Several patterns emerge from the racial hoax cases:

- Approximately two-thirds of all cases involved White-on-Black hoaxes.
- Hoaxes were most frequently fabricated to allege assault, murder, and rape.
- Less than one-half of the hoaxes were revealed as fabrications in less than one week.
- Hoax perpetrators were charged with filing a false police report in approximately 45 percent of the cases.
- In 25 percent of the cases, an innocent person was stopped, questioned, or arrested for the alleged crime.
- Hoaxes were perpetrated by people representing all races, classes, and geographic regions.
- In 12 percent of the cases, hoax perpetrators were under the age of twenty-one.

White-on-Black Hoaxes

Sordid Details. In several cases, the hoax was created with great attention to detail, sometimes bordering on a malevolent fantasy:

- A White woman in Pennsylvania reported that she had been attacked by a thirty-something, muscular Black man with a crew cut. She told police that the knife-wielding attacker used the weapon to play a game of tic-tac-toe on her arm. The woman claimed that the same man returned two months later to terrorize her. (Lisa Tanczos)
- A White female college student reported that another White female student had been raped at knifepoint by two young Black men. The attackers were described as having "particularly bad body odor." Within days the woman admitted to making up the entire story. (Miriam Kashani)
- A forty-seven-year-old White man told police that he had been robbed at gunpoint by a Black man, with "light-colored hair, 6 to 8 inch braids, a deformed pupil in one eye, acne scars on his cheeks, and one or two missing front teeth." (Paul Veach)

- A White woman reported that while she was at a bank machine she and her two-year-old daughter were approached by a Black man wielding a gun. The woman told police that the man "put a gun to [her] child's head while he laughed." (Maryrose Posner)

These cases provide actual examples of how different White people have visualized the *criminalblackman*. These images, generated by television, newspapers, radio, and American lore, create a menacing caricature of young Black men. Interestingly, in these hoaxes, it was not enough for the perpetrators to describe the fictional assailant as Black; they added menacing, demonlike details. Many White-on-Black hoaxes are successful because society buys the much-stated connection between Blackness and crime.

In one hoax incident that defies classification, a White Louisiana woman told police that she had been sexually assaulted by a Black man. She said the attacker had a tattoo of a serpent on his arm. A police sketch of the rapist was widely circulated in Baton Rouge. In a bizarre twist, *twenty-eight* other women notified the police that they, too, had been assaulted by the imaginary "serpent man." The high number of copycat victims suggests more than the usual hysteria associated with criminals on the loose. Within days, the alleged victim confessed that she had made up the rape story (Unnamed, Louisiana).

Police and Judicial Officials. Many of the cases involve hoaxes committed by legal officials. In a little more than 12 percent of the cases, the hoax perpetrator was a police officer or officer of the court:

- A White deputy sheriff told police that while he and his wife were out walking, they were accosted by two Black men. Both the sheriff and his wife were shot. His wife died following the attack, and he sustained a flesh wound. It was later discovered that the sheriff had hired a hit man to kill his wife to cash in on her insurance policy. (Thomas DiBartolo)
- A Delaware state trooper reported that she had been shot by a Black teenager. She said her attacker was named "Willy" and described him as a light-skinned Black male, between sixteen and nineteen years old, six feet tall, and weighing 160 to 170 pounds. After a two-month investigation, the officer admitted that she had

made up the story. The hoax was designed to cover up the fact that she had accidentally shot herself in the arm with her service revolver. (Dawn Frakes)

- A New Jersey prosecutor claimed that someone was trying to kill him. He reported that two Black men chased him and shot at his car. He later confessed to making up the attempted-murder story. (Samuel Asbell)

- Two New York City police officers got into a physical fight over who would file a police report in a fire incident to which both men had responded. The altercation left both officers with extensive cuts and bruises. To hide the fact that they had been fighting, the White officers filed a police report stating that one of them had been assaulted by a Black man. At least six officers were involved in the cover-up. Two weeks following the incident, an officer who had witnessed the fight informed authorities of the hoax. (Thomas Drogan and Louis Papaleo).

- A White court deputy told police that a Black man had attempted to rape her in the hallway of a federal courthouse. Several Black male courthouse employees were questioned about the attack. After extensive questioning by the FBI, the alleged victim confessed to fabricating the attack. (Lisa Wight)

All-Purpose Suspects. The majority of White-on-Black hoaxes are concocted to shift criminal responsibility, as in the Susan Smith case. A handful of cases involve insurance scams. In one case, Robert Harris told police that he and his fiancée had been shot and robbed on a quiet Baltimore street. Harris's fiancée died from her gunshot wounds. Harris described the attacker as a Black man who was wearing a camouflage jacket and black-and-white pants. Based on the mistaken belief that he was the named beneficiary on his fiancée's $250,000 insurance policy, Harris had hired a White hit man to kill her.

In another murder-for-money case, Jesse Anderson told police that he and his wife had been attacked by Black assailants in a restaurant parking lot. Anderson's wife was stabbed twenty-one times and died following the assault. After a five-day search for the nonexistent Black assailants, Anderson was charged and ultimately convicted of his wife's murder. Police learned that Anderson had called his wife's insurance company, one month prior to her murder, and asked whether her policy was in effect. (*See also* Matthew Gayle.)

Sometimes hoaxes are devised for more mundane reasons. In the case of the "runaway bride," Jennifer Wilbanks created an elaborate tale to avoid her upcoming wedding. Wilbanks, a White woman, disappeared from her Duluth, Georgia, home days before the scheduled ceremony. Family members and friends suspected foul play and notified authorities. A few days later the missing woman called her fiancé and told him that she was in Albuquerque, New Mexico. She said she had been kidnapped by a Hispanic man and White woman and that the couple had sexually assaulted her. She repeated the same tale to law enforcement officers. Wilbanks told authorities that she was under stress about her upcoming wedding and that she had purchased a bus ticket in the week prior to her wedding. Wilbanks pled no contest to giving authorities false information. She was sentenced to two years probation, required to perform 120 hours of community service, and fined $2,250. This case is the most prominent one in which a Hispanic was falsely accused in a hoax incident. It is unclear why Wilbanks added this racial twist to her story; perhaps she believed it would boost her credibility and evoke sympathy.

Other rationales behind hoaxes run the gamut from the mundane to the silly. Excuses include the desire to get time off from work, to win attention from a spouse, to garner sympathy, and to avoid parental discipline for violating curfew. Here are some of the more remarkable hoax stories:

- A White man reported that he had been carjacked by a Black man. He told police that he was forced at knifepoint to drive his kidnapper from Philadelphia to Atlantic City. After intense questioning, the man admitted that he had devised the story to avoid further car payments. (Dennis Pittman)
- A nineteen-year-old White woman told police that she had been kidnapped from a mall and raped by an armed Black man. Within two days, she admitted to making up the story as a cover for the fact that she stayed out all night with her boyfriend. (Kelli McGuire)
- A White New Jersey man told police that he saw a Black man running into a wooded area carrying a small White child. Based on his statement, an extensive air and land search was mounted. The next day, the man admitted to making up the story. Apparently the story had been concocted so he could get the afternoon off from work. (Michael Shaw)

- A White woman told police that she had been kidnapped from
  a shopping mall by three Black men. She said she was raped and
  forced to take drugs. She later confessed that she had made up
  the story to avoid getting into trouble for staying out past her
  curfew. (Janet Maxwell)

Multiple Perpetrators. White-on-Black hoaxes are often perpetrated by
more than one offender. Thus, hoaxes cannot be dismissed as the work
of loners. These multiple-perpetrator hoaxes have been used to cover up
a variety of offenses, including accidental shootings (Adam Baisley, Tonya
Gibson, et al.), a work-related scuffle (Thomas Drogan and Louis Papaleo), domestic violence (Tina Gateley and William Karaffa), and a planned
crime (Joshua Green, Neva Veitch, and David Craig).

The Interracial Rape Hoax. Several of the White-on-Black hoaxes are based
on fabricated claims of rape (25 percent) by a White woman who said she
was assaulted by a Black man. For many Blacks, particularly those over a
certain age, the mention of interracial rape taps into age-old allegations
of Black men forcing themselves on innocent White females. Historically,
protecting the virtue of White women was placed on a legal pedestal. The
fear of Black male sexual assault against White women was the stated impetus behind the lynch laws. Given this backdrop, it is not surprising that
so many White women have created Black male rapists as their fictional
criminals.

Throughout history, rape has been the most common criminal hoax
played on Black men. The case of the Scottsboro Boys is perhaps the best-
known example of Black men being used as racial scapegoats. In 1931,
Victoria Price and Ruby Bates, two young White women, alleged that they
had been assaulted and raped by nine "Negro boys." Following a swift legal process, eight of the Black boys were sentenced to death. The final case
resulted in a hung jury. The press portrayed Bates and Price as symbols of
Southern White womanhood. Eventually, Bates recanted her story.[5]

A racial hoax also triggered the 1923 massacre in Rosewood, Florida.
A false claim by a White woman that she had been raped and beaten by
a Black man led Whites in Sumter, Florida (an adjoining town), to go on
a killing rampage and burn down the all-Black Rosewood. According to
official estimates, six Blacks and two Whites were killed. Unofficial estimates are that between 40 and 150 Blacks were killed. In 1994, seven decades later, a court awarded Rosewood family descendants more than $2
million in reparations.[6]

Black-on-White Hoaxes

The nineteen Black-on-White hoaxes are an interesting counterpoint to the White-on-Black hoaxes. Most Blacks who carried out hoaxes created a scenario in which they were victimized because of their race. Most of these were staged as hate crimes. A hate crime was typically used as a cover for an insurance scam (e.g., Tracy Birt, DeWayne Byrdsong, and Persey Harris et al.). Apparently these hoax perpetrators believed that a hate crime would be the most believable offense that a White person could commit against a Black person. The frequency of hate-crime hoaxes underscores the prevailing view: except for hate crimes, most of us have difficulty imagining someone White committing a random act of violence against someone Black.

Black-on-White hate-crime hoaxes contrast sharply with White-on-Black racial hoaxes. The latter are typically created as random acts of Black violence against Whites, which matches with the public perception that Blacks run amok committing depraved, unprovoked acts of violence against Whites, while the only Whites who commit violent crimes against Blacks are racial extremists. As is true for White-on-Black hoaxes, the motivations for Black-on-White hoaxes are varied. Some Black-on-White hoaxes are perpetrated as insurance scams and some to make a social statement, and still others are fabricated to evoke sympathy. Oftentimes these hoaxes are triggered by a combination of factors.

The Duke Lacrosse and Tawana Brawley Cases. Until the 2006–2007 Duke lacrosse rape case, the Tawana Brawley case was the most well-known Black-on-White hoax. In 1987 Brawley, a fifteen-year-old Black girl from Wappingers Falls, New York, told police that she had been abducted and raped by six White men. Brawley said that the men were police officers. She also said she was smeared with feces, placed in a plastic bag, and left in a gutter. The story drew national attention. After convening for seven months, the grand jury declined to issue any indictments in the case. Although Brawley stands by her original account, the incident has been widely discredited as a hoax.

Two decades later, three members of the Duke University lacrosse team were accused of raping an exotic dancer. Team members hosted a party and hired exotic dancers to provide entertainment. Two dancers, both Black, were hired to perform at the event hosted by the White collegiate team. The young women arrived at the house and left a short time later, after hearing some harsh language directed at them by some of the young men at the party.[7] Some of the other partygoers, however, managed to persuade the women to go back inside to finish the show. The dancers returned to the house and performed for the young men. After the young women left, one of them called the police and said that she had been forced into a bathroom and sexually assaulted by three team members at the party.

This explosive allegation led to heated and rancorous debates about a multitude of topics, including race, economic inequality, sex work, college sports, the South, sexism, White privilege, elite universities, Black female sexuality, the criminal justice system (particularly the power of the prosecutor's office), "jungle fever," the credibility of rape victims, historically Black colleges, elite sports, race relations, the media, and the Tawana Brawley case.

Many people felt that members of the lacrosse team had been unjustly set up by a scheming Black woman. Others believed the young woman and felt that she was not being taken seriously because she was Black and because she was a stripper. Still others felt the case presented an opportunity to address the harms of the "boys will be boys" mentality, regardless of whether a rape occurred at the party. The case also highlighted the squeamishness that many people have toward exotic dancers: many feel that strippers stand barely one rung above prostitutes. Some media figures, including radio talk-show host Rush Limbaugh—who called the young woman accuser a "ho"—openly questioned the woman's allegations, in part based on her choice of employment. Nationwide, people wore wristbands to show their support for the elite athletic team. The royal blue bands were available for purchase on the Internet. They were inscribed, "Innocent! #6, #13, #45—Duke Lacrosse 2006."[8] The proceeds went to the legal defense fund established for the three young men.

From the beginning, the criminal case appeared to have holes in it. For instance, one of the young men who had been identified as an attacker appeared to have a credible alibi. A taxicab driver said he had picked up the young man from the party and taken him, as directed, to an automated teller machine. There were also inconsistencies in the young woman's story regarding the timeline, the nature of the attack, and the number of people involved in the assault (and their physical descriptions). Adding to this, the second exotic dancer initially stated that she did not believe that a rape had taken place. From the beginning of the case, there were questions about the judgment and motives of the district attorney, Mike Nifong. Some people speculated that he used the case to secure the Black vote in

Durham, North Carolina, and ride to re-election. More than one year after the initial allegations made headlines, the rape charges were dropped and the district attorney faced numerous counts of professional ethics violations. Nifong was disbarred, forced to resign from his job, and later declared bankruptcy. No false report charges were filed against the accuser.

Comparing Harms: Black-on-White versus White-on-Black Racial Hoaxes

Several features distinguish White-on-Black from Black-on-White hoaxes. First, as discussed earlier, Black-on-White hoaxes are almost always drawn as hate crimes. When Whites create imaginary crimes, they are unlikely to use hate crime as a ruse. Second, the White-on-Black hoax causes greater social damage and harm than the Black-on-White hoaxes. This is primarily because Black-on-White hoaxes are less likely to receive national attention. Third, in hoaxes involving an interracial crime, a White person who claims to have been victimized by a Black person is much more likely to be believed than a Black person who claims to have been victimized by a White person.

An Aggrieved Community. The social and legal response to hoaxes differs according to the race of the person alleging that a crime has occurred. For example, Charles Stuart's claim that he had been shot by a Black jogger led to a full-scale police invasion of Boston's Mission Hill. Blacks in Boston, as well as many Blacks nationwide, felt some sense of responsibility for the crimes committed by the fictional Black criminal. Although the police department of Union, South Carolina, handled the Susan Smith case much differently, the town's Black community still felt betrayed by the hoax, as did many other Blacks. The same sense of community betrayal does not exist with Black-on-White hoaxes. There was no "White community" that bore comparable responsibility or group shame in the Tawana Brawley, Sabrina Collins, or Reggie Rivera cases. Nor was there a White community that was placed under siege after Brawley and Collins made their allegations.

In the Jesse Anderson, Susan Smith, Miriam Kashani, and Charles Stuart cases, there were calls for an apology to the Black community. This suggests that the response to and perception of racial hoaxes varies according to the race of the perpetrator. The demands for an apology

indicate that many Blacks believed the racial hoax had created a communal injury. Although Susan Smith's brother offered an apology to the Black
community, Ray Flynn, the mayor of Boston at the time of the Charles
Stuart case, declined to issue an apology.

Because Black criminals are perceived as more menacing than White
criminals, hoaxes created with a Black villain are treated differently than
are hoaxes created with a White villain. Greater social harm results when
someone White falsely accuses someone Black of a crime than when the
reverse occurs. This is not to suggest that there is no social harm associated with Black-on-White hoaxes. Black-on-White hoaxes make it easier
for Whites to dismiss claims of White racism. However, the greatest harm
of White-on-Black hoaxes is that they create negative racial stereotypes
for a new generation of young people. The case of Lucille Magrone offers
an example of this effect. Magrone, a White woman living in upstate New
York, sent out letters purportedly written by a Black man. The letters, sent
to neighborhood Whites, threatened them with rape and murder if they
did not move from the area: "You white people cannot live here. I will see
you dead."[9] After Magrone's hoax was unmasked, one of her White neighbors stated,

> Small children in the neighborhood have been introduced to racism that
> was never there before. Now it is in their minds that black people are
> bad, that black people are trying to break in—that there's a bogeyman, a
> black bogeyman out there who is going to get [them].[10]

Another indicator that the criminal stereotypes of Blacks are having an
impact on young people is the number of racial hoaxes involving a perpetrator under the age of twenty-one. In several cases White youths fabricated a crime against someone Black (e.g., Kendra Gillis, Edward O'Brien,
and Toby Campbell). In one case, a seven-year-old girl made up an assault charge against a Black man (Unnamed, Maine).

Whites who fabricate crimes against Whites have not caused the same
hysteria as Whites do when they fabricate crimes against Blacks. A comparison of the Susan Smith case with the Darlie Routier case is instruc-
tive. Routier claimed that a White male intruder had entered her home
and attacked her and her two boys. Both boys, ages five and six, died following the brutal attack, and Routier was severely wounded. Within days,
police began to suspect Routier in the deaths, and she was eventually
charged with both murders. Although Routier received an outpouring of

support, it does not compare with the attention and support received by Susan Smith.

Credibility. The public appears to be more willing to believe a White person who claims to have been victimized by someone Black than a Black person who to have been victimized by someone White. The Tawana Brawley and Duke Lacrosse cases are examples of this difference. From the beginning, many people suspected that the Brawley and Duke Lacrosse allegations were fabrications. By contrast, the stories of Susan Smith and Charles Stuart cases were readily believed. The reluctance to believe the Brawley and Duke lacrosse claims, though, may be partly due to the fact that they involved criminal allegations against protected communities (the police and an elite athletic team).

Additionally, Black-on-White hoaxes often end without a clear resolution. In the Brawley case, for instance, it was the grand jury's refusal to issue an indictment against law enforcement officials that caused her claim to be widely considered a hoax. Similarly, in the Duke Lacrosse case, the accuser stands by her story that she was sexually assaulted by members of the lacrosse team. In the first instance the case was "closed" based on the findings of an independent judicial body. In the second, as details of the district attorney's case surfaced (including the fact that he never actually interviewed the accuser), many people concluded that the case was a hoax. Unfortunately, in these cases Blacks and Whites remained divided. Many Blacks claimed that there was a cover-up, and many Whites claimed that there was a hoax.

Another indication of the tension created by these cases is the amount of litigation they spark. Following the Brawley investigation, a $30 million defamation suit was brought against her and her advisers. A default judgment was entered against Brawley, and a few years later, one of her lead attorneys was disbarred. The case has continued to dog the Reverend Al Sharpton, who has stated that at the time of the allegations he believed Brawley's story, as did many others. He has since worked with numerous families victimized by police brutality and in 2004 ran for president.

False Report Charges. There does not appear to be a rhyme or method that explains whether a hoax perpetrator will face charges for filing a false report. As table 6.1 indicates, some perpetrators are charged, and others are not. The seriousness of the offense does not appear to be determinative, since some perpetrators charged with murder faced false report charges (e.g., Thomas DiBartolo) whereas others did not (e.g., Donald Cherry, Susan Smith). For some prosecutors it may be that adding false report charges to a murder case is perceived as excessive. Notably, in many of the cases involving money scams, false report charges were filed (e.g., Sonia James, Daniel Mayo and Philip LaForest, Jaelyn Sealey). Further, whether someone fabricated a crime or used a hoax to cover up a real crime does not appear to be linked with whether they are charged with filing a false police report. Also, in several cases, though hoax perpetrators did not face false report charges, they did face other criminal charges for their hoax—for example, Alicia Hardin (felony disorderly conduct).

Equating Black-on-White with White-on-Black hoaxes ignores the different social reaction to these hoaxes. Black men have always been perceived as a physical threat; however, until recently, that threat was portrayed in sexual terms. In the past twenty years, the image of the Black male as rapist has evolved into the image of the Black male as the symbolic pillager of all that is good. The *criminalblackman* stereotype persists, despite the fact that the majority of people arrested each year are White. The negative perceptions of Black men affect how Blacks and Whites, as individuals and as group members, are affected by racial hoaxes.

White-on-Black hoaxes follow a standard pattern. First, law enforcement officials are called into action. They are asked to protect an innocent White person from further harm and to apprehend a widely perceived threat, a menacing Black man. Second, the incident arouses sympathy and results in calls for swift and stiff punishment. Third, even after the hoax is uncovered, the image of the *criminalblackman* lingers and becomes more embedded in our collective racial consciousness.

Other Cases and Patterns

Campus Hoaxes. One of the most striking patterns that has emerged since my initial analysis of racial hoaxes is the number of cases that involve college students. Eleven of the cases (12.5 percent) involved a university. For a variety of reasons a college campus is fertile ground for hoaxes: One, for some students, college is the first interaction they have had with members of other racial and ethnic groups. Two, for many students, college provides their first exposure to student activism and political dissent. Three, for some students, college may represent a first in-depth exploration of sociopolitical issues, including race.

Both Blacks and Whites have perpetrated university hoaxes. A number of these hoaxes were designed to "send a message," to make a social or political statement about an issue of importance to the hoax perpetrator. The following cases are representative:

- A young White female student at the University of Montana told police that she had been robbed by a Black man. She said her attacker took one hundred dollars. She described him as six foot three with a dark or Black complexion. After discovering several inconsistencies in her story, police charged her with filing a false police report. (Emily Clark, Josephine Lupus)
- A Black student at Trinity International sent out hate mail to Black and Latino students. The letters threatened violence. As a precautionary response, school officials moved all minority students off-campus to hotels. After two weeks of campus turmoil, Alicia Hardin admitted that she had sent the letters. She wanted to transfer to another school and thought this tactic would make her parents believe that Trinity International was not a safe school for minority students. (Alicia Hardin)
- A White female student at George Washington University reported that another White female had been raped by two Black men with "particularly bad body odor." The perpetrator later claimed that the hoax was staged to "highlight the problems of safety for women . . . [and was] never meant to hurt anyone or racially offend anyone." (Miriam Kashani)

Perhaps the most unusual campus hoax is the one involving Keri Dunn, who in 2004 was a visiting professor at Claremont McKenna College. Dunn, who is White, claimed that she was attacked one evening as she returned to her car. She had just given a lecture on hate crime. Dunn said that her vehicle had been spray-painted with racist and anti-Semitic slurs ("kike whore" and "nigger lover"). A campus uproar followed, and classes were canceled for one day. Officials later concluded that Dunn had staged the hoax herself. She was sentenced to one year in prison and restitution of twenty thousand dollars, the cost of investigating the incident. This case is unusual in that Dunn is White and she perpetrated a hoax that implicated Whites.

Miscellaneous Hoaxes. A number of hoaxes defy easy categorization. Sometimes cases are not discovered to be hoaxes until years or decades later. In one instance, a twenty-year-old racial hoax was uncovered by police. In 1982, Mark Mangelsdorf was involved with a married woman, Melinda Raisch. Raisch, who was part of a religious community and worked at a Bible college, did not want to suffer the stigma of a divorce, so she and Mangelsdorf conspired to kill her husband, David Harmon. The pair killed Harmon with a crowbar while he lay sleeping. At the time, Raisch blamed the murder on Black intruders into the Harmon home. After police reopened the case in 2001, both Mangelsdorf and Raisch were convicted of second-degree murder in Harmon's death. In 2006, both received sentences of ten to twenty years in prison.

In another twist on the traditional racial hoax, Donald Cherry, a White father of two, told police that his two-year-old son had been killed by Black youths, following a traffic dispute. According to Cherry, following the traffic encounter, the youths fired shots at his car after he made an obscene gesture at them. Within one week, Cherry told police that he had been involved not in a traffic dispute but rather in a drug deal gone awry. Cherry had driven across town to purchase crack cocaine. His small children were in the back seat of the vehicle. As it turned out, the suspect, who admitted to firing the shot, is Black. The case is unusual because Cherry attempted to portray himself as an innocent victim of random Black crime, thereby attempting to make the actions committed by the Black youth appear even more sinister.

There were two incidents in which White assailants robbed White victims and demanded that they tell the police that the assailants were Black. In one case, a gang of White thieves robbed a man and threatened to kill his family unless he told police that the robbers were Black. In another case, a White man robbed an elderly couple of $2,850 and told them to blame the crime on a Black man. These cases mirror the rationale behind the racial hoax cases: to play on racial stereotypes and avoid criminal responsibility.

In another case, a nineteen-year-old White man, David Mazziotti, used face paint to disguise his race. The Philadelphia man also hid a pillow under his clothes to make himself appear obese. Mazziotti had created this obese Black man disguise so that he could rob banks. In one South Africa case, a gang of White robbers wore mud masks to disguise their race and trick their victims into believing and reporting that the perpetrators were Blacks. Because Mazziotti was arrested before he could carry out the crime, the case does not classify as a typical racial hoax. However, Mazziotti's perceptions and beliefs about race and crime are identical to those of perpetrators of successful hoaxes.

Based on the uncorroborated testimony of a lone undercover agent, police in Tulia, Texas, arrested more than forty African American residents, approximately 16 percent of the town's Black population. This undercover drug sting operation, by a White officer, resulted in numerous convictions and sentences. An investigation by a special prosecutor revealed that the evidence was unreliable, and all the convictions were voided. By itself, this incident represents more than forty separate racial hoaxes.

In each of these hoaxes, it is clear that the goal was to have someone Black singled out and held responsible for a crime he or she did not commit. These cases, when added to the others, make a compelling argument for publicizing the prevalence and harms of hoaxes. That some people have gone to the extreme of using Blackface to avoid criminal responsibility demonstrates the strength of the perceived link between Blackness and crime.

Economics of the Racial Hoax

Beyond causing social injury, the racial hoax also exacts a financial toll. Untold resources have been wasted on efforts to locate fictional Black criminals. The following comment illuminates the varied harms of racial hoaxes:

> [A racial hoax] accusation affects us all. It terrorizes a community and discriminates against a race of people. And it is the kind of crime that costs taxpayers thousands of dollars to launch massive, futile investigations.[11]

Indeed, the economic consequences of many hoax cases—for example, Susan Smith, Charles Stuart, Duke lacrosse, and Jennifer Wilbanks—underscore this point. Each of these cases triggered massive searches and investigations by police departments and sometimes involved multiple law enforcement agencies. The costs of these cases ran into the tens of thousands of dollars.

Increasingly hoax perpetrators are being required to pay investigative costs. In one case, a White college student falsely claimed that she had been raped by a Black man. After confessing to the fabrication, she had to repay the police for the costs of investigating her case (Michele Yentes). Several other cases have imposed restitution on hoax perpetrators (Keri Dunn, Sonia James, and Jennifer Wilbanks).

A Legal Response: The Law and the Logistics

False Report Statutes. Though they are on the books, false report laws are not always used to punish racial hoax offenders. Just over half of the hoax perpetrators were charged with filing a false police report. False reporting charges are most often filed in cases involving less-serious offenses. The fact that false report charges are not uniformly sought renders them an ineffective deterrent against future hoaxes. Further, most false report statutes constitute misdemeanors, which also undercuts their deterrence value. On the one hand, adding a false report charge to a murder case such as Susan Smith's might appear to be overkill. At the other extreme, pursuing a false police-report charge against someone like Miriam Kashani might seem like a waste of the prosecutor's time and resources. The failure to punish racial hoaxes, however, only makes it more likely that they will continue.

The Law on Hate Crimes. Hate-crime statutes can be divided into two types. First, some statutes treat hate crimes as independent criminal offenses. These are referred to as "pure bias" statutes. The Minnesota statute at issue in *R.A.V. v. St. Paul* is an example of this type.[12] In this 1992 case, the U.S. Supreme Court held that the state's bias-crime law impermissibly criminalized certain forms of hate speech, in violation of the First Amendment.

A second kind of hate-crime statute provides a "penalty enhancement" for crimes motivated by bias. Under these statutes, when the court finds that the offender has committed a crime against a person because of his or her race, it may impose additional penalties. In some states, for example, a person convicted of assault could face one year behind bars, but if the assault was racially motivated, the penalty could be increased to two years. A number of states have adopted the Model Bias Crime provision, drafted by the Anti-Defamation League. The federal government has also enacted penalty-enhancement legislation.

Penalty-enhancement statutes have been upheld by the U.S. Supreme Court. In *Wisconsin v. Mitchell* a Black defendant challenged the state's penalty-enhancement statute.[13] Mitchell, who had been convicted of assaulting a fourteen-year-old White youth, faced an increased prison sentence of five years because the crime was motivated by bias. Finding the state law constitutional, the Supreme Court noted that "bias-inspired conduct" is an appropriate arena for penalty enhancement because it is "thought to inflict greater individual and societal harm."[14] Further, the Court observed, such conduct is likely to provoke "retaliatory crimes, inflict distinct emotional harm on their victims, and incite community unrest."[15] A racial hoax law could be framed as either a pure bias-crime statute or as a penalty enhancement. Given that the Supreme Court has upheld bias-crime enhancement, this looks to be the safer constitutional route.

The Racial Hoax as Crime: Constitutional Concerns

The road to making the racial hoax a crime is, constitutionally speaking, a much smoother road than the one that earlier hate-crime legislation had to travel. This is primarily because First Amendment concerns do not pose a barrier to making the racial hoax a crime.[16] It is a longstanding principle of constitutional law that when speech involves imminent lawless action, it is not accorded First Amendment protection. Thus, one does not have the right to yell "fire" in a crowded video store.[17]

When one uses a racial hoax to mislead law enforcement, a chain of predictable responses follows. The speech element ("A Black man harmed me") of the racial hoax triggers numerous actions, including the deployment of police officers to particular neighborhoods to locate potential suspects, the creation of "wanted" posters, the dissemination of information about the crime to the media, the announcement of all-points bulletins, and meetings by the police and community groups to discuss what actions should be taken. The person uttering the words of a racial hoax has done more than simply speak. He or she has pointed a finger at a community of people, with the goal of thwarting justice. By design, the speech of the racial hoax is actually lawless conduct, which is unprotected by the First Amendment.

It could be argued as well that given the historically fraught relationship between the African American community and law enforcement that Black-on-White hoaxes, in particular, have the potential to result in violence. Arguably, then, they represent "true threats" that suggest that the hoax perpetrator intends to commit an act of violence against the victim —by triggering police action. In *Virginia v. Black*, the Supreme Court determined that the state legislation that punishes speech on the basis of its content is permissible in some instances, particularly for speech with a long and historical connection to violence.[18]

Proposed Legislation

In 1995, New Jersey congressperson Shirley Turner drafted legislation designed to punish racial hoaxes. Although the proposed state law, False Reports to Law Enforcement Authorities, was not signed into law, it offers a look at how a racial hoax law might be framed:

- *Falsely Incriminating Another.* A person who knowingly gives or causes to be given false information or a description of a fictitious person to any law enforcement officer with purpose to implicate another because of race, color, religion, sexual orientation or ethnicity commits a crime of the third degree (punishable by three to five years in prison and/or $15,000 fine).
- *Fictitious Reports.* A person who files a fictitious report is guilty of a crime of the fourth degree if the person acted with purpose to implicate another because of race, color, religion, sexual orientation, or ethnicity (punishable by eighteen months in prison and/or $10,000 fine).
- *Restitution.* In addition to any other fine, fee, or assessment imposed, any person convicted of an offense under this section is to reimburse the governing body of the municipality for the costs incurred in investigating the false information or the fictitious report.[19]

Since 1996, New Jersey senator Shirley Turner has introduced racial hoax legislation every few years. Notably, the proposed law distinguishes between a hoax used to cover up an actual crime (false incrimination) and one used to mask a fake crime (fictitious reports) and attaches a harsher penalty to the former offense. This proposed law will serve as a reference for the following discussion on the ideal components of a racial hoax law.

The Offender. Regardless of race, a hoax law should apply to anyone who perpetrates a hoax against someone Black or other person of color. The foregoing discussion and analysis support this approach. The damage done by a fabricated claim is so great that there should be no exclusion as to who can be punished. Harm occurs irrespective of whether a hoax perpetrator is White or Black.

Community responses and harms may differ depending on the race of the perpetrator. When a White offender points the finger at a Black person, it acts to further polarize Black and White communities. As a result, Blacks feel more vulnerable to indiscriminate police practices, and Whites feel more vulnerable to crime by Blacks. Conversely, when the hoax perpetrator is Black and the victim is Black, it is probable that the alleged crime will not be taken as seriously. The police are unlikely to respond as quickly to a Black person claiming harm as they would to a White person claiming harm. White-on-Black hoaxes receive much more media attention than Black-on-Black hoaxes, and Black-on-Black hoaxes are less likely to be uncovered because such a fabrication would appear to represent the status quo: the erroneous belief that the majority of crime in the United States involves a Black offender. In fact, Whites comprise the majority of the people arrested for crime in any given year. Furthermore, more than 80 percent of all crime is intraracial, involving a victim and offender of the same race. Both the Black-on-Black and the White-on-Black hoax should be sanctioned because they perpetuate the *criminalblackman* stereotype.

Professor Mari Matsuda, in a compelling argument for criminalizing race-based hate speech, contends that only Whites can be offenders. She states that the harm of racist speech is greatest when the speech reinforces a "historically vertical relationship."[20] Likewise, professor Marc Fleischauer argues that penalty enhancement should only attach in cases involving a White offender. Without this "White-only" rule, "minorities will be subjected to enhanced penalties at a disproportionate rate compared to Whites because it is the nature of society for the majorities to prosecute minorities more frequently and with more vigor than vice versa."[21] The fact that *Wisconsin v. Mitchell*—the only hate-crime sentencing-enhancement case decided by the U.S. Supreme Court—involved a Black defendant supports Fleischauer's observations.

Although Fleischauer and Matsuda make strong arguments, the race-of-the-perpetrator/race-of-the-victim line that they draw should not be applied to a racial hoax law. First, unlike the victim of racist hate speech, the victim of a racial hoax is not directly assaulted by the offender. Second, it is not just one person who is harmed by a racial hoax but an entire community. Given the harm done by pointing a false finger at a Black person, anyone of any race who perpetrates a hoax against someone Black should be penalized. The proposed New Jersey legislation correctly makes no distinction based on the race of the perpetrator.

Targets and Victims. With regard to who is classified as a victim for the racial hoax, two questions arise. First, should a racial hoax law mandate an identifiable, named victim, a "Willie Bennett requirement"? Willie Bennett is the Black man whom Charles Stuart identified as the person who shot and robbed him and his wife. Since current false report statutes do not require an identifiable victim, there should be no such requirement for a racial hoax law. The goal of false report statutes is to punish intentional efforts to thwart law enforcement. Whether there exists an identifiable victim or not, the racial hoax causes harm. A penalty is also justified by the communal harm it causes.

Professor Frederick Lawrence, in a discussion of the breadth of harm caused by hate crimes, states, "The victim suffers for being singled out on the basis of race, and the general community of the target racial group is harmed as well."[22] As applied to the racial hoax, once a "victim" says "a Black guy did it," he or she has hurled a racial epithet that is actionable. Given the predictable responses of law enforcement, the hoax is a kind of physical harassment, solely on the basis of race. It is as if Susan Smith and all the other hoax perpetrators called every Black man a "low life," "hoodlum," or "criminal" *because* of his race. The racial hoax exemplifies philosopher Ludwig Wittgenstein's assertion that "words are also deeds."[23]

The proposed New Jersey legislation penalizes people who use a racial hoax to target a specific person because of his race ("False Incrimination") as well as those who use a hoax to create a nonexistent villain ("Fictitious Persons"). Assuming there is a legally cognizable crime, a second question arises: Which racial groups should receive protection under a racial hoax law? A strong argument can be made for applicability only when there is a Black victim. Ideally, a racial hoax law would be actionable only when the finger has been pointed at someone Black.

Fleischauer, in his discussion of Florida's hate-crime statute, argues that it would be constitutional to make minorities the only protected group.[24] He observes that one of the explicit goals of hate-crime legislation is to curb racism and empower minorities. To allow a racial hoax law to encompass both White-on-Black hoaxes *and* Black-on-White hoaxes unfairly accords the two equal weight. Beyond the individual harm that a racial hoax may cause a targeted Black person, it brings harm to Blacks as a group and creates more tension between Blacks and Whites. A look at the hoax cases establishes that the harm of a White-on-Black hoax is not comparable to the harm of either a White-on-White or Black-on-White hoax. The proposed New Jersey legislation is silent with regard to the victim's race, implying that a hoax victim may be of any race.

The Equal Protection Clause presents the biggest roadblock to the proposed construction of who qualifies as a victim under a racial hoax law, but making a distinction between victims of different races is legally justified because White-on-Black hoaxes cause more harm than Black-on-White hoaxes. False reporting laws are an adequate penalty for Black-on-White hoaxes. White-on-White hoaxes, though they do occur, do not pose the same societal problems as those in which the victim is Black. Considering the U.S. Supreme Court's race-neutral leanings, however, the safest route is to draft hoax legislation that would protect a victim of any race. This legal compromise, however, does not provide adequate protection to Blacks as a group.

Intent. A racial hoax law could be written to require either specific or general intent on the part of the perpetrator. A distinction could be made between whether the perpetrator acted "knowingly" or "purposely." If the requirement is that the perpetrator acted "knowingly," the prosecution would have to show only that the hoax perpetrator was "practically certain" that law enforcement forces would respond and that some harm would occur as a result of the perpetrator's race labeling. If the requirement is that the perpetrator acted "purposely," prosecutors would have to prove that the hoax perpetrator had as a conscious objective causing the particular result: triggering a manhunt *and* harming a specific Black person or Blacks as a group. This higher standard of intent should not be required for a racial hoax law.

The New Jersey legislation appears to impose a general-intent requirement. Under the proposed law, one could be charged with false incrimination on the basis of race, when one "knowingly" gives false information to a police officer with the goal of implicating someone because of his or her race. To avoid the problem of attempting to determine whether the hoax perpetrator intended to cause harm to Blacks as a group or to any particular Black person, specific intent should not be an element of a racial hoax offense. The very fact that a racial hoax has been employed means that existing stereotypes have been reinforced and racial dissension furthered. Professor Charles Lawrence elaborates:

> Traditional notions of intent do not reflect the fact that decisions about racial matters are influenced in large part by factors that can be characterized as neither intentional—in the sense that certain outcomes are self-consciously sought—nor unintentional—in the sense that the outcomes

are random, fortuitous, and uninfluenced by the decisionmaker's beliefs, desires, and wishes.[25]

Prosecutors should not be required to establish that a hoax perpetrator is a racist or that he or she intended to mislead law enforcement. As set forth in the proposed New Jersey law, it is sufficient that the perpetrator has blamed someone *because* of his or her race. The reasons behind the racial finger-pointing should be irrelevant.

Legal Sanctions. Perpetrating a racial hoax should be a felony offense because it is a serious crime and has ramifications beyond any one particular case. Further, a penalty must be imposed that would deter others from employing hoaxes. A state could decide to impose a criminal fine and prison time. Beyond a prison term, a racial hoax perpetrator should be required to pay restitution. The New Jersey provision requires restitution in the amount of law enforcement costs for wasted resources. Additionally, payment of court costs and restitution to any identifiable victims should be imposed.

Moral Sanctions: An Apology. In addition to imposing criminal penalties and restitution, the hoax offender should be required to publicly apologize for playing on racial stereotypes. An apology would be one step toward healing a racially divided community. In recent years, some criminal-court judges have strongly encouraged offenders to apologize (e.g., batterers, drunk drivers, corporate polluters). Regardless of whether a hoax case reaches trial, the mayor, police chief, or other official could ask perpetrators to apologize to the community.

Following Susan Smith's confession, there were numerous calls for an apology. Columnist William Raspberry commented, "This may be difficult for non-minorities to accept, but black people do feel specially violated by Susan Smith's lie."[26] At the same time that the Black community is injured, so are other racial communities of color. And so are Whites. An apology, therefore, is due the entire community.

Reporting Requirement. In the same way that the law imposes reporting requirements for bias crimes, there should be reporting requirements for racial hoaxes. It is impossible to estimate the annual frequency of racial hoaxes because there is no database for this information. A national repository should be created that tracks information on racial hoaxes, including the race, sex, and age of the offender and victim; the underlying hoax offense; the number of days of the hoax; and the estimated cost of investigating the hoax. These data could be compiled as a part of the information collected for the Hate Crime Statistics Act.

Conclusion

The racial hoax should be subject to criminal penalty. With the exception of the proposed New Jersey legislation, there has been a deafening legal silence about the ravages of the racial hoax. The legal analysis makes clear that a racial hoax law is constitutionally permissible. A racial hoax law provides a legal route for addressing this country's racial past as it is played out today in perceptions of crime. As important, given that hate-crime statutes are similar to antidiscrimination laws, a racial hoax law is a natural and necessary extension of redress for legally recognized racial harms. In sum, a racial hoax law acknowledges American racial history, the power of negative stereotypes based on this history, and the need for legal redress.

Absent a specific legal intervention, people will continue to use hoaxes to play the race card and avoid criminal liability. In the absence of a law, we are in effect encouraging people to employ racial hoaxes. Enactment of racial hoax legislation would send a message, both functional and symbolic, that the wide-ranging and deleterious impact of racial hoaxes will not be tolerated.

7

White Crime

No one focuses on White crime or sees it as a problem. In fact, the very category "White crime" sounds funny, like some sort of debater's trick.　　　　　　　　　　　　—Richard Delgado[1]

It has been said that you can tell a lot about how something is valued in a culture by the number of types or models it has been given. For instance, the automobile has many names; it has hundreds of makes and models. The same is true for a variety of things, such as trees, colors, movies, architecture, books, computers, desserts, and so forth. Given the perceived prevalence of and fear associated with Black crime, perhaps it is not surprising that there are a plethora of labels for it. It is sometimes referred to as "Black offending," "Black-on-Black crime," or "Black criminality." Additionally, terms such as "urban crime," "inner-city crime," "metropolitan crime," "big-city crime," and "street crime" refer to Black crime. There are also offense-specific markers for Black crime, such as gang-related offenses, carjackings, and sexual-assault crimes. Given the various names for Black crime, we would expect that the criminal that most Americans "see" happens to be Black. This reality challenges the popular public fantasy that we are "color-blind" or that we "don't see race."

Given how crime is labeled and in light of society's emphasis on street crimes, which Blacks disproportionately commit, it is no surprise that Blacks, Latinos, Whites, Native Americans, and Asian Americans alike visualize crime in Blackface. A person would have to live as a hermit—avoid watching television, reading the newspaper, or engaging in public conversation—to escape seeing crime portrayed in shades of Black. Our language of crime, however, does not include terms such as "White crime," "White criminality," or "White-on-White crime." In some instances, crime is racialized in other colors besides Black—for example, references to

Latino gangs or Asian gangs. No other group, however, is as closely linked to crime by language as African Americans are.

Although portraying crime in Blackface is widespread within the media, social scientists who study crime also portray crime in varied hues of Black. Social scientists rely heavily on terms that spotlight crimes associated with Blacks. At the same time, however, they do not use similar labels to describe the crimes committed by Whites. The work of academics suggests that they are no better at putting a realistic color on the face of crime than the lay public is.[2]

This chapter looks at crime data by race, with an emphasis on White crime. The first section examines the amount of White involvement in the criminal justice system, as measured by arrests and prison. This is followed by a discussion of whether social scientists should use terms to highlight offenses by Whites, including "White crime" and "White criminality." There is also a consideration of whether the use of racial labels is affected by the small number of minority criminologists. One downside of the way we currently talk about crime and race is that it supports partial truths. The chapter ends with a detailed discussion of this problem, using James Q. Wilson's "Black crime causes White racism" thesis as an example. The chapter concludes that half facts skew our perception and thereby our understanding of the relationship between race and crime.

The Study of White Crime

Contrary to popular belief, Whites are arrested more than members of other racial groups. As table 7.1 indicates, this is not a new trend, nor is it particularly surprising given that Whites are more than two-thirds of

TABLE 7.1
*Black and White Arrests, Percentage Distribution
for All Crimes, 2000–2006*

	Black	White
2000	27.9%	69.7%
2001	28.1%	69.5%
2002	26.9%	70.7%
2003	27.0%	70.6%
2004	27.1%	70.5%
2005	27.8%	69.8%
2006	28.0%	69.7%

Source: Bureau of Justice Statistics, *Sourcebook of Criminal Justice
Statistics (2000–2005) (2006).*

TABLE 7.2
Total Arrests, Distribution by Race, 2006

Offense Charged	Number of Arrests					Percentage Distribution				
	Total	White	Black	American Indian or Alaskan Native	Asian or Pacific Islander	Total	White	Black	American Indian or Alaskan Native	Asian or Pacific Islander
All crimes	10,437,620	7,270,214	2,924,724	130,589	112,093	100.0	69.7	28.0	1.3	1.1
Murder and nonnegligent manslaughter	9,801	4,595	4,990	110	106	100.0	46.9	50.9	1.1	1.1
Forcible rape	17,042	11,122	5,536	195	189	100.0	65.3	32.5	1.1	1.1
Robbery	93,393	39,419	52,541	611	822	100.0	42.2	56.3	0.7	0.9
Aggravated assault	326,721	206,417	112,645	3,949	3,710	100.0	63.2	34.5	1.2	1.1
Burglary	221,732	152,965	64,655	2,123	1,989	100.0	69.0	29.2	1.0	0.9
Larceny-theft	798,983	548,057	230,980	9,377	10,569	100.0	68.6	28.9	1.2	1.3
Motor-vehicle theft	100,612	63,090	35,116	978	1,428	100.0	62.7	34.9	1.0	1.4
Arson	11,972	9,101	2,591	116	164	100.0	76.0	21.6	1.0	1.4
Violent crime	446,957	261,553	175,712	4,865	4,827	100.0	58.5	39.3	1.1	1.1
Property crime	1,133,299	773,213	333,342	12,594	14,150	100.0	68.2	29.4	1.1	1.2
Other assaults	949,940	619,825	306,078	13,097	10,940	100.0	65.2	32.2	1.4	1.2
Forgery and counterfeiting	79,258	55,562	22,337	433	926	100.0	70.1	28.2	0.5	1.2
Fraud	196,930	135,329	59,087	1,213	1,301	100.0	68.7	30.0	0.6	0.7
Embezzlement	14,705	9,668	4,741	82	214	100.0	65.7	32.2	0.6	1.5
Stolen property: buying, receiving, possessing	89,850	58,066	30,267	670	847	100.0	64.6	33.7	0.7	0.9
Vandalism	219,652	165,518	48,781	2,987	2,366	100.0	75.4	22.2	1.4	1.1
Weapons: carrying, possessing, etc.	147,312	84,929	59,863	1,134	1,386	100.0	57.7	40.6	0.8	0.9
Prostitution and commercialized vice	59,616	33,827	23,612	569	1,608	100.0	56.7	39.6	1.0	2.7
Sex offenses (except forcible rape and prostitution)	63,048	46,194	15,465	640	749	100.0	73.3	24.5	1.0	1.2

Drug-abuse violations	1,376,792	875,1C1	483,886	8,198	9,607	100.0	63.6	35.1	0.6	0.7
Gambling	9,001	2,358	6,467	12	164	100.0	26.2	71.8	0.1	1.8
Offenses against the family and children	91,618	61,278	28,086	1,678	576	100.0	66.9	30.7	1.8	0.6
Driving under the influence	1,034,651	914,225	95,260	13,484	11,681	100.0	88.4	9.2	1.3	1.1
Liquor laws	466,323	393,068	50,035	12,831	5,389	100.0	85.4	10.7	2.8	1.2
Drunkenness	408,439	344,155	54,113	7,884	2,287	100.0	84.3	13.2	1.9	0.6
Disorderly conduct	517,264	325,991	179,733	7,606	3,934	100.0	63.0	34.7	1.5	0.8
Vagrancy	27,016	15,303	11,238	333	137	100.0	56.7	41.6	1.2	0.5
All other offenses (except traffic)	2,906,311	1,962,017	872,571	37,935	33,788	100.0	67.5	30.0	1.3	1.2
Suspicion	1,723	1,01_	658	41	13	100.0	58.7	38.2	2.4	0.8
Curfew and loitering-law violations	114,166	69,624	42,496	814	1,232	100.0	61.0	37.2	0.7	1.1
Runaways	83,749	57,393	20,896	1,489	3,971	100.0	68.5	25.0	1.8	4.7

Source: FBI, Uniform Crime Reports 2005, U.S. Department of Justice (2006).

TABLE 7.3

Black and White Arrest and Incarceration Figures, 2005

	Arrested	In Prison	In Jail
White*	7,117,040 (69.8%)	800,400 (54.8%)	442,900 (59.2%)
Black	2,830,778 (27.8%)	577,100 (39.5%)	290,500 (38.9%)
Other	241,873 (2.3%)	83,600 (5.7%)	14,129 (1.9%)
Total	10,189,691 (100%)	1,461,100 (100%)	747,529 (100%)

Source: Bureau of Justice Statistics, "Prisoners in 2005," NCJ 215092 (2006); Bureau of Justice Statistics, "Demographic Trends in Jail Populations."
  * Latinos are included in the White category.

the U.S. population. Table 7.2, which provides a racial breakdown of arrests for 2006, shows that in three offense categories Whites account for approximately 80 percent of those arrested: DUI (88.4 percent), liquor-law violations (85.4 percent), and drunkenness (84.3 percent). For these three crimes, White arrest rates are on par with their percentage in the population. Table 7.2 also indicates that Whites have high rates of arrest for several other offenses, including arson (76 percent), vandalism (75.4 percent), sex offenses (73.3 percent), and forgery and counterfeiting (70.1 percent).

Not only do Whites represent the majority of all those arrested in any given year; they also make up the majority of the incarcerated population. For 2005, Whites comprised 55 percent of the total incarcerated population—those in prison or jail—1.2 million of the 2.2 million behind bars (table 7.3). They also constitute 55 percent of the people in prison, 800,000 out of 1.4 million. What is often left unsaid is that White criminal representation, though not disproportionate, is quite high. A public discussion about crime and race necessarily means discussing White crime. One outcome of the fact that race has become synonymous with being Black is that White crime is rarely labeled—and rarely discussed.

Public Beliefs about Race and Crime

There is a widespread belief that Blacks both disproportionately commit crime and are responsible for the majority of crime. The first belief is true; the second is not. The second belief, that Blacks commit most crime, is an extension of the first. Though distinct, these perceptions, one fact and one fiction, are jumbled in the public mind. The public's inaccurate picture of the amount of Black crime is partly media driven, since television in particular focuses to a great extent on street crime. Although each year two-thirds of the people arrested for street crimes are White, Blacks continue to represent the public face of street crime.

The perception that crime is violent, Black, and male has converged to create the *criminalblackman* (see chapter 1). By itself, this mythical criminal Black symbol is scary enough. The figure has become even more ominous, however, because we do not have anything with which compare him. There is no *criminalwhiteman*. There is every reason to believe that if more images of White criminals and White criminality were put in the media spotlight, the public image of crime would shift. The damage of the crime-equals-Black stereotype, however, cannot be undone simply by highlighting White crime. The media and the academic community will also have to expose the *criminalblackman* image as a misrepresentation.

Invisible Labels: A Look at the Research

Disproportionately high rates of crime by Blacks cannot be used to explain why we rarely see crime represented in other colors. Our discussion of race and crime is not so much segregated as one-dimensional. Nobel Prize laureate Toni Morrison has keenly observed that the racial presentation of crime reinforces "racial half-truths. . . . Unless you can intelligently use the phrase 'White on White crime,' you can't use the phrase 'Black on Black crime.'"[3] A review of newspapers, law review articles, and social science articles indicates that when the picture of crime and deviance is assigned a color, it is usually Black.

LexisNexis, a computerized database that catalogs news stories from more than fifty-six hundred sources, lists few articles that use terms such as "White crime" or "White-on-White crime." Notably, most of these articles reference White crime in comparison with Black crime, not as an independent phenomenon. By comparison, it is not hard to find articles that use some variation of "Black crime." The grossly disparate use of the term "Black crime" cannot be completely explained by the different crime rates for Blacks and Whites. When discussing race and crime, legal analysts and journalists have a hard time seeing White crime.

The virtual absence of articles on White crime suggests that in our individual and collective minds "White" and "crime" simply do not go together. By way of example, when I presented a draft of this chapter at a conference, the moderator introduced me by stating my name, my university affiliation, and the title of my paper, "White-Collar Crime"! He never caught his mistake, that he had added the word "collar" to the title of my paper. At the outset of my talk, I mentioned the error and suggested that it underscored the racialized ways in which we think and talk about crime. For most of us, White crime is rarely conceptualized as a separate phenomenon, one unhooked from Black crime. As Richard Delgado observes in the epigraph to this chapter, "White crime" sounds "funny."

In addition to journalists and law professors, criminologists have managed to overlook White crime. A review of five top-ranked criminology journals between 2001 and 2005 revealed few journal articles explicitly devoted to "White crime."[4] White crime is being studied, yet it is not called White crime. The numerous academic articles that focus on the deviance of White adults and White youths avoid using terms such as "White criminality." The nonacknowledgment of White crime contrasts sharply with the pervasive labeling of Black crime.

Scores of academic articles refer to Black crime. In addition to those that use terms such as "Black crime," "Black criminality," and "Black-on-Black crime" (or use the term "African American"), many articles use ostensibly race-neutral words. These terms include "inner city," "street crime," and "urban." Code words such as these widen the extent to which Black crime is labeled by social scientists.

The skewed focus of journalists and academics on Black offending may simply mirror society's skewed concern with street crime. By this reasoning, because Blacks are responsible for a disproportionate amount of street crime, they receive a disproportionate amount of attention by academics and the media. Such reasoning, however, rings only partially true. Disproportionate offending by Blacks may explain why research centers on Black crime, but it does not explain why so little research and media attention focuses on White street crime. Also, it does not explain why crime by Whites is rarely referred to as "White crime." Finally, a look at the history of race and crime suggests that offenses committed by Blacks have always received extraordinary attention. This was true long before "disproportionality" and "disparity" became part of the public lexicon on crime.

Crime in Whiteface: Some Examples

Several areas of research could be classified as "White crime," including white-collar, rural and suburban, and hate crime.

White-Collar Crime. White-collar crime, as defined by Edwin Sutherland, is "crime committed by a person of respectability and high social status in the course of his occupation."5 Researchers have observed that Whites have disproportionate opportunities to commit high-status offenses because they are more likely to hold high-status jobs. With the exception of fraud and embezzlement, white-collar offenses are not collected as part of the Uniform Crime Reports. Although white-collar criminality may never produce the same degree of fear as street crime, its impact on society is substantial. Many researchers have observed that white-collar crime is associated with violence and imposes moral damage on society.6 Researchers Francis Cullen and Michael Benson state, "the costs of white collar crime —the violence it entails, the money it transfers illegally, its damage to the moral fabric—may well outstrip the costs of traditional street crimes."7 Some researchers estimate that white-collar crime costs ten times as much as street crime. It remains a mystery why there is no annual count of white-collar crimes. Cullen and Benson suggest that white-collar crime is downplayed because criminologists do not view it as real crime:

> [C]riminologists secretly may believe what . . . politicians are saying [that street crime is more serious than white-collar crime]. At the very least, their raised consciousness does not dispose them to place knowledge about white-collar crime on an equal footing with knowledge about street crime.[8]

These perceptions signal our fears of who the real criminals are. They also indicate who we think belongs in prison. As important, they reflect our definitions of "criminal justice."

Rural and Suburban Crime. We regularly hear reports that Blacks, who live predominantly in urban areas, offend disproportionately in these areas. It is also worthwhile to hear reports that Whites, who live mostly in rural and suburban areas, offend in these communities at rates close to their percentage in the population. In nonmetropolitan areas (rural), Whites comprise a disproportionately high percentage of the arrests for all crimes (table 7.4). For numerous offenses, including arson, auto theft, burglary, embezzlement, forgery, larceny, liquor-law violations, sex offenses, and vandalism, Whites account for more than 80 percent of the arrests. For Whites who live in suburban areas, the arrest rates are higher than 75 percent for a number of offenses including arson, drunkenness, vandalism, and burglary (table 7.5).

TABLE 7.4
Total Nonmetropolitan County Arrests, Distribution by Race, 2006

Offense Charged	Number of Arrests					Percentage Distribution				
	Total	White	Black	American Indian or Alaskan Native	Asian or Pacific Islander	Total	White	Black	American Indian or Alaskan Native	Asian or Pacific Islander
All crimes	779,872	644,643	107,129	21,056	7,044	100.0	82.7	13.7	2.7	0.9
Murder and nonnegligent manslaughter	622	401	189	29	3	100.0	64.5	30.4	4.7	0.5
Forcible rape	1,536	1,226	258	46	6	100.0	79.8	16.8	3.0	0.4
Robbery	1,988	1,110	801	59	18	100.0	55.8	40.3	3.0	0.9
Aggravated assault	20,312	15,299	3,987	904	122	100.0	75.3	19.6	4.5	0.6
Burglary	18,253	15,106	2,441	592	114	100.0	82.8	13.4	3.2	0.6
Larceny-theft	29,429	24,242	4,137	741	309	100.0	82.4	14.1	2.5	1.0
Motor-vehicle theft	5,068	4,247	567	178	76	100.0	83.8	11.2	3.5	1.5
Arson	968	828	104	28	8	100.0	85.5	10.7	2.9	0.8
Violent crime	24,458	18,036	5,235	1,038	149	100.0	73.7	21.4	4.2	0.6
Property crime	53,718	44,423	7,249	1,539	507	100.0	82.7	13.5	2.9	0.9
Other assaults	67,440	53,609	11,153	2,179	499	100.0	79.5	16.5	3.2	0.7
Forgery and counterfeiting	5,117	4,236	795	52	34	100.0	82.8	15.5	1.0	0.7
Fraud	29,364	23,113	5,838	335	78	100.0	78.7	19.9	1.1	0.3
Embezzlement	765	633	111	12	9	100.0	82.7	14.5	1.6	1.2
Stolen property: buying, receiving, possessing	5,047	4,103	817	108	19	100.0	81.3	16.2	2.1	0.4
Vandalism	12,750	10,905	1,329	435	81	100.0	85.5	10.4	3.4	0.6
Weapons: carrying, possessing, etc.	7,171	5,430	1,444	246	51	100.0	75.7	20.1	3.4	0.7
Prostitution and commercialized vice	227	166	37	2	22	100.0	73.1	16.3	0.9	9.7
Sex offenses (except forcible rape and prostitution)	5,048	4,490	427	106	25	100.0	88.9	8.5	2.1	0.5
Drug-abuse violations	92,014	74,340	15,422	1,499	753	100.0	80.8	16.8	1.6	0.8
Gambling	506	325	166	6	9	100.0	64.2	32.8	1.2	1.8

Offense Charged	Total	White	Black	American Indian or Alaskan Native	Asian or Pacific Islander	Total	White	Black	American Indian or Alaskan Native	Asian or Pacific Islander
Offenses against the family and children	12,576	8,878	2,913	765	20	100.0	70.6	23.2	6.1	0.2
Driving under the influence	149,706	133,764	10,765	3,453	1,684	100.0	89.4	7.2	2.3	1.1
Liquor laws	35,736	33,175	1,344	989	228	100.0	92.8	3.8	2.8	0.6
Drunkenness	18,029	15,982	1,336	662	49	100.0	88.6	7.4	3.7	0.3
Disorderly conduct	21,714	16,957	3,786	878	93	100.0	78.1	17.4	4.0	0.4
Vagrancy	168	124	36	8	0	100.0	73.8	21.4	4.8	0.0
All other offenses (except traffic)	232,784	187,537	36,508	6,536	2,203	100.0	80.6	15.7	2.8	0.9
Suspicion	185	125	22	38	0	100.0	67.6	11.9	20.5	0.0
Curfew and loitering-law violations	533	483	18	17	15	100.0	90.6	3.4	3.2	2.8
Runaways	4,816	3,809	378	113	516	100.0	79.1	7.8	2.3	10.7

Source: FBI, Uniform Crime Reports 2006, U.S. Department of Justice (2006).

TABLE 7.5

Total Suburban Arrests, Distribution by Race, 2006

	Number of Arrests					Percentage Distribution				
Offense Charged	Total	White	Black	American Indian or Alaskan Native	Asian or Pacific Islander	Total	White	Black	American Indian or Alaskan Native	Asian or Pacific Islander
All crimes	4,105,074	3,119,705	925,822	29,289	30,258	100.0	76.0	22.6	0.7	0.7
Murder and nonnegligent manslaughter	3,073	1,775	1,254	26	18	100.0	57.8	40.8	0.8	0.6
Forcible rape	6,534	4,782	1,656	53	43	100.0	73.2	25.3	0.8	0.7
Robbery	26,578	13,057	13,238	117	166	100.0	49.1	49.8	0.4	0.6
Aggravated assault	117,565	83,484	32,189	921	971	100.0	71.0	27.4	0.8	0.8
Burglary	82,916	62,896	18,944	482	594	100.0	75.9	22.8	0.6	0.7
Larceny-theft	302,288	215,585	81,351	2,205	3,107	100.0	71.3	26.9	0.7	1.0
Motor-vehicle theft	31,243	23,258	7,574	179	232	100.0	74.4	24.2	0.6	0.7
Arson	5,261	4,297	886	23	55	100.0	81.7	16.8	0.4	1.0
Violent crime	153,750	103,098	48,337	1,117	1,198	100.0	67.1	31.4	0.7	0.8
Property crime	421,708	306,036	108,795	2,889	3,988	100.0	72.6	25.8	0.7	0.9

(*continued*)

TABLE 7.5 (continued)

Offense Charged	Number of Arrests					Percentage Distribution				
	Total	White	Black	American Indian or Alaskan Native	Asian or Pacific Islander	Total	White	Black	American Indian or Alaskan Native	Asian or Pacific Islander
Other assaults	361,321	263,017	92,780	2,721	2,803	100.0	72.8	25.7	0.8	0.8
Forgery and counterfeiting	32,325	23,591	8,341	103	290	100.0	73.0	25.8	0.3	0.9
Fraud	96,872	68,071	28,017	270	514	100.0	70.3	28.9	0.3	0.5
Embezzlement	5,907	3,885	1,945	18	59	100.0	65.8	32.9	0.3	1.0
Stolen property: buying, receiving, possessing	37,602	26,500	10,621	207	274	100.0	70.5	28.2	0.6	0.7
Vandalism	86,493	70,887	14,413	592	601	100.0	82.0	16.7	0.7	0.7
Weapons: carrying, possessing, etc.	49,077	32,765	15,589	273	450	100.0	66.8	31.8	0.6	0.9
Prostitution and commercialized vice	6,263	4,056	1,784	25	398	100.0	64.8	28.5	0.4	6.4
Sex offenses (except forcible rape and prostitution)	23,732	18,931	4,434	156	211	100.0	79.8	18.7	0.7	0.9
Drug-abuse violations	491,999	365,791	121,184	2,224	2,800	100.0	74.3	24.6	0.5	0.6
Gambling	1,554	942	545	2	65	100.0	60.6	35.1	0.1	4.2
Offenses against the family and children	50,024	33,185	16,214	380	245	100.0	66.3	32.4	0.8	0.5
Driving under the influence	483,197	434,381	41,600	3,306	3,910	100.0	89.9	8.6	0.7	0.8
Liquor laws	196,333	176,212	14,930	2,893	2,298	100.0	89.8	7.6	1.5	1.2
Drunkenness	142,756	127,333	13,537	1,198	688	100.0	89.2	9.5	0.8	0.5
Disorderly conduct	195,112	140,866	51,400	1,386	1,460	100.0	72.2	26.3	0.7	0.7
Vagrancy	6,060	3,860	2,166	11	23	100.0	63.7	35.7	0.2	0.4
All other offenses (except traffic)	1,208,571	874,192	317,758	9,097	7,524	100.0	72.3	26.3	0.8	0.6
Suspicion	987	581	396	1	9	100.0	58.9	40.1	0.1	0.9
Curfew and loitering-law violations	23,337	18,407	4,655	90	185	100.0	78.9	19.9	0.4	0.8
Runaways	30,094	23,118	6,381	330	265	100.0	76.8	21.2	1.1	0.9

Source: FBI, Uniform Crime Reports 2006, U.S. Department of Justice (2006).

Hate Crimes and Ethnicity. Crimes motivated by hate could also be placed under the umbrella of "White crime." These offenses range in severity and include murder, rape, assault, vandalism, and intimidation. In 2006, more than one-half of all hate-crime incidents—7,720—involved racial bias. Two-thirds of these crimes were motivated by anti-Black bias. Also, the majority of the offenses involving ethnic bias were anti-Hispanic. Notably, Whites make up 58 percent of all hate-crime offenders.[9]

In response to the media and research emphasis on Black crime, researchers have observed that there is little empirical attention given to the differences between White ethnic groups. To address this research gap, some researchers propose conducting research that compares the successes and failures of the fifteen White ethnic groups denoted by the U.S. Census. Political science professor Andrew Hacker observes, somewhat tongue-in-cheek, that if some researchers can insist on examining Blacks and low achievement, the same can be done with Whites. His research indicates that French-Canadian and Dutch Whites are much less likely to complete college than Russian and Scottish Whites.[10]

Calling Names. Race and criminal law are inextricably linked, and therefore, the phenomenon of Black crime cannot be discussed without a discussion of the phenomenon of White crime. If Black crime is labeled, then by this logic, White crime should be given a label. In fact race labels could be imposed for all crime. For instance, when journalists refer to crime in rural areas, it could be labeled White crime. In this way, "rural" crime would be used to denote race in the same way that "inner-city" crime is used. Another example would be to catalog the crimes of White militia groups as White crime.

Another option, to eliminate labels altogether, is unrealistic since they are already in widespread use. Further, if race labels were discouraged, some researchers and journalists might rely more frequently on code words, which would not solve the underlying problem.

Perhaps the biggest concern with using racial labels, however, is the implication that there is something about crime that is race specific. Without a comparable language that defines and analyzes White crime, the implicit message is that Blackness somehow "explains" criminality. Thus, labeling Black crime may cause some people to conclude, improperly, that Black people are genetically predisposed to commit crime. That race is a social rather than biological reality unmasks the fallacy of racial determinism. Further, due to the history of colonialism and slavery and mixed-race liaisons, many Blacks are only Black because we still rely on the "one-drop" rule. It has been estimated that 75 percent of Blacks have some White ancestry.[11]

Those Who Study Race and Crime: A Look at the Numbers

Between 1995 and 2005 only 55 Blacks in the nation were awarded doctorates in criminology or criminal justice. During the same period, 430 Whites received criminology doctorates. In 2005, 611 people received doctoral degrees in criminology. Of these, 501 were White (82 percent), 55 were Black (9 percent), 20 were Latino (3.3 percent), 16 were Asian (2.6 percent), and 4 were American Indian (less than 1 percent). Between 1995 and 2005, Whites were the only racial group to have double-digit graduates in any of the ten years (table 7.6).

There is no threshold number of Black criminologists that would be satisfactory. Less than one hundred, however, may be too few to have a substantial impact on how crime and race are discussed, analyzed, and researched. The small number of Blacks in criminology, the behavioral science that focuses predominantly on street crime, is problematic in view of the disproportionate rates of Black arrests, conviction, and incarceration. Studies indicate that to some degree a researcher's race is correlated with his or her ideology and areas of research interest. If so, the racial makeup

TABLE 7.6
Criminology Doctoral Degrees Awarded, by Race, 1995–2005
(U.S. Citizens and Permanent Visas Only)

	American Indian	Unknown Race	Asian	Latino/ Hispanic	Black	White	All Races
1995	1	1	1	1	8	29	41
1996	1	1	2	2	4	44	54
1997	0	1	2	3	4	36	46
1998	0	1	1	5	7	34	48
1999	0	2	2	2	4	38	48
2000	0	1	0	2	6	51	60
2001	1	2	3	1	0	47	54
2002	0	2	0	0	4	44	50
2003	0	1	2	1	5	50	59
2004	0	1	2	1	5	57	66
2005	1	2	1	2	8	71	85
1995–2005 Total	4	15	16	20	55	501	611
1995–2005 Percentage	0.7%	2.5%	2.6%	3.3%	9%	82%	100%

Source: National Science Foundation et al., "Survey of Earned Doctorates (1995–2005)" (2006).

of the profession is relevant. A look at journalism and law, two other arenas that affect research and public discussion on the criminal justice system, also reveals a pattern of Black underrepresentation. For 2005, Blacks constituted 5 percent of the U.S. attorneys and 6 percent of the U.S. journalists.[12] An increase in the number of Black criminologists might hasten the development of useful theories to explain Black overinvolvement in crime and shift the focus from Black crime to White crime.[13]

Implications and Future Possibilities

The issue of whether racial labels should be attached to crime and criminals raises several questions. First, when is a racial label appropriate? If disproportionality is used as the standard, then labels of "White crime" and "Black crime" have to be used. Another possible standard would be also to use a racial label whenever a crime involves an offender and a victim of the same race. Thus, crimes involving White offenders and White victims would be called "White-on-White crime" or "White crime." Intraracial crime involving Latinos, Native Americans, Blacks, Asian Americans, and other racial and ethnic groups would be similarly labeled. This standard still does not resolve the question of how to label interracial crimes—for example, one involving an Asian American offender and a Latino victim. As a general rule, it is the race of the offender that determines the race of the crime—for instance, whether it will be labeled a "Black" crime.

The issue of labeling crimes by race is problematic beyond the straightforward concern about fairness and accuracy. Historically, crimes committed by Blacks were singled out as the ultimate example of deviance. As detailed earlier (see chapter 3), this was particularly true for crimes involving Black offenders and White victims. A Black person who committed an offense was subject to a harsher penalty than a White person who committed the same offense. Today, the widespread practice of highlighting crimes by Blacks and overlooking those by Whites underscores this history.

By every yardstick, the general public has a distorted picture of the racial makeup of crime in the United States. As a result, academics and journalists have a heightened responsibility to present a picture of crime and race that bears some semblance to reality. C. Wright Mills cautioned, "All social scientists, by the fact of their existence, are involved in the struggle between enlightenment and obscurantism. In such a world as ours, to practice social science is, first of all, to practice the politics of truth."[14] If Mills is correct, social scientists have an obligation to shed light on the phenomenon of White crime. This duty also requires us to discuss crime and race in ways that do not perpetuate inaccurate stereotypes.

Too often, the disproportionate rate of Black crime is used as the whipping boy for U.S. racial ills. The next section examines and critiques an example of this phenomenon: public policy professor James Q. Wilson's thesis that Black crime causes White racism. As detailed below, Wilson's conclusions are wide of the mark in analyzing how race, racism, and crime are interlinked.

Fearful, Angry White People: The "Black Crime Causes White Fear" Thesis

Whether it is shock-jock Don Imus's racist and sexist comments about the Rutgers women's basketball team, allegations that baseball player Barry Bonds took steroids, allegations that members of the mostly White Duke University men's lacrosse team raped a Black woman, or Hurricane Katrina, Whites and Blacks see the world very differently. Unfortunately, as noted earlier, we know little about how other groups of color view these events because the media is fixated on the Black-White racial divide. Racism and its prevalence is the thread that unites and reinforces these group-based views. Whites are much less likely to believe that racism still exists than are African Americans.

The din coming from both racial camps is at times deafening. Let us, however, examine one thesis about White racism, James Q. Wilson's thesis that "Black crime causes White racism." In 1992 Wilson wrote an editorial that argued that if Blacks would stop committing so much crime, there would not be so much White racism. His thesis, developed in subsequent writings, is that White racism and White fear of Black and Latino men are justified because Black and Latino men have high rates of crime.[15] It is fear, Wilson contends, not racism that accounts for the negative perceptions that White people have of Black and Latino men. In fact, Wilson states, "fear can produce behavior that is indistinguishable from racism."[16] His tacit conclusion is that the current level of White racism is acceptable, so long as it coexists with the current level of Black and Latino crime. At first read, Wilson's argument sounds vaguely tenable or at least difficult to dismiss. A careful consideration of his underlying premise, however, indicates that his thesis raises more questions than it answers.

At core, Wilson argues the following one-directional relationship:

$$\text{Black crime rates} \rightarrow \text{White racism}$$

Two major assumptions underlie Wilson's hypothesis. First, the Black crime rate is the primary source of White racism. Second, solving the Black crime problem rests almost entirely with the Black community.

White Fear and White Racism

According to Wilson, "The best way to reduce racism real or imagined is to reduce the black crime rate to equal the white crime rate."[17] It is not clear what Wilson means by "imagined." He points out that Black men offend at a rate six to eight times greater than the rate for Whites. Accordingly, it is reasonable to expect that White racism will persist until Blacks and Whites offend at an equal rate. Awaiting such a drop in the Black crime rate is neither the best nor the quickest way to reduce White racism. Ignoring the interconnection between crime, poverty, and education, Wilson exhorts Blacks to rise above their circumstances before they can ask for a reduction in White racism. This is a tall order.

Not only does Wilson imply that the Black crime rate is the sole source of White racism; he also places the onus of eradicating White racism on Blacks. Even if the Black crime rate were reduced to equal the White crime rate, how would this affect the *amount* of White racism? Is Wilson suggesting that if Black and White crime rates were equal, or nearly proportionate, that White racism would disappear completely? Drop by one-half? Wilson implies that White racism will wither away or decline substantially if the rate of Black crime were equal to the rate of White crime. Wilson provides neither theoretical nor empirical support for this sweeping assertion. In fact, he could not, as there are no such data available.

Wilson also offers an incomplete analysis of the role of fear. His hypothesis suggests that fear is a one-dimensional variable. White fear, however, has at least four related, though distinct, components: the fear of crime, the fear of losing jobs, the fear of cultural demise, and the fear of Black revolt. Wilson overlooks the fact that the generalized White fear of Black crime encompasses these other fears.

Studies show that the closer Whites live to Blacks, the more fearful they are of crime. This fear is justified since Whites who live near Blacks also face the greatest threat of victimization by Blacks.[18] Although levels of neighborhood integration may explain why Whites who live in urban areas are fearful of Black crime, it does not justify the general, nationwide White fear of Blacks, particularly of Black men. Most Whites do not live close to Blacks, which is not surprising given that Blacks are a relatively small percentage of the U.S. population (13 percent). Furthermore, given the fact that more than 80 percent of all crime is *intra*racial, White fear of Black crime is inexplicably high. It may be that Whites translate their discomfort about race relations into attitudes about crime.[19]

Jesse Jackson has remarked that he is sad that Black crime has reached such epidemic proportions, that when he walks down the street at night he is actually relieved to discover that the person coming toward him is White.[20] Many White commentators pointed to Jackson's comments as "proof" that White fear of Black crime is justified.[21] However, this argument overlooks the fact that, statistically speaking, the greatest crime threat to Jesse Jackson *is* another Black man. On the other hand, the greatest crime threat to someone White is another White person, because most crime is intraracial. At least Jackson's fears are factually based.

The fear of victimization at the hand of a Black criminal has led some researchers to study the link between abortion and crime. Professors John Donohue and Stephen Levitt note that abortion is most common for poor, minority women and find that "legalized abortion can account for about half of the observed decline in crime in the United States between 1991 and 1997."[22] Levitt is the coauthor of the best-selling book *Freakonomics*. This research inspired former secretary of education Bill Bennett to comment, "If you wanted to reduce crime . . . you could abort every black baby in this country, and your crime rate would go down."[23]

There exists an economic component to White fear of Blacks. This fear is commonly couched in terms of affirmative action. There has been a lot of talk about "qualified" Whites losing jobs, government contracts, or university admissions slots to "unqualified" Blacks. Many Whites believe that Blacks, and similarly, Latinos and recent immigrants, pose a serious threat to their economic well-being. Affirmative action is perceived as a threat by many Whites, who fear losing their privileged status. Although many Whites have legitimate fears about the state of the economy, blaming Blacks for downsizing and global economic decline misses the mark. Andrew Hacker observes that Whiteness has been devalued, and "for the first time in this country's history, [Whites have been] made to feel they no longer come first."[24] The media's response to this fear has created more heat than light. It has failed to report the obvious: it is statistically impossible for Blacks, who constitute less than one-sixth of the population, to take most of the jobs, government contracts, and college, graduate, and professional school admissions spots.

Another type of fear that Whites have of Blacks is a cultural one. Some Whites view Black culture as the antithesis of American culture. This fear manifests itself when Black culture crosses over into White culture, such as in music, clothing, hair styles, speech patterns, and posture. Loud cries of cultural decline are heard when White youths mimic and adopt aspects of Black culture (e.g., music preferences, interracial dating, slang, and speech patterns). Specifically, calls for school dress codes, record-label warnings, standard English, and music morality are sounded when Black culture and other cultures of color contaminate Whites. The creation of moral panics to marginalize a racial or ethnic group from the mainstream is not new.[25]

Other fears include the fear of losing majority status and the fear of a Black revolt. The fear that Blacks will become the majority race and in turn use their power to pay Whites back for centuries of slavery was expressed as early as the year 1751.[26] More than two hundred years later, conservative pundit William F. Buckley commented that many Whites favor abortion to ensure that Blacks do not overpopulate the country.

Referring to the fear of "racial revenge,"[27] Andrew Hacker states, "There is a fear in White America of this second nation, this Black nation. There is fear of rebellion."[28] Some people have speculated that this fear drives popular support for abolishing welfare and affirmative action.

As the foregoing discussion makes clear, most of the fears that Whites have of Blacks are not rational. Wilson's dichotomous treatment of White fear obscures its dimensions and its irrationality. For Wilson, White fear is a typical, therefore justifiable, response to Black crime. Wilson's analysis glosses over the fact that although it may be commonplace for Whites to fear Blacks, it is not necessarily reasonable. Fear is not always a rational emotion; however, to use fear to justify racism, which Wilson does, the fear must be grounded in reality. A great deal of White fear—of crime, of economic loss, of cultural demise—has been a knee-jerk response to media stories. By all indicators, Wilson is correct when he says that Whites are fearful of Blacks, yet his analysis jumps past the fundamental question of the logic of White fear. Why does this matter? Whether or not White fear is justified, whether White fear is used to cloak prejudice, has *everything* to do with determining the relationship between White racism and Black crime. A generalized, empirically insupportable White fear of Black crime cannot be used to excuse White racism.

Let us consider the practical, harmful consequences of this twisted logic. During Hurricane Katrina, one of the most salient racialized images involved two photographs, both depicting storm victims trudging through high flood waters, carrying food and water. One of the pictures featured a Black man; the other, a White couple. The Black man was described as a "looter," whereas the White couple were said to have found the bread and water they were carrying.[29] The language of "looting" evokes criminality, whereas "finding" suggests a desperation and justification for actions taken. Wilson's thesis encourages us to "see" Black looters but not White ones; thus, we privilege some crimes and diminish others. Another way of looking at this effect is that we do not see the humanity of the Black person who "finds" food, but we are able to when the face is White.

The problem with allowing White fear to justify White racism is driven home when we consider Black fear of Whites. Although rarely acknowledged publicly, many Blacks, as well as members of other minority groups, are fearful of Whites. They are fearful of becoming victims of a hate crime. There is also a more general fear of White violence and assault—against the poor, against urban dwellers, and against the disenfranchised generally, such as within the criminal justice system. Black fear of Whites may stem from the fact that Whites are at the helm of every American institution. The office of the president, Congress, the Supreme Court, and the private sector, including owners of the "fourth estate" (media) all show a White face. Black fears of White power and its abuses, however, do not justify Black racism against Whites. Are Blacks "excused" from being racist because they fear Whites? Wilson says no.[30] Wilson characterizes Black outrage at the verdict in the LAPD/Rodney King trial as "appalling racist bigotry." How is it that Wilson allows Whites to leap blindly from fear to racism, yet this same leap is impermissible for Blacks? Wilson's "White-only" fear-racism link speaks volumes.

White Racism or Black Crime Rates: Which Came First?

Wilson offers little historical support for his assumption that high Black crime rates trigger White racism. Considering the fact that Whites kidnapped Africans and brought them to this country in chains, it would be a safe bet that White racism existed centuries before disproportionate rates of Black crime. For proof of this supposition, one need only review the slave codes and Black codes for blatant examples of White racism enshrined into early American criminal law. Wilson's thesis conveniently ignores this history.

Derrick Bell provides an interesting counterpoint to Wilson's thesis. In his book *And We Are Not Saved*, Bell considers what would happen if Black crime magically disappeared. Bell describes a hypothetical scenario in which magic stones have been discovered. Once ingested, the stones eliminate all desire to engage in crime. The stones, whose power only works for Blacks, are distributed throughout the country. However, now that "blacks had forsaken crime and begun fighting it, the doors of opportunity, long closed to them because of their 'criminal tendencies,' were not opened more than a crack."[31] The fact that there was no longer a crime excuse did not reduce the barriers to racial equality. Bell's hypothetical, based on historical fact, is much closer to reality than Wilson's suggestion that White racism surfaced only in response to high Black crime rates.

Whose Fault Is It Anyway?

Wilson draws an interesting configuration. He assigns Whites a passive role in the Black-crime/White-racism dynamic. Simply put, he blames Blacks for White racism. Wilson has asserted that Blacks unfairly use racism as an excuse for criminal activity. According to Wilson, racism that is "imagined" by Blacks will disappear if the Black crime rate declines. Wilson never tells us what "imagined" racism is. The reader is left to surmise that this is racism that only exists in the minds of Blacks. How is it that a reduction in the Black crime rate will cause a reduction in imagined racism? Wilson does not tell us this either. Rather than holding Whites accountable for their racism, Wilson allows them to claim victim status: they are victimized by Black crime. Wilson allows the blame for White racism to be placed entirely on Black shoulders. Yet he charges that Blacks unfairly place all the blame for the Black crime rate on Whites. This smacks of a double standard.

Another troublesome aspect of Wilson's argument is that it encourages us to think along racially segregated tracks about crime and other societal problems. His argument is that Blacks are responsible for Black crime and that White racism is part of the larger racial finger-pointing that persists. None of this, however, reduces the crime rate or diminishes racial divisions. The net result is that Blacks blame Whites for their lack of progress, and Whites blame Blacks for all social ills. As detailed in the first part of this chapter, the overemphasis on Black crime makes it difficult to see that "race and crime" is not synonymous with "Blacks and crime." More must be done to present the public with an accurate racial picture of crime, including White crime.

One of the biggest roadblocks to an informed discussion about crime and race is the perpetuation of half facts. Half facts are statements or propositions about crime that are discussed in a vacuum, divorced from their context. Wilson's discussion of the relationship between White racism and Black crime exemplifies this phenomenon.

Conclusion

This chapter argues that crime has many colors. The language of crime matters and affects how we see crime. Specifically, it influences how we define offenses and which ones deserve sanction by the criminal law. If we agree that it is acceptable to label crime by race for Blacks, the same should be true for other racial groups. Otherwise, a message is sent that there is something unique about Black crime that is different and more loathsome than crime committed by Whites, Latinos, Asian Americans, Native Americans, or members of other racial groups.

8

Race and Crime Literacy

Looking Back

When I was in graduate school studying criminology, "race" seemed to be shorthand for African Americans. Most of the books and articles we read cast Blacks either as offenders or as victims of crime, primarily at the hands of Black offenders. Assigned readings focused on "Black crime" and "Black-on-Black" crime as a unique phenomenon with specific theoretical causes, such as the "culture of poverty." At the same time, however, there was no discussion of the causes of "White crime" or any acknowledgment that there was any such phenomenon (see chapter 7). Adding insult to injury, very little of the research we read had been written by academics of color. For example, we never studied *The Philadelphia Negro*, W. E. B. Du Bois's seminal work—considered by many scholars to be the sociological ancestor of the famed Chicago School of sociology.[1] Sociologist Monroe Work's research was another glaring omission from the curriculum. Further, there was very little discussion of systemic discrimination or other factors that would explain, or at least contextualize, Black offending. Along with many of my fellow students, I was left with the unstated yet unmistakable impression that crime and Blackness go hand in hand. Had I not known better, I might have come to the conclusion that there is a link—a genetic one—between Blacks and criminality.

When I was in my first year of law school, one of my professors declared, "Poor people are programmed to default." He made this pronouncement as we discussed the facts of *Williams v. Walker-Thomas Furniture*, a 1965 case.[2] The case involved a Black woman named Ora Lee Williams, who lived in Washington, D.C. She had signed an installment contract to purchase furniture. Under the agreement the store could demand payment in full at any time. When Williams fell behind on her monthly bill, the store sued her, seeking to recover the outstanding balance and the furniture. The appeals court found the contract language "unconscionable" and voided Williams's contract with the store. My professor took great issue with this decision. In his class lecture he made no mention of race or the intersection of race and class. Though race was not explicitly referenced, the lecture and discussion hinted at Williams's race (including the fact that it was a District of Columbia case). The professor did not address segregation, redlining, poverty, or employment discrimination against Blacks, some of which would have given the case some historical perspective. As presented, the discussion of the case drew a bold line connecting Blackness with deviance.

Both of these academic experiences took place while I was in my twenties. At the time, I had neither the knowledge nor the language, in history or research, to debate or rebut the half truths that were being presented as facts. Even if I had, it is unlikely that I would have challenged a professor on his facts. Unfortunately, my educational experiences are not unique. In academia (and elsewhere) issues of race are often ignored, dismissed as irrelevant, or used as code for "Black." I believe that most of the racial silence I witnessed was due to benign neglect. Regardless, the overall failure to address racial issues within the academic curriculum does harm to all of us, not just students of color.

Where and how do we begin to make changes? Is it students' fault that they appear to know so little about the relationship between race and crime? We often bemoan the "ignorance" of students. We are told that they cannot find Asia on a map, that they do not know who the founding fathers are, that they have not read the Greek classics, or that they do not know how to use the library. Students aside, however, perhaps educators are a more important focal point. They should not be let off the hook. For the most part, teachers teach what they themselves have been taught. So whatever knowledge gaps a teacher has will likely be passed along to his or her students. An interruption of the status quo cycle of missed educational opportunities is in order. This brings us to the focus of this chapter, sociological literacy.

Sociological Literacy

Judith Shapiro, former president of Barnard College, uses the term "sociological illiteracy" to describe the lack of knowledge most students have regarding historical issues of race, gender, and class. She observes that many of us are focused on our immediate and personal experiences and are unable (or unwilling) to see how they are shaped by social and historical forces. This inability reflects a lack of what sociologist C. Wright Mills called "the sociological imagination." Shapiro continues,

> When people are ignorant about quantum mechanics or medieval literature, they are generally aware of their ignorance, readily admit it, and understand that the remedy for their ignorance is serious and systematic study. When however, the subject is how societies operate, or why people behave the way they do, the situation is different. Confusing their folk beliefs with knowledge, people typically don't realize their ignorance.[3]

Shapiro's conception of sociological literacy offers a valuable and much-needed reformulation of E. D. Hirsch Jr.'s "cultural literacy." His book, *Cultural Literacy: What Every American Needs to Know*, argues that there is an identifiable set of historical, contemporary, and social facts that culturally literate Americans should know. To this end, the book includes an index of more than five thousand names, phrases, dates, and concepts considered by Hirsch to be "essential." This thesis was criticized as elitist and ahistorical. Many people argued that Hirsch's list reflected dominant ideologies about race, class, and gender—that what was included on the list was as important to examine as what was not included on the list. Critics noted that the philosophies, writings, events, and art of people of color were largely overlooked.

There are several places to begin the literacy project as called for by Shapiro. Given the salience of race and crime issues, there is an obvious need to develop a sociological literacy to address the knowledge gaps in this area. We do not have a well-developed language on race and crime. Instead we have only a collection of words, a series of phrases, and a few names. These signifiers are used as shorthand for larger themes and issues involving race. This terminology includes such words and phrases as "affirmative action," "racism," "reverse discrimination," "Tawana Brawley," "diversity," "I'm colorblind, I don't see race," "O. J. Simpson," "We need border security," "It's the system's fault," and "I'm not a racist." A few oft-repeated words and expressions, however, do not make a language. And without a language, there can be no dialogue.

Working Myths

A sociological literacy project is a lot harder to undertake than it appears. To a large extent, we are happy with our race and crime myths; they work for us.[4] Myths are easy to perpetuate, and they do not require us to think critically. And most importantly they signal our membership in the group of believers. We are all in the gang of myths. We repeat what we have heard, pass it along, and believe we have done no harm. In this large-scale version of the children's game of telephone, what is ultimately repeated as fact is a caricature of the initial truth. Mythmaking makes it easier for us to collectively treat Blackness as a signifier of criminality, deviance, and general unworthiness. The bottom line is that we have a set of deeply held myths about race, Blackness in particular. However, we have no language with which to discuss them. Not surprisingly, then, myths rule. Let us consider two examples. The first involves racial preferences based on visual cues, and the second involves racial representations and interpretations of good and bad.

The Implicit Association Test

The Implicit Association Test (IAT) is an interesting psychological test that measures the degree to which someone has a preference for a particular racial group.[5] One version of the test evaluates one's preferences for Blacks and Whites. In his best-selling book, *Blink*, Malcolm Gladwell, who is Black, notes that he was startled to find that his IAT score indicated that he showed a "low to moderate preference for Whites."[6] The online test presents a series of photographs and words on the screen, and the test taker is required to categorize them as Black, White, good, or bad. My results were less remarkable than Gladwell's. My score indicated "little to no automatic preference between Black and White people." The majority of all IAT test takers (54 percent) placed within the "strong" or "moderate" automatic preference for Whites. These findings may simply reflect the race of the test taker or may tell us something more: that when given a choice people, regardless of race, prefer Whites over African Americans.

Doll Tests

Psychologists' Kenneth and Mamie Clark's famous study, conducted in the 1940s, was designed to evaluate the psychological impact of racial segregation on Black children. Their "doll test" used plastic, diapered dolls that were identical, except for skin color. Black children between three and nine years old were shown the dolls and asked questions about racial preference and perception. The directions included, "Show me the doll that you like best" and "Show me the doll that looks 'bad.'" The children were also asked to select the White doll, select the colored doll, and select the doll that looked most like them. The majority of the kids chose the White doll as the one they liked best and chose the brown doll as the one that looked "bad." The Clarks, whose research was cited by the U.S. Supreme Court in *Brown v. Board of Education*, concluded that "segregation of white and colored children in public schools has a detrimental effect upon the colored children."[7]

In a stunning replication of the Clarks' study, Kiri Davis interviewed twenty-one preschool-aged Black kids.[8] Davis, who was sixteen when she conducted her study, wanted to see whether anything had changed in the intervening fifty years since the first doll tests. After placing a White doll and Black doll on a table, Davis asked each child to point to the doll that they liked the most and asked them which doll they looked the most like. She, too, found that the Black children greatly preferred the White dolls over the Black ones. The seven-minute film of the interviews painfully affirms the Clarks' findings and demonstrates how very young children have already learned to associate images of Blackness with something bad and Whiteness with something good.

These are only two of the many examples of how Blackness is perceived. The results of the doll study are particularly troubling since they involve the impressions of young children. As has been discussed throughout this book, racial portrayals have been fairly consistent in presenting Black skin as deviant, as criminal, or as a curiosity. Though contemporary portraits are more nuanced and diverse than in the past, the overriding images have not changed. How else can we explain the results of the Clarks' doll tests and the same results by Davis fifty years later?

Building Race and Crime Literacy

What follows is a preliminary draft of a list of items that would appear on a social literacy list designed to highlight information on race and crime. The list identifies terms, names, and concepts that focus on African Americans and Whites. It is intended to be illustrative, not exhaustive. The list should be used to generate more detailed discussion and curriculum on race.

RACE AND CRIME LITERACY:
NAMES, CONCEPTS, AND TERMS

Abu-Jamal, Mumia
Affirmative action
An American Dilemma (book)
Attica Prison
Bakke v. U.C. Regents
Batson v. Kentucky
Bell Curve, The (book)
Birth of a Nation (movie)
Black codes
Blackface
Black Muslims
Black Panthers
Bloody Sunday
Brawley, Tawana
Brown v. Board of Education
Central Park jogger case
Chicago School
Civil disobedience
Civil Rights Act of 1964
Civil Rights Amendments
Civil Rights Cases (1883)
Civil War
Convict-lease system
Corporate crime
Crime Control Act of 1994
Culture of poverty
Davis, Angela Y.
De facto segregation
De jure segregation
Diallo, Amadou
Driving while Black
Due Process Clause
Duke lacrosse case
Enron
Equal Protection Clause
Federal crack law
Federal Housing Authority

One-drop rule
Patriot Act
Philadelphia Negro, The (book)
Pioneer Fund
Plessy v. Ferguson
Police brutality
Powell v. Alabama
Pratt, Geronimo
Prison industrial complex
Prisons for profit
Racial hoax
Racial profiling
Racial steering
Reconstruction
Redlining
Rockefeller drug laws
Rosewood massacre
Scottsboro Boys
Sharpton, Al
Simpson, O. J.
Slave codes
Slave patrols
Southern strategy
Statistical discrimination
Stop snitching campaign
"Strange Fruit" (song)
Strauder v. West Virginia
Stuart, Charles
Sundown towns
Superpredators
Thomas, Clarence
Three-fifths clause
Till, Emmett
Title VII
Traffic Stops Statistics Study Act
Tulsa Race Riot
Unconscious racism
Uniform Crime Reports
Vagrancy laws

Voting Rights Act of 1965
War on Drugs
Washington v. Davis
Watts Riot
Wells, Ida B.
White-collar crime
White flight
White privilege
Whren v. United States
Wilkins v. Maryland State Troopers
Wilson, Genarlow
Work, Monroe
X, Malcolm

These 128 items should be part of the core of teaching about race, crime, and justice. They form part of the shell of a body of history and research in this area. Developing a lexicon is an important step in building a general understanding of the importance and breadth of the undertaking of a sociological literacy project. The sheer number of entries makes clear that inserting a race-and-crime "moment" in a history or criminal law course is inadequate. A more holistic curricula approach is necessary to ensure that these topics are integrated and discussed as part of American history.

Hurricane Katrina and Sociological Illiteracy

Hurricane Katrina and its aftermath provide perhaps the best contemporary example of what can happen when we do nothing about our general ignorance about race, poverty, and crime. The perfect storm of events that ended in Katrina would not have been possible if we did not connect Blackness with deviance. The pervasive media message that Blackness is something to be feared, something to be admonished, and something to be controlled is widespread and unmistakable. Society's racial tableau depicts a system in which achieving "justice" is a fleeting quest, one partly dependent on one's racial group membership. One of the many things that Katrina starkly uncovered was a general willingness—indeed readiness—to blame victims who fall into the cracks of race, crime, and justice. To borrow professor Derrick Bell's language, the "faces at the bottom of the well"[9] are victimized by our inattention, ignorance, and inaction. Let us consider several interrelated parts of the Katrina story.

Evacuation. When the levees broke, homes were flooded, people were thrashed into rising tidewaters—resulting in death, missing persons, relocated families, destroyed homes, dashed careers, lost animals, and flooded vehicles. The Gulf Coast was decimated. It was the worst of times. After watching news reports of the unfolding devastation wrought by Hurricane Katrina, many people asked, "Why didn't they evacuate?" It seemed simple enough. Those who remained were betting the odds and lost. It was their fault.

A closer examination, however, reveals a much more complex set of factors at work. The evacuation warnings were issued late, leaving little time for people to receive word of the warnings and organize themselves to leave town before the hurricane hit land. Further, the people who lived in the poorest sections of town were the ones least likely to have transportation. Many of these same people had no place to evacuate *to* or money to leave the city. Still others who wanted to leave could not because they had family members who would not or could not leave the city: some were incapacitated (in a hospital or in jail), some were elderly or infirm, and some were essential government employees and had to report to work. We learned later that the media's snapshot image of those left behind as irresponsible was inaccurate.

Katrina's Crimes. In the days following Katrina, there were widespread stories of rapes. The New Orleans police chief, Eddie Compass, reported that he had been told that children were being raped at the Superdome, where thousands of the evacuees were being held. He repeated the unverified rape reports when interviewed for the *Oprah Winfrey Show,* just days after the hurricane's landfall. Within weeks it was determined that there was no evidence to support the claims: nobody had come forward to report either being victimized by or having witnessed a sexual assault in the hurricane's aftermath. Compass, who later said that he had "erred on the side of caution,"[10] was forced to resign. The tales of Superdome rapes were urban legends that spread like wildfire through a receptive general public, who—already inculcated with the myth of the *criminalblackman*—could easily imagine such horrors.

The fact that the truth ultimately came out is in some ways too little too late. Similar to what happens in racial hoax cases (see chapter 6), the damage has already been done. There are still many people who believe that there were an epidemic number of rape cases following Katrina and that Black men were to blame. The fact that the police chief was forced to resign does not alter the persistent image of Black male criminality.

Looting is another crime that received widespread media attention after the storm. There is no question that some of the people who survived the storm used it as an opportunity to steal. What is also true, however, is that many people looted as a life-saving measure—to steal water, food, clothes, and diapers. As discussed earlier (see chapter 2) the racially skewed depiction of looting is highlighted by two well-circulated photographs: one of a Black man treading water, carrying what appears to be a garbage bag filled with soda, and another of a White couple trudging through high tide waters with water bottles. In the first photograph, the man is described as a "looter," whereas the couple in the second photograph is said to have "found" its bounty.[11]

Katrina's Other Crimes

The examples in the preceding section sharply reflect the skewed racial visions that permeated Katrina and its aftermath. They offer snapshots of our deep-seated views of race and justice. There are, however, other prisms through which we can see the storm. A critical reading of Katrina reveals that there were many acts of injustice that were not acknowledged as harms and, therefore, were not remedied.[12] These include numerous incidents of negligence, including the delay in the search-and-rescue efforts for hurricane victims; inadequate police, fire, and rescue efforts; the failure to construct an adequate levy system; and the failure to implement a feasible evacuation plan. One of the more striking instances of racial mistreatment involved the Crescent City Connection bridge.

The Bridge to Gretna. The story of the Gretna bridge incident is almost impossible to understand without knowledge of this country's historical relationship and link between Blackness and crime. In the wake of the storm, thousands of people, mostly African American, tried to flee from New Orleans's rising floodwaters. Their attempts to walk across the Crescent City Connection bridge, a public bridge over the Mississippi River, were thwarted. The would-be evacuees were confronted with armed police officers. Officers representing three jurisdictions blocked access to the bridge to Gretna, a mostly White, suburban bedroom community. The people who were present on the bridge stated that officers fired warning shots in the air and that almost all the thousands of people who sought safe passage were turned away. Apparently some of the officers indicated that Gretna officials did not want Blacks to seek refuge in their town—for fear it would become "another New Orleans."[13]

In 2005, two of the women who sought passageway out of New Orleans via the Crescent City Connection bridge, Tracy and Dorothy Dickerson, filed a lawsuit against the City of Gretna.[14] Among other things, they argued that their constitutional rights to equal protection and freedom of travel were denied. Because there were many others who were also denied access to the bridge, they sought to have their case brought as a class-action lawsuit. The district court found that although the right to interstate travel is widely recognized, there is no recognized right to *intra*state travel. This decision highlights the fact that law and justice are not synonymous. It is lunacy to have a right to travel out of state without having a right to travel within a state. In order for the right to interstate travel to have any practical effect, one needs to have the right of intrastate travel protected. The court also denied the request for class-action certification.

Closing Comment

The Katrina narratives of blameworthiness were established early on. As the saying goes, you cannot unring a bell. The bell that we all heard was one that signaled to us that the victims of Katrina, particularly those in New Orleans, were criminals. Initially many of us were tricked by our knee-jerk reflexes, those that equate Black skin with bad people. We were fooled into believing that Katrina was simply a sad, unfortunate, unavoidable event: a natural disaster. Had more of us been armed with substantive knowledge about how race and racism operate structurally, however, a preemptive strike would have been possible. Katrina will forever represent an instance in which our national ignorance became deadly. Now that we know better, can we do better?

Appendix A

Traffic Stops Statistics Study Act of 2000
(Proposed, HR 1443, 106th Congress,
2nd Session)

The Attorney General shall conduct a nationwide study of stops for traffic violations by law enforcement officers. The Attorney General shall perform an initial analysis of existing data, including complaints alleging and other information concerning traffic stops motivated by race and other bias. After completion of the initial analysis . . . the Attorney General shall then gather the following data on traffic stops from a nationwide sample of jurisdictions, including jurisdictions identified in the initial analysis:

- The traffic infraction alleged to have been committed that led to the stop.
- Identifying characteristics of the driver stopped, including the race, gender, ethnicity, and approximate age of the driver.
- Whether immigration status was questioned, immigration documents were requested, or an inquiry was made to the Immigration and Naturalization Service with regard to any person in the vehicle.
- The number of the individuals in the stopped vehicle.
- Whether a search was instituted as a result of the stop and whether consent was requested for the search.
- Any alleged criminal behavior by the driver that justified the search.
- Any items seized, including contraband or money.
- Whether any warning or citation was issued as a result of the stop.

- Whether an arrest was made as a result of either the stop or the search and the justification for the arrest.
- The duration of the stop.

Information released pursuant to section 2 shall not reveal the identity of any individual who is stopped or any law enforcement officer involved in a traffic stop.

For purposes of this Act: the term "law enforcement agency" means an agency of a State or political subdivision of a State, authorized by law or by a Federal, State, or local government agency to engage in or supervise the prevention, detection, or investigation of violations of criminal laws, or a federally recognized Indian tribe.[1]

Appendix B

Racial Hoaxes: Summaries of Ninety-Two Cases (1987–2006, Alphabetical Listing)[1]

BRADLEY ADAMS

In February 1995, Molly Sullivan was killed. Her fiancé, Bradley Adams, was arrested five months after the murder. Adams told police that a group of Black men was responsible for Sullivan's death. He later admitted that Sullivan, who suffered from a degenerative muscle disease, died after he sat on her chest. Adams was convicted of murder and sentenced to seventy years in prison.

STEVIE ALLMAN

In March 1997, the home of Stevie Allman was torched. It was believed that Allman, an antidrug activist in Oakland, California, had been targeted because of her efforts to remove drug dealers. Allman was White, and the suspected arsonists were believed to be Black. The case received widespread publicity. The governor at the time, Pete Wilson, put up a fifty-thousand dollar reward, neighbors raised almost five thousand dollars, and the nation's drug czar expressed concern. Four months later it was discovered that Allman's sister Sarah had killed her, placed her body in a freezer, and fire bombed the home to cover up the murder. Police believe that Sarah, who had assumed Stevie's identity, planned to cash in on her sister's insurance policy.

JESSE ANDERSON

In April 1992, Jesse Anderson, a White man, told the police that he and his wife had been attacked in a restaurant parking lot in suburban Milwaukee. Anderson said two Black men stabbed him and his wife. His wife, who suffered twenty-one stabs to her chest, died following the attack. Anderson received superficial wounds. Following a week-long search for the fictional criminals, Anderson was arrested and charged with murder. He had planned the murder and devised the hoax to cash in on his wife's $250,000 insurance policy. Anderson was convicted of first-degree murder. In 1994, Anderson was murdered in prison along with serial killer Jeffrey Dahmer, causing some people to speculate that he was killed because of the racial upheaval that his hoax caused.

TISHA ANDERSON AND WILLIAM LEE

In December 1995, Tisha Anderson, a Black woman, and her White boyfriend, William Lee, told police that they had received death threats and that their apartment had been defaced with racial slurs. It was subsequently determined that Anderson and Lee had staged the hate crime to get out of their apartment lease.

SAMUEL ASBELL

In January 1990, Samuel Asbell, a White New Jersey prosecutor, told police that he had been involved in a car chase with two Black men. Asbell, who reported that the chase had reached speeds up to 100 mph, said that the assailants had fired at his car with an automatic rifle. After a police investigation established that the incident could not have happened the way Asbell described it, Asbell admitted that he had shot at his own car. He later said that he had been under stress and checked himself into a psychiatric clinic. Asbell pled guilty to filing a false police report, and his license to practice law was suspended for two years.

ANTHONY AVENT

In 1994, Anthony Avent, a player for the Orlando Magic basketball team, told police that he had been stabbed by three White men on an Orlando street. Avent, who is Black, sustained injuries requiring thirty stitches. He later recanted his tale, telling police that he made up the story to protect the identity of a friend, with whom he had had a fight. The Orlando Magic fined Avent three thousand dollars.

ADAM BAISLEY

In 1996, Adam Baisley and three other White teenagers decided to cut school and have a party. At the party, a gun was passed around. The firearm accidentally discharged, and a bullet hit one of the boys in the cheek. After the shooting the boys cleaned up the area with bleach. They told police that a Black man, wearing a dark sweatshirt and carrying a semiautomatic handgun, had committed the crime. The boys later admitted that they had lied.

TRACY BIRT

In 1996, Tracy Birt, a Black man who was a former courthouse employee, admitted to vandalizing a judge's chambers. Birt used red paint to write racial epithets and symbols in the Little Rock, Arkansas, courthouse. He was charged and convicted of criminal mischief.

DANIEL BOLDUC

In April 1995, Daniel Bolduc, a White police officer from Hartford, Connecticut, filed a police report, wherein he stated that three Black men had smashed the windshield of a vehicle. Bolduc's report stated that the vehicle was a police car that was permanently out of service. When it was determined that the police report was false, Bolduc was suspended for one day and placed on sick leave pending psychological exams.

TAWANA BRAWLEY

In 1987, Tawana Brawley told police that she had been kidnapped and raped by six White men. Brawley, a Black fifteen-year-old, said that the men were law enforcement officers who wore badges. She said she was smeared with feces, placed in a plastic bag, and left in a gutter. The grand jury charged with investigating the case found no basis for issuing criminal indictments. Over the years, Brawley has stood by her initial claims. Today, however, the case is widely believed to have been a hoax.

DWAYNE BYRDSONG

Dwayne Byrdsong, of Coraville, Iowa, fabricated a hate crime. Byrdsong, who is Black, painted his Mercedes Benz with racial slurs, including "Go Back to Africa" and "KKK." The Black community mobilized to collect funds for Byrdsong, who is a minister. Byrdsong was convicted of filing a false police report.

TOBY CAMPBELL

In 1995, Toby Campbell, a White convenience-store clerk in South Carolina, told police that he had been robbed. Campbell said that two Black men had held him up at knifepoint. According to Campbell, the robbers took a dozen cartons of cigarettes. He provided detailed descriptions of the two Black men, including that one man wore earrings depicting a marijuana leaf and a bull. Campbell later admitted that he had stolen the cigarettes.

DONALD CHERRY

In 1996, Donald Cherry told police that following a traffic dispute, Black youths shot and killed his two-year-old son, who was seated in the back of his car. Cherry later admitted that he had gone to purchase drugs and that while there, he had a dispute with the dealer over payment. When Cherry attempted to leave without paying for the drugs, the dealer shot into his vehicle, killing the boy. Cherry was convicted of reckless aggravated assault and reckless endangerment. He was sentenced to five years in prison.

EMILY CLARK

In 2004, Emily Clark, a young White female who was a student at the University of Montana, told police that she was a robbery victim. She described her attacker as six foot three with dark or black complexion and said the man grabbed one hundred dollars from her as she approached her dormitory. After interviewing Clark's friends, the police discovered several inconsistencies in her account. She was charged with filing a false police report.

GARRICK CLEMENTE

In 1996, Garrick Clemente, a Black man, gave a neighbor four hundred dollars to paint a racial slur on his apartment door. Clemente's plan was to fake a hate crime. The motive for the hoax is unclear.

SABRINA COLLINS

In 1990, Sabrina Collins, a Black freshman at Emory University, claimed that she was a victim of racial harassment. Collins told police that she had received a death threat and that someone had scrawled racial slurs on her dormitory walls. Several weeks later Collins admitted that she had written the death threat and scrawled the slurs. Her claims of racial harassment triggered protests by students and civil rights leaders on campus and in Atlanta.

HENRY CRANE

On New Year's Eve in 1995, Henry Crane notified police that he had been carjacked at gunpoint. He said the assailants were three Black men. After hearing a police broadcast about the incident, another police officer spotted the car and pulled it over. The woman driving the car told police that she and Crane had just had sex at a hotel. Crane fabricated the hoax to avoid having his wife learn that he had been with another woman.

TANYA DACRI

In January 1989, Tanya Dacri, a White women from Philadelphia, reported to the police that her two-month-old son, Zachary, had been snatched from her in the parking lot of a shopping mall. According to her report, two Black men had kidnapped the infant. Police later learned that Dacri and her husband fabricated the story after murdering and dismembering the child and throwing his remains in a river. The child's crying upset the parents. Dacri is serving a life sentence for murder.

THOMAS DIBARTOLO

In 1996, Thomas DiBartolo was an eighteen-year veteran with the Spokane County Sheriff's Department. Sheriff DiBartolo notified officials that he and his wife had been shot by two armed Black gunmen. According to DiBartolo, the attempted robbery resulted in a shooting; he sustained a flesh wound and his wife died following the attack. Early on, police were suspicious of DiBartolo's story and did not release a sketch of the suspects. Three months after the death of his wife of nineteen years, DiBartolo was charged and ultimately convicted of first-degree murder. At trial, there was evidence that he carried out the murder to cash in on his wife's life insurance and to avoid a costly divorce. One woman testified that she had sex with him on the day of his wife's funeral. DiBartolo was sentenced to twenty six years in prison and restitution in the amount of eleven thousand dollars.

THOMAS DROGAN AND LOUIS PAPALEO

In March 1993, two Yonkers, New York, police officers, Thomas Drogan and Louis Papaleo, got into a physical fight in the police station. The officers fought over who would file a report on a car fire to which both had responded earlier in the day. The fight left both officers with extensive cuts and bruises. In an attempt to cover up their altercation, they invented a story that they were assaulted by a Black man wearing a blue jacket and sneakers. They said their attacker had evaded capture. The hoax was finally revealed by a fellow police officer who witnessed the fight in the police station house. Officer Drogan was fired from the police force, and Officer Papaleo was suspended for sixty days and put on probation for a year.

DUKE LACROSSE CASE (RACIAL HOAX VICTIM'S NAME)

In 2006, members of the Duke University men's lacrosse team held a party. Two strippers were hired as part of the entertainment. Following the party, one of the women said that she had been raped by members of the lacrosse team. This allegation, brought by a Black woman against the White athletic team, led to a firestorm of controversy and media attention. Over several months the prosecution's case began to fall apart. There were questions about the victim's credibility and incompatible DNA evidence. A new district attorney took over the case, and the charges were dropped. The initial prosecutor, Mike Nifong, was charged with several ethics violations. The panel reviewing the case instituted the ultimate sanction, disbarment—the first for a sitting district attorney in the history of North Carolina.

KERRI DUNN

In 2004, Kerri Dunn was a visiting psychology professor at Claremont McKenna College. One evening, following a lecture she had given on hate crimes, Dunn returned to her car to discover that it had been vandalized. The vehicle had been spray painted with racist and anti-Semitic slurs ("kike whore" and "nigger lover") and the tires had been slashed and the windows broken. McKenna, who is White, notified authorities, who classified the case as a hate crime. The racial assault led supporters of McKenna to hold antiracism protests, and the college was shut down for one day. After talking with witnesses, police and prosecutors concluded that Dunn staged the hoax herself. She was convicted of filing a false police report and insurance fraud and was sentenced to one year in prison and restitution in the amount of twenty thousand dollars.

DAWN FRAKES

In December 1995, Dawn Frakes, a White state trooper, told police that she had been shot by a Black teenager. In fact, Frakes had accidentally shot herself in the arm. Officer Frakes gave police a detailed description of her attacker, saying that he went by the name "Willy." Frakes was suspended after it was determined that her story was a hoax.

TINA GATELEY AND WILLIAM KARAFFA

In 1993, Tina Gateley and her boyfriend, William Karaffa, both White, claimed that several Black youths had beaten up Gateley and taken her purse. Gateley was hospitalized for three days with broken ribs and other injuries. The pair told their story on local television and urged neighbors to call on police to make arrests in the case. Police investigators determined that the story was fabricated to cover up an incident of domestic violence. Karaffa had beaten up Gateley.

MATTHEW GAYLE

In 1995, Matthew Gayle told police that his wife had been killed by a Black man wearing baggy pants and a red-and-white sweatshirt. According to Gayle, his wife was shot as the couple drove through an Orlando neighborhood. It was later determined that Gayle had paid a hit man ten thousand dollars to kill his wife. He concocted the hoax to collect on his wife's $150,000 insurance policy. Gayle was sentenced to life in prison.

TONYA GIBSON, TYNNUSH BUSH, CLAYTON HENLEY, WILLIAM GIBSON, AND GARY SNYDER

In August 1996, five White friends agreed on a racial hoax scheme. They decided to blame an accidental shooting on a fictional Black man. The men informed police that a Black man had broken into their apartment and fired, hitting one of the five. Based on a description of the attacker, the police questioned and arrested John Harris, a Black man. Harris was taken to the scene of the shooting, and he was positively identified as the armed assailant. After police told the men that their friend who had been hospitalized after the shooting would survive and that Harris had a solid alibi, they admitted to making up the story.

KENDRA GILLIS

In November 1994, Kendra Gillis, a White female student at SUNY-Albany, reported that she had been attacked by a Black man wielding a knife. After police questioned her about inconsistencies in her story, Kendra admitted that she had fabricated the story. She had created the tale to protect her father, David Gillis, who had physically abused her. Gillis apologized for the false accusation. No false report charges were filed against her.

JOSHUA GREEN, DANIEL PRATT, AND MICHAEL CROWLEY

In December 1994, three White men reported that they had been robbed of thirty-five hundred dollars at the carwash where they worked. They told police that the assailant was a gun-toting Black man. Less than a week later, the police discovered that the story was part of a plan the three men had devised to rob the carwash. All three men were arrested for larceny. Green and Crowley were also charged with filing a false report.

ALICIA HARDIN

In 2005, Alicia Hardin was a nineteen-year-old student at Trinity International College. Hardin, who is Black, used campus mail to send threatening, racist messages to other minority students. As a precaution, the university evacuated all minority students from the campus dormitories. Hardin devised the ruse to convince her parents that Trinity was not safe, hoping that they would then let her transfer to another university. She pled guilty to felony disorderly conduct and was sentenced to two years probation, two hundred hours of community service, and two thousand dollars in restitution.

PERSEY HARRIS, ANN VIGIL, AND CARYN HARRIS

In 1996, Persey Harris, a Black man, was sentenced to fifteen days in jail for filing a false police report. Harris and his cohorts told police that a restaurant owner had threatened them with a four-foot stick and shouted racial epithets at them. Harris later admitted that the fabricated incident was to be the basis of a civil lawsuit.

ROBERT HARRIS

In January 1996, Robert Harris, a White man, claimed that he and his fiancée had been shot and robbed on a quiet Baltimore street. Harris said that the assailant was an armed Black man, wearing a camouflage jacket and black-and-white pants. Harris's fiancée died from her gunshot wounds. Within three days, Harris confessed that he had hired a hit man to rob the pair and kill his fiancée. Harris was motivated by the mistaken belief that he was the beneficiary of his fiancée's $250,000 insurance policy.

JEFFREY HEBERT

In August 1995, Jeffrey Hebert told police that three Black men had broken into his home, assaulted everyone there, and set the house on fire. Hebert, who is White, was the only survivor. He told police that following the attack, the Black assailants ran into the woods nearby. Police became suspicious when they discovered contradictions in Hebert's story. Police also observed that the wounds on Hebert's wrists were consistent with a suicide attempt. Hebert, who pled guilty to murder and arson, was sentenced to two life terms behind bars.

BRENDA HUENEKE

In 1995, Brenda Hueneke told police that a Black man had robbed her at knifepoint. She later admitted to making up the story. Hueneke was charged with filing a false police report.

FRANK IRVINE

In 1994, Frank Irvine, a White police officer, told police that he had been attacked by a Black customer at a convenience store. A videotape of the North Miami incident indicated that Irvine had assaulted the customer. Irvine resigned his post and pled no contest to misdemeanor battery and filing a false report. He received one year on probation.

ANGELA JACKSON

In November 1996, Angela Jackson, a twenty-seven-year-old Black woman, sent herself packages containing damaged goods and scrawled with racial slurs. To draw attention and enhance the legitimacy of her insurance scam, Jackson also sent defaced mail packages to several Black officials, including Jesse Jackson (no relation). Jackson, a law student, blamed United Parcel Service for the racist hate mail and sought $150,000 compensation. Police traced the packages to Jackson, and she was charged and convicted of mail and wire fraud. She was sentenced to five years in federal prison.

SONIA JAMES

In April 1996, Sonia James told police that her home had been vandalized and defaced with racial slurs. James, who is Black, claimed that furniture, clothing, and personal belongings had been destroyed by intruders. Community residents took up her cause and raised more than five thousand dollars for her and her infant son. James later told police that she had fabricated the scheme to cash in on her home insurance policy. James was sentenced to nine months in jail and ordered to pay twenty-six thousand dollars in restitution.

KATHLEEN JOHNSTON

In September 1994, Kathleen Johnston, a White female, reported that she had been assaulted and robbed at the high school where she was a physical education instructor. The Maryland woman said that two Black males had attacked her. Two months later, Johnston admitted that her wounds were self-inflicted and recanted her story. Johnston later resigned from her teaching position.

MIRIAM KASHANI

In 1990, Miriam Kashani, a student at George Washington University, reported that another White female student had been raped by two young Black men, with "particularly bad body odor." The day after press reports about the crime, Kashani admitted that she had made up the story. She said her goal was to "highlight the problems of safety for women."

MARK LAMBIRTH

In 1995, Mark Lambirth, a White man, claimed that an American Indian man had forced him at gunpoint to drive from North Carolina to Colorado. Lambirth reported that in Colorado the car got stuck in the snow in a remote area. He also told police that his kidnapper then burned the car and made him walk up a mountain. After investigating the story, police concluded that it was a hoax. Among other things, police found only one set of foot tracks in the snow where Lambirth was allegedly taken.

MARK LEWIS

In August 1993, Mark Lewis, a White, thirteen-year veteran of the Lake Worth, Florida, police department, filed a report stating that he had been hit on the head with a wrench. Lewis said that his attacker was a Black man. After investigating the case, police officials concluded that the incident was a hoax. The incident was staged to garner sympathy for a demotion that Lewis had recently received and to support a claim that he experienced on-the-job injuries.

MARCY LIMOS

A White woman from Reno, Marcy Limos, told police that she had been raped by two Black men. According to Limos, while on her way to meet her husband for dinner, she was approached by the men. She said the men dragged her and her one-year-old daughter into the SUV. They were taken to a park, where she was sexually assaulted, and then she was allowed to go free. Limos later admitted that she had fabricated the tale to hide her drug problem from her husband. She was charged with filing a false report.

JOSEPHINE LUPUS

In November 1994, Josephine Lupus, a student at State College at Old Westbury in New York, told police that she had been robbed by a Black man. The twenty-one-year-old White woman said that the attacker had slashed her face and stabbed her in the stomach as she walked to her car following an evening class. Lupus went on television and displayed her injuries. Lupus, who later confessed to making up the whole story, was charged with filing a false police report. The district attorney refused a plea bargain because "he felt strongly about the aspect of trying to blame a black man."

LUCILLE MAGRONE

In 1990, White residents in Islip Terrace, New York, began receiving death threats. The letters, allegedly written by a Black man, threatened them with rape, robbery, and murder. One letter threatened, "You people are all dead in 24 hours." White residents became fearful: some purchased dogs, some slept with baseball bats at their bedside, and some believed that they saw intruders in their yard. Five months after the first threatening letter had appeared, Lucille Magrone, a forty-eight-year-old White woman, admitted to writing the letters. She said that the incident was the result of stress she suffered from an assault, months earlier, by a Black man.

RAMON MARTINEZ, LUIS MENDEZ, AND JOSEPH DEGROS

In January 1996, Ramon Martinez, an eighteen year-old from Manchester, New Hampshire, told authorities that he had been shot in the foot. He said that a Black man had shot him after a traffic dispute on a highway. Martinez's story was corroborated by Luis Mendez and Joseph Degros, who said that they were with Martinez and witnessed the assault. Martinez later admitted that he had accidentally shot himself. The men were charged with filing a false police report.

JANET MAXWELL

In 1993, Janet Maxwell, a twenty-six-year-old White woman, claimed that she had been abducted at gunpoint from a shopping mall. She said her attackers were three Black men. Maxwell told police that she was driven around in her car for ten hours, forced to take drugs, then raped. Police later determined that Maxwell made up the story so that her parents would not be angry with her for staying out all night. Maxwell was charged with filing a false police report.

DANIEL MAYO AND PHILIP LAFOREST

In 1997, two White teenagers, Daniel Mayo and Philip LaForest, told police that they had discovered hate graffiti on the walls of a building they were patrolling. The messages included "KILL WHITY" and "KILL SECURITY." Both Mayo and LaForest, who confessed to spray painting the messages, were security guards in a Worcester, Massachusetts, apartment complex for elderly residents. The men hoped that the incident would generate publicity and result in a pay raise. They were charged with destruction of property, making a false police report, and intimidation based on race, color, religion, or national origin.

CECIL MCCOOL

In 1995, Cecil McCool, a White man, accused two Black police officers of leaving his friend, Richard Will, another White man, stranded in a dangerous Chicago neighborhood. Will was later found beaten and burned to death. In fact, McCool and Will were driving through the neighborhood to purchase drugs when police pulled McCool over for a traffic violation. Police took McCool into custody because he had an outstanding warrant. They directed Will to a pay phone three blocks away. Instead Will walked to a crack house, where he was later killed. McCool later admitted that he and Will had been trying to buy drugs and that they had never asked police officers for assistance.

KELLI MCGUIRE

In July 1997, nineteen-year-old Kelli Maguire told police that she had been abducted and raped by a Black man. She said she had been forced from a shopping mall and assaulted by an armed gunman. Based on McGuire's description, Fort Lauderdale police released a sketch of the attacker. Within two days Maguire admitted to making up the story as a cover for staying out all night with her boyfriend.

MILTON METCALFE

In April 1993, Milton Metcalfe, a Black man from Cincinnati, reported that he and his girlfriend had been abducted and held at knifepoint. Metcalfe said that the crime had occurred after he had offered a ride to two

Black men. After 911 records revealed that Metcalfe was not at the location that was indicated in his police report, he was charged with and later convicted of filing a false report. Metcalfe spent one night in jail, and his thirty-day jail sentence was suspended.

RICHARD MILAM

In January 1994, Richard Milam told police that his wife had been murdered and that he had been stabbed. According to Milam, a masked Black man attacked and robbed the couple outside a restaurant. Police became suspicious of Milam's story when they discovered that his wife's death made him the beneficiary of a large insurance settlement. Nearly two years after the murder, police located a co-worker of Milam's who said Milam had offered him money to kill his wife. Police took Milam into custody, whereupon he confessed to the murder.

PHILLIP MILLER

In February 1994, Phillip Miller, a White convenience-store clerk, reported that he had been a crime victim. The North Carolina man said that two Black men had come into the store and robbed him at gunpoint. A week later, Miller was charged with stealing the money and filing a false report.

DEANTRIOUS MITCHELL

DeAntrious Mitchell was a computer science student at Iowa State University and also worked as a security guard. He told police that while making his rounds one evening, he was attacked by eight White men. He said that the men also shouted racial epithets at him. It was later determined that Mitchell fabricated the attack. He was charged with making a false police report.

RICHARD NICOLAS

In July 1996, Richard Nicolas, a Black man, claimed that while driving on a rural Maryland road with his two-year-old daughter, he was rammed from behind by another car. The driver of that car, a White man with long hair, pulled alongside Nicholas's car and fired a shot that killed his daughter. Nicolas was charged and convicted of first-degree murder. Months prior to his daughter's death, he had taken out a fifteen-thousand-dollar insurance policy in her name, listing himself as the sole beneficiary.

EDWARD O'BRIEN

In July 1995, Edward O'Brien, a White teenager, reported that he had been robbed and knifed by two men. He said that one of his attackers was Black and that the other was Hispanic. A police investigation indicated that O'Brien had sustained the cuts while murdering his neighbor, whom he stabbed more than sixty times.

BRIAN PATTERSON

In March 1996, a White man told police that he had seen a Black man throw a White person off a bridge. Police searched the area and the river but did not locate a body. Patterson eventually told police that he had fabricated the story.

DENNIS PITTMAN

In April 1996, Dennis Pittman, a White man, told police that he had been carjacked. He said that a Black assailant pointed a knife at him and forced him to drive from Philadelphia to Atlantic City. The carjacker then left in his car. Shortly after the incident, Pittman admitted that he had made up the story so that he would no longer have to make car payments.

MARYROSE POSNER

In February 1994, Maryrose Posner told police that she was robbed at an ATM. Posner said that she was with her two-year-old daughter when she was accosted by a Black man. According to Posner, the man held a gun to her daughter's head, laughed, and demanded that she withdraw two hundred dollars from her account. After police questioning, Posner admitted that she had used the ploy to get attention from her husband and to cover up the fact that she had purchased an expensive shirt for her father. Days later she said that the police had coerced her into signing a confession and stood by her original story. Posner was charged with filing a false report.

CHRISTOPHER PRINCE (RACIAL HOAX VICTIM'S NAME)

In 1994, a twelve-year-old White girl from Virginia told police that a Black man had broken into her family's home and attempted to rape her. The girl identified her attacker as Christopher Prince, a twenty-one-year-old Black man. Prince, who was arrested, charged with, and convicted of burglary and attempted rape, was sentenced to a twelve-year prison term. After the girl recanted, Prince was released, having served fifteen months in prison. In 1995, Prince was pardoned by the governor, and in 1997, the Virginia Senate voted unanimously to award him forty-five thousand dollars for wrongful imprisonment. A short time later this award was deemed "illegal," and no other compensation was approved for Prince.

LORETTA REED

In July 1997, Loretta Reed, a twenty-eight-year-old White woman, told police that she had been carjacked by a Black man. Reed told Sarasota police that the man had grabbed her hair and forced her onto the ground. Later she said she made up the story to "protect herself." Reed had given a man her car in exchange for drugs.

REGGIE RIVERA (RACIAL HOAX VICTIM'S NAME)

In 1993, four New York livery-van drivers and a mechanic, all of whom were Black, accused a White police officer, Reggie Rivera, of raping them. A two-year police investigation found that the men, some of whom worked in the unlicensed van trade business, made the false allegations as part of a plot to get Rivera fired because he had been ticketing unlicensed van drivers.

KATHARINE ROBB

In 2001, Katharine Robb, a White Iowa State University student, claimed that she had been kidnapped and sexually assaulted by four Black men. She said that she was abducted from a campus bus stop by an armed man and then assaulted by the other men. Days later Robb admitted to fabricating the story. Members of the campus community, including Blacks and victims of sexual assault, expressed outrage at Robb's tale. Robb was charged with filing a false police report.

DARLIE ROUTIER

In 1996, Darlie Routier, a White mother of three, told police that a White man, wearing dark clothes and a baseball cap, broke into her home. According to Routier, the attacker stabbed her and two of her sleeping children. Routier received superficial stab wounds in the assault. In 1997, Routier was convicted of capital murder in the death of her youngest child.

JUDY RUSSELL

In 1988, Judy Russell, a White federal prosecutor in New Jersey, reported that she had received death threats from two alleged terrorists who faced extradition to India. She later admitted that she had written and sent the letters to herself. Her actions were part of a scheme to further incriminate the men at their extradition hearing, a case that Russell was prosecuting. In 1989, Russell was acquitted of obstruction of justice charges, based on her insanity plea. The court recommended psychological counseling for Russell because tests indicated that she had multiple personality disorder.

ZHALEH SARABAKHSH

In October 1995, Zhaleh Sarabakhsh claimed that she had been bound, slashed, and left to die in a fire at her family's restaurant in Fargo, North Dakota. Sarabakhsh was found outside the restaurant, bound and with a swastika carved into her abdomen. News of the assault erupted in protests by community members, who denounced the act as a hate crime. Police determined that the wounds were self-inflicted and that she had staged the hate crime herself. She faced several charges, including arson and filing a false police report.

ED SATTERLY

In 2004, a process server for juvenile court shot himself and blamed a fictitious Black man. Ed Satterly of Louisville told police that a man had approached and shot him as he sat in his car reviewing paperwork. Satterly said that the man had blue and white beads in his braided hair. Police discovered a bullet lodged in the bulletproof vest that Satterly was wearing. After police received information from the crime lab that the bullet matched the gun found in Satterly's trunk, he admitted that he had shot himself and fabricated the entire story.

JAY B. SAULS

In April 1997, Jay Sauls, a parking-lot security guard, told police that he had been beaten and robbed. He said he was attacked after walking in on two people having sex in a stairwell. Sauls said that he was then assaulted by the man, whom he described as a Black male, five foot ten. Several police officers spent hours searching for the fictional Black male attacker. Two weeks following the alleged attack, Sauls admitted making up the story. He was charged with filing a false police report.

SHAWNDA SCRUGGS

In February 1996, Shawnda Scruggs, a Sunday-school teacher, told police that her home had been vandalized and burglarized. Racial slurs were painted on her walls. She said she would pray for the thieves and turn the other cheek. The thirty-two-year-old Black woman filed an insurance claim for more than fifty thousand dollars. Her story began to fall apart after inconsistencies were discovered. One of her neighbors reported seeing her china cabinet empty days earlier, and her most expensive possessions were not spray painted.

JAELYN SEALEY

In 2000, Jaelyn Sealey told police that her car had been burned and her driveway scrawled with "Go home nigger." The Huntersville, North Carolina, case sparked an outpouring of support for Sealey: more than three hundred people attended a rally in support of her and her family. Sealey, who is Black, later admitted that she torched her vehicle to collect insurance money. She pled guilty to making false statements to police investigators and to mail and wire fraud. Sealey was sentenced to six months in prison, two years probation, and was required to pay five thousand dollars in restitution.

DORNE SHAVER

In 2000, Dorne Shaver told police that several White men had attacked him and shouted racial slurs at him while he was selling magazines and books door-to-door in DuPage County, Illinois. Shaver was charged with felony disorderly conduct for filing a false police report.

MICHAEL SHAW

In January 1995, Michael Shaw, a twenty-one-year-old White man from Maple Shade, New Jersey, reported that a White toddler had been kidnapped by a Black man. According to Shaw, the young girl's mouth had been bound with duct tape. The police quickly mounted an extensive air and land search for the child. One day later, Shaw admitted that the story was false. Police believe he came up with the tale to get the afternoon off from work. Shaw was charged with making a false report to the police.

CARLTON SKIPPER

In October 1997, Carlton Skipper, a retired D.C. police officer who is Black, told police that he had been assaulted and robbed by two armed Black men. The fifty-year-old officer said that while out on his morning run he was accosted, required to strip off his clothing, and thrown down an embankment. It was later determined that Skipper was suffering from depression and may have had a failed suicide attempt.

SUSAN SMITH

In 1994, Susan Smith, a White women, told police that a young Black man carjacked her and drove off with her two young sons. Nine days after massive federal and state searches had been launched, Smith confessed to drowning her two boys in a South Carolina lake. Smith was depressed over a recent breakup with a boyfriend who did not want to raise children. Smith was convicted of murder and sentenced to life in prison. She will be eligible for parole in 2025.

MOUNIR SOLIMAN

In November 1994, Mounir Soliman, a convenience-store manager, claimed that two Black men had robbed him of ten thousand dollars while he was taking the money to the bank. The description that Soliman gave police was used to draw a composite sketch. The Texas man ultimately confessed that he had taken the money. He was charged with filing a false report.

CHARLES STUART

In 1989, Charles Stuart told police that he and his pregnant wife had been shot by a Black jogger on their way home after a birthing class. Stuart's wife and the unborn child died as a result of the gunshot wounds. Stuart identified a Black man from a police line-up as the criminal. The Boston case made national and international headlines. Police ransacked Mission Hill, a predominantly Black neighborhood, in search of the murderer. Stuart's brother Matthew informed police that Charles had concocted the hoax as a murderous scheme to collect his wife's insurance money. When Stuart learned that the police were going to question him as a murder suspect, he committed suicide.

LISA TANCZOS

In September 1995, Lisa Tanczos told police that she had been assaulted by a gun- and knife-wielding man. Tanczos, a thirty-year-old White woman, described her attacker as a muscular Black man in his late thirties. The Allentown, Pennsylvania, woman claimed the assailant scratched her with the knife and used it to play a game of tic-tac-toe on her arm. Two months later, Tanczos said that the same man attacked her at her home and again cut her with a knife. DNA evidence was used to show that Tanczos had fabricated the hoax (DNA was taken from the envelope of a card allegedly sent by the attacker to Tanczos's boss). Tanczos was sentenced to 350 hours of community service at a local Black church.

HARRY TICKNOR

In 1997, Harry Ticknor told police that he had been robbed at a gas station by an armed Black man. Ticknor, who is White, later confessed to making up the story. He did not want his girlfriend to find out that he had lost sixty-seven dollars He was charged with filing a false police report.

TULIA, TEXAS

In 1999, more than forty African Americans were arrested in Tulia, Texas. They were arrested based on the word of a lone undercover agent who said that they were all involved in the drug trade. Many of the charges resulted in convictions and lengthy sentences. An investigation by a special prosecutor determined that the evidence in these cases was not reliable, and all the convictions were voided.

PAUL VEACH

In May 1995, Paul Veach, a forty-seven-year-old White man from Des Moines, claimed that he had been robbed at gunpoint by a Black man with "light-colored hair in six-to-eight-inch braids, a deformed pupil in one eye, acne scars on his cheeks, and one or two missing front teeth." Veach said he had been forced to drive around for six hours before being put out of his car. A police investigation revealed that Veach had made several ATM transactions at a local horse track. Veach subsequently admitted that he came up with the story to hide gambling losses, totaling $390.

NEVA VEITCH AND DAVID CRAIG

In 1989, Billy Joe Veitch was brutally murdered. His wife, Neva, told police that she and her husband had been kidnapped by two Black men, who killed her husband and tried to rape her. It was believed that Neva and her husband were targeted by Blacks because they were both KKK members. Neva Veitch told her story at numerous Klan rallies. Two years later, David Craig, Veitch's lover (also a Klansman), confessed to police that he and Neva had killed her husband. The lovers had hoped to cash in on Billy Veitch's insurance. Both were tried for murder. Craig, who was found guilty, committed suicide in prison.

CANDICE WAGNER

In November 1995, Candice Wagner, a twenty-four-year-old White woman, reported that she had been kidnapped at gunpoint from a shopping-mall parking lot. Her attacker, described as a "short, slender Black man with a bad complexion," forced her to drive to an isolated area, where he raped her. Wagner told police that she escaped by kicking her attacker in the groin and driving to a friend's home, from which she called the police. After police told her that parts of her story were inconsistent, she admitted that her story was false.

LISA WIGHT

In January 1996, Lisa Wight told police that a Black man had attempted to rape her. Wight, a White woman employed as a courthouse deputy, claimed that she had been assaulted in a hallway of the federal courthouse where she worked. After intense questioning by the FBI, Wight admitted that she made up the story. Wight was forced to resign her post.

JENNIFER WILBANKS

Also known as the "runaway bride," Jennifer Wilbanks was engaged to be married to John Mason in Duluth, Georgia. Days before their 2005 wedding, Wilbanks disappeared. Her disappearance was a big news story. Mason and Wilbanks were expecting six hundred guests and friends at their nuptials. Family members could think of no reason that the bride would voluntarily flee. Three days later, Wilbanks called her fiancé from Albuquerque, New Mexico, claiming that she had been kidnapped and sexually assaulted by a couple, a Hispanic man and a White woman. Wilbanks repeated the same claims to law enforcement officials. A short time later, though, she admitted that she had made up the tale because she was under great stress—her pending nuptials. One week prior to her wedding she had purchased the bus ticket to travel west to Las Vegas and then Albuquerque. Wilbanks pled no contest to giving false information to the police. She was sentenced to two years probation and 120 hours of community service and fined $2,250 in restitution.

MICHELE YENTES

In 1990, Michele Yentes claimed that she had been raped on the campus of Ohio State University. Yentes, who is White, told police that her assailant was Black. Police spent hours investigating her claim. Yentes later admitted that she had fabricated the rape. Yentes was charged with filing a false police report and fined fifteen thousand dollars.

SOLOMON YOUSHEI

In 1995, Solomon Youshei, a jewelry-store owner, told police that he was robbed of five hundred thousand dollars in jewelry and twenty-seven hundred dollars in cash. Youshei said that the robbers were two well-dressed Black men wearing White gloves. Police determined that Youshei and his brother made up the story as part of an insurance scheme.

Unnamed Racial Hoaxes, Alphabetical by State

UNNAMED, FLORIDA (1)

In 1994, a White seventeen-year-old high school student claimed that a young White male, with long brown hair and wearing a Metallica T-shirt, kidnapped her at gunpoint outside a library at the University of South Florida and took her to a remote area, where she was raped. Two days later, the young woman recanted her story. At the time of the alleged offense, the girl was at the home of her boyfriend, whom her parents had forbidden her to see.

UNNAMED, FLORIDA (2)

In July 1996, a White Florida woman claimed that she was the victim of a sexual assault. She told police that two Black men followed her into her home and slashed her with a steak knife. It was later determined that the story was a hoax.

UNNAMED, KENTUCKY

A Louisville girl told police that she had been kidnapped. The fifteen-year-old said that a Black man wearing dark clothing and a hooded sweat-shirt had tried to force her from her bus stop early one morning. She said that the man grabbed and pulled her and that she was only able to free herself by kicking him in the groin. After receiving her report, school officials issued warnings throughout the county. Police gave chase to a Black man who was seen in the area. Later the same day police determined that there were numerous inconsistencies in the minor's story and dismissed it as a hoax.

UNNAMED, LOUISIANA

In 1994, a White woman in Baton Rouge told police that she had been sexually assaulted by a Black man who had a tattoo of a serpent on his arm. Police released a composite sketch of the "serpent man." As many as twenty-eight other women reported that they had seen or had been attacked by the pictured assailant. When the woman admitted to making up the story, police had already fingered a suspect whom they planned to arrest.

UNNAMED, MAINE

In October 1994, a seven-year-old White girl told police that she had been assaulted by a Black man while she walked across a parking lot with two friends. Her friends corroborated her story. After initiating a state-wide search for the assailant, the police discovered that the girls had made up the story of the attack.

UNNAMED, NEW JERSEY

In March 1994, a young White women reported that she and her seventy-one-year-old mother-in-law had been attacked by a Black male intruder. The police investigation revealed that the woman had been in a fight with another woman and had come up with the story as a cover-up.

UNNAMED, VIRGINIA

In May 1995, a thirty-nine-year-old White man claimed that two Black men had cut him with his own knife and then stolen his van at a traffic light in Fairfax County. The man later admitted that he had parked the van and cut himself with his knife.

UNNAMED, WISCONSIN

In March 1996, a White woman in Madison told police that a Black man had dragged her off the sidewalk and raped her. She later admitted that the story was a fabrication. She was not charged with filing a false report.

Notes

NOTES TO THE INTRODUCTION

1. Nelson Mandela, *A Prisoner in the Garden* (Viking, 2005), 9.

2. Thelma Golden, "My Brother," in *Black Male: Representations of Masculinity in Contemporary American Art* (Whitney Museum of American Art, 1994), 19.

NOTES TO CHAPTER 1

1. Marshall McLuhan, *Understanding Media: The Extensions of Man* (Signet Books, 1964), 23.

2. *See generally*, Philip Deloria, *Indians in Unexpected Places* (University Press of Kansas, 2004).

3. *See* C. Richard King and Charles Frueling Springwood, *Team Spirits* (University of Nebraska Press, 2001).

4. *See, e.g.*, Andrew Adam Newman, "Nike Adds Indian Artifacts to Its Swoosh," *New York Times*, October 3, 2007, p. C4.

5. *See, e.g., Ebony*, September 2007. The cover story features models Tyra Banks, Alek Wek, Iman, and Kimora Simmons. The title is "Black Is Black: The Players, the Clothes, the History."

6. Quoted in Vanessa Hua, "Survivor Winner Hopes He Shattered Some Asian Stereotypes," *San Francisco Chronicle*, December 18, 2006.

7. *See, generally*, Jeff Adachi's documentary, *Slanted Screen* (2006).

8. *See, generally*, the television documentary *Black History: Lost, Stolen, or Strayed* (1968); Berkeley Art Center Association, *Ethnic Notions: Black Images in the White Imagination* (text and documentary, 1982).

9. *E.g.*, comedians Chelsea Sandler, Sarah Silverman, and Rosie O'Donnell.

10. *Cohen v. California*, 403 U.S. 15, 25 (1971).

11. Spike Lee, *Do the Right Thing* (Universal Pictures, 1989).

12. Teresa Wiltz, "A Part Colored by History," *Washington Post*, June 23, 2007, p. C1.

13. *Id.*

14. Music and lyrics by Jordan Houston, Cedric Coleman, and Paul Beauregard.

NOTES TO CHAPTER 2

1. The video can be viewed on YouTube, http://www.youtube.com/watch?v= U3RjiVcIlhY (accessed January 17, 2008).

2. "O'Reilly Surprised 'There Was No Difference' between Harlem Restaurant and Other New York Restaurants," *MediaMatters.org,* http://mediamatters. org/items/200709210007 (accessed January 17, 2008).

3. www.Mediamatters.org, April 4, 2007.

4. *See, e.g.,* Cornelia Dean, "Nobel Winner Issues Apology for Comments about Blacks," *New York Times,* October 19, 2007, p. A21.

5. Peggy Davis, "The Law as Microaggression," *Yale Law Journal* 98 (1989): 1559, 1565.

6. "President Clinton's Weekly Radio Address," Federal News Service, March 29, 1997.

7. Darryl Fears, "Nooses Seen More Frequently after Louisiana Town's Strife," *Washington Post,* October 20, 2007, p. A1.

8. Angela Onwuachi-Willig and Mario Barnes, "By Any Other Name? On Being "Regarded as" Black, and Why Title VII Should Apply Even If Lakisha and Jamal Are White," *Wisconsin Law Review* (2005): 1283.

9. *Id.* at 1304.

10. Steven Levitt and Stephen Dubner, *Freakonomics: A Rogue Economist Explores the Hidden Side of Everything* (William Morrow, 2005), 187.

11. *Id.*

12. Michael Eric Dyson, *Is Bill Cosby Right? Or Has the Black Middle Class Lost Its Mind?* (Basic Books, 2005), 103.

13. *See, e.g.,* Dawn Smalls, "Linguistic Profiling and the Law," *Stanford Law and Policy Review* 15 (2004): 579.

14. *See, e.g.,* Lis Wiehl, " 'Sounding Black' in the Courtroom: Court-Sanctioned Racial Stereotyping," *Harvard Blackletter Law Journal* 18 (2002): 185.

15. Derrick Bell, "The Space Traders," in *Faces at the Bottom of the Well* (Basic Books, 1992), 163.

16. *See, e.g.,* Michael Coyle, "Race and Class Penalties in Crack Cocaine Sentencing" (The Sentencing Project, 2002).

17. *See Kimbrough v. United States,* 128 S.Ct. 558 (2007).

18. Lauren Glaze and Thomas Bonczar "Probation and Parole in the United States, 2005," Bureau of Justice Statistics, NCJ 215091 (2007).

19. Paige Harrison and Allen Beck, "Prisoners in 2005," Bureau of Justice Statistics, NCJ 215092 (2006).

NOTES TO CHAPTER 3

1. A. Leon Higginbotham Jr., *In the Matter of Color* (Oxford University Press, 1978), 28–29.

2. F. James Davis, *Who Is Black?* (Pennsylvania State University Press, 1991), 5.

3. *See, generally,* J. Clay Smith, "Justice and Jurisprudence and the Black Lawyer," *Notre Dame Law Review* 69 (1994): 1105.

4. Michael Hindus, *Prison and Plantation* (University of North Carolina Press, 1980), 145.

5. *State v. Maner,* 2 Hill 355 (S.C. 1834) ("The criminal offense of assault and battery cannot at common law be committed on the person of a slave").

6. *See* Thomas Morris, *Southern Slavery and the Law, 1619–1860* (University of North Carolina Press, 1996), 306.

7. A. Leon Higginbotham Jr. and Anne Jacobs, "'The Law Only as Enemy': The Legitimization of Racial Powerlessness through the Colonial and Ante-Bellum Criminal Laws of Virginia," *North Carolina Law Review* 70 (1992): 969, 1958.

8. *See, e.g.,* Emily Field Van Tassel, "Freedom: Personal Liberty and Private Law: 'Only the Law Would Rule between Us," *Chicago-Kent Law Review* 70 (1995): 873.

9. Higginbotham, *In the Matter of Color,* 23–24.

10. Higginbotham and Jacobs, "Law Only as Enemy," 1056.

11. Some states did make the rape of a slave girl under the age of twelve a criminal offense. *See, e.g.,* Morris, *Southern Slavery,* 306 (discussion of *State v. Jones,* involving Mississippi statute that punished the rape or attempted rape of a mulatto or Black female by a mulatto or Black male).

12. *See, generally,* J. Clay Smith, "Justice and Jurisprudence."

13. *See, e.g., id.* at 1107 (citing Mississippi Code penalty for helping a slave obtain freedom); Higginbotham and Jacobs, "Law Only as Enemy," 1021 (discussing Virginia law).

14. Smith, "Justice and Jurisprudence," 1117.

15. *Id.* at 1110.

16. *See, e.g.,* Kenneth Stampp, *The Peculiar Institution* (Vintage Books, 1956), 214–215; Marvin Dulaney, *Black Police in America* (Indiana University Press, 1996), 2.

17. Smith, "Justice and Jurisprudence," 1108.

18. Eric Foner, *Reconstruction: America's Unfinished Revolution, 1863–1877* (Harper and Row, 1988), 198.

19. Jason Gilmer, "*U.S. v. Clary*: Equal Protection and the Crack Statute," *American University Law Review* 45 (1995): 597, 538 (citing "An Act to Amend the Vagrant Laws of the State").

20. Douglas Colbert, "Challenging the Challenge: Thirteenth Amendment as

a Prohibition against Racial Use of Peremptory Challenges," *Cornell Law Review* 76 (1990): 1, 41.

21. *United States v. Cruikshank*, 25 F. Cas. 707 (1875), aff'd 92 U.S. 542 (1875). *See also* Colbert, "Challenging the Challenge," 60–61.

22. Walter White states that prior to 1902 there were reports of lynchings of Chinese, Japanese, Mexicans, and Italians. As redress, between 1887 and 1901, the United States paid almost $500,000 to the governments of China, Mexico, Italy, and Great Britain for the mob attacks.

23. Gunnar Myrdal, *An American Dilemma* (1944; repr., Transaction, 1996), 562.

24. W. E. B. Du Bois, *Dusk of Dawn* (Harcourt, 1940), 251.

25. *See* Orlando Patterson, *Rituals of Blood* (Civitas, 1999).

26. Ida B. Wells-Barnett, *On Lynchings* (Humanity Books, 2002).

27. U.S. Bureau of the Census, *Historical Statistics of the United States, Colonial Times to 1970, Bicentennial Edition, Part 2* (1975), 422.

28. Hilton Als, John Lewis, Leon Litwack, and James Allen, *Without Sanctuary: Lynching Photography in America* (Twin Palms, 2000), 25–26.

29. *See, e.g.*, Sherrilyn Ifill, *On the Courthouse Lawn* (Beacon, 2007), 7–8 ("Between 1900 and 1935, courthouse lawns on the Eastern Shore [Maryland] were routinely the sites of lynchings or near lynchings, involving the participation of hundreds and sometimes thousands of White onlookers.").

30. *Id.* at 198.

31. *Id.*

32. "Apologizing to the victims of lynching and the descendants of those victims for the failure of the Senate to enact anti-lynching legislation," S. Res. 39, 109th Cong., 1st sess. (2005).

33. One example is James Byrd, a Black man who was tied to the back of a truck and dragged to his death in 1998. Three White men were convicted of his murder; two were sentenced to death and one to life in prison.

34. California Civil Code, section 60 (Deering Supp. 1905).

35. 4 Cal. 198 (1854).

36. *See, generally,* Stetson Kennedy, *Jim Crow Guide: The Way It Was* (Florida Atlantic University Press, 1959).

37. *Loving V. Virginia*, 388 U.S. 1, 5 (1967).

38. Montgomery, Alabama, Ordinance 15-57 (1957).

39. James Loewen, *Sundown Towns: A Hidden Dimension of American Racism* (New Press, 2005).

NOTES TO CHAPTER 4

1. Ronald Weitzer and Steven Tuch, "Racially Biased Policing: Determinants of Citizen Perceptions," *Social Forces* 83 (2005): 1009.

2. The question of disproportionality raises the issue of racial classification. The Uniform Crime Reports lists five racial categories: White, Black, Asian, Native American, and Other. It treats Hispanic as an ethnicity. Because the arrest rate for Hispanics in included with other racial groups, this may result in inflated figures for White and Black rates. The U.S. Census Bureau classifies Hispanics as a racial group. This difference in classification makes for problematic analyses when using both these sources.

3. Marvin Wolfgang and Bernard Cohen, *Crime and Race* (Institute of Human Relations Press, 1970), 30–31.

4. See, e.g., John Reitzel and Alex Piquero, "Does It Exist? Studying Citizens' Attitudes of Racial Profiling," *Police Quarterly* 9 (2006): 161.

5. Alfred Blumstein, "Racial Disproportionality of U.S. Prison Populations Revisited," *University of Colorado Law Review* 64 (1993): 743.

6. *Id.* at 759.

7. Office of Applied Studies, "NSDUH Report, Illicit Drug Use, by Race/Ethnicity, in Metropolitan and Non-Metropolitan Counties: 2004 and 2005" (2007), available online at www.oas.samhsa.gov (accessed January 17, 2008).

8. The Sentencing Project, "Federal Crack Cocaine Sentencing" (The Sentencing Project, 2008).

9. 517 U.S. 456 (1996).

10. Daniel Georges-Abeyie, "The Myth of a Racist Criminal Justice System?" in Brian MacLean and Dragan Milovanovic, eds., *Racism, Empiricism and Criminal Justice* (Collective Press, 1990).

11. See, e.g., Sheri Johnson, "Racial Derogation in Prosecutors' Closing Arguments," in Dragan Milovanovic and Katheryn Russell, eds., *Petit Apartheid in the Criminal Justice System* (Carolina Academic Press, 2001).

12. Erving Goffman, The *Presentation of Self in Everyday Life* (Overlook Press, 1973), 112.

13. See the website of The Innocence Project, www.innocenceproject.org (accessed January 17, 2008).

14. For a more detailed discussion of petit apartheid, see Katheryn Russell-Brown, *Underground Codes: Race, Crime and Related Fires* (New York University Press, 2007), 5–19.

15. See, e.g., Dennis Roddy, "Young Black Males Taught Lesson in Caution: Instruction on Dealing with Police Commonplace," *Pittsburgh Post-Gazette*, November 5, 1995, p. A1.

16. See, e.g., Rod Brunson, "'Police Don't Like Black People': African-American Young Men's Accumulated Police Experiences," *Journal of Criminology and Public Policy* 6 (2007): 71.

17. Jerome McCristal Culp Jr., "Notes from California: Rodney King and the Race Question," *Denver University Law Review* 70 (1993): 199, 200.

18. David Dante Troutt, "The Race Industry, Brutality, and the Law of Moth-

ers," in Jabari Asim, ed., *Not Guilty: Twelve Black Men Speak Out on Law, Justice and Life* (Amistad, 2001).

19. *See, e.g.,* Robert Worden and Robin Shepard, "Demeanor, Crime and Police Behavior: A Reexamination of the Police Serves Study Data," *Criminology* 34 (1996): 83.

20. *See, e.g.,* Ronald Weitzer and Stephen Tuch, *Race and Policing in America: Conflict and Reform* (Cambridge University Press, 2006); Reitzel and Piquero, "Does It Exist?" 161.

21. Gunnar Myrdal, *An American Dilemma* (1944; repr., Transaction, 1996), 542.

22. *See* Malcolm Gladwell, *Blink* (Little, Brown, 2005), 89–244 (chap. 7, "Seven Seconds in the Bronx").

23. Arthur Colbert (college student pulled over by Philadelphia police and gun placed to his head); Joseph Gould (homeless man killed by White off-duty Chicago police officer); Malice Green (killed by Detroit police); Don Jackson (Long Beach, California, police officer who secretly videotaped a police assault against him; Jackson's head was slammed through a glass window); Rodney King (after high-speed chase, King was beaten by four Los Angeles police officers as other officers watched); Arthur McDuffie (Miami motorist who was beaten and killed by a police officer; the officer's acquittal led to days of Miami riots); Desmond Robinson (undercover New York Transit officer who was shot in the back by a White officer who mistook him for a criminal); Brian Rooney (Wall Street businessman detained overnight with his sixty-four-year-old mother after New York Transit police mistakenly believed he had entered the station without paying); and Ron Settles (college football star found dead in jail cell after being arrested for speeding. His family was awarded $760,000 in a wrongful-death suit; the movie *The Glass Shield* was partly inspired by this incident). *See, e.g.,* Pierre Thomas, "Police Brutality: An Issue Rekindled," *Washington Post,* December 6, 1995, p. 1.

24. 517 U.S. 806 (1996)

25. John Cloud, "What's Race Got to Do with It?" *Time,* July 30, 2001.

26. Bureau of Justice Statistics, "Contacts between Police and the Public, 2005," NCJ 215243 (April 2007).

27. *Traffic Stops Statistics Act of 1997,* H.R. 118, 105th Cong., 1st sess. (January 7, 1997).

28. General Accounting Office, "U.S. Customs Service: Better Targeting of Airline Passengers for Personal Searches Could Produce Better Results" (GAO, 2000).

29. Criminal Intelligence Report, State of Maryland, Maryland State Police, dated April 27, 1992 (*Wilkins v. Maryland State Police,* Civil Action No. MJG-93468).

30. STIF officer John Appleby was forced to resign after an undercover operation revealed that he was stealing drug money. *See, e.g.,* "Ex-State Trooper Caught

in Police Sting to Serve 18-Month Sentence for Theft," *Baltimore Sun*, May 13, 1997, p. 2B.

31. Quoted in Tanya Jones, "Race Based Searches Prohibited," *Baltimore Sun*, January 15, 1995, p. 1B.

32. Culp, "Notes from California," 206.

33. Brunson, "Police Don't Like Black People," 71.

NOTES TO CHAPTER 5

1. Darryl Fears, "Black Opinion on Simpson Shifts: African Americans Now More Likely to Say He Murdered Ex-Wife, Her Friend," *Washington Post*, September 27, 2007, p. A3.

2. Mark Terrill, "Text of the Simpson Letter," *Chicago Sun-Times*, June 18, 1994, p. 7.

3. Humphrey Taylor, "Public Belief in O.J. Simpson's Guilt or Innocence Varies Greatly Not Just with Race but Also with Age, Education and Income," Harris Poll no. 21 (1995).

4. Christopher Caldwell, "Why the Simpson Case Endures," *Weekly Standard*, July 29, 1996, p. 22 (emphasis added).

5. *Id.*

6. *See, e.g.*, David Margolick, "What the Tapes in the Simpson Case Say," *New York Times*, August 23, 1995, p. A14.

7. William Raspberry, "Where's the Outrage from White America? Black Americans Put Their Faith in the System. They Were Let Down," *Washington Post*, May 1, 1992, p. A27.

8. For a detailed, book-length discussion of Black protectionism, *see* Katheryn Russell-Brown, *Protecting Our Own: Race, Crime and African Americans* (Rowman and Littlefield, 2006).

9. Quoted in Meri Nana-Ama Danquah, "Why We Really Root for O.J.: The Superstar Suspect Embodies the Illusion of a Colorblind America," *Washington Post*, July 3, 1994, p. C1.

10. *See, e.g.*, Larry Dorman, "We'll Be Right Back after This Hip and Distorted Commercial Break," *New York Times*, September 1, 1996, p. 13 (Tiger Woods indicates that he does not want to be limited to being a "Black" golfer).

11. Rachel Swarns, "So Far, Obama Can't Take Black Vote for Granted," *New York Times*, February 2, 2007.

12. Michael Eric Dyson, *Race Rules: Navigating the Color Line* (Vintage Books, 1997), 30.

13. Harry Edwards, "We Must Let O.J. Go: Separating Fact from Image," *Sport* 86 (1995): 80.

14. Regina Austin, "Deviance, Resistance, and Love," *Utah Law Review* (1994): 179, 180.

15. Clarence Thomas's full statement was,

And from my standpoint as a black American, it is a high-tech lynching for uppity blacks who in a way [*sic*] deign to think for themselves, to do for themselves, to have different ideas, and it is a message that unless you kowtow to an old order, that it is what will happen to you. You will be lynched, destroyed, caricatured by a committee of the U.S. Senate rather than hung from a tree.

Reuters, *New York Times*, October 12, 1991, p. 12.

16. Bill Carter, "In Interview, Simpson Appeals for Privacy," *New York Times*, January 26, 1996, p. A16.

17. W. E. B. Du Bois, *The Souls of Black Folk*, in *Three Negro Classics* (Avon Books, 1965), 215.

18. "Essay: American Mix," *NewsHour with Jim Lehrer*, PBS, December 19, 1995, transcript no. 5422.

19. *See, e.g.,* Cynthia Kwei Yung Lee, "Beyond Black and White: Racializing Asian Americans in a Society Obsessed with O. J.," *Hastings Women's Law Journal* 6 (1995): 165.

20. Quoted in Louis Aguilar, "Latinos, Asians Seek a Voice in Emerging National Discussion on Race," *Washington Post*, October 15, 1995, p. A24.

21. Gregory Rodriguez, "Latinos Written Out of the Script in LA's Latest Racial Drama," *JINN*, October 6, 1995, available online at http://www.pacificnews.org/jinn/stories/columns/california/951006-la-oj.html (accessed April 13, 2008).

NOTES TO CHAPTER 6

1. Quoted in Richard Grant, "Mother of All Crimes," *Independent*, February 25, 1995, p. 16.

2. Michael Grunwald, "For Boston, Harsh Reminder: Five Years Ago, Stuart's Racist Hoax Was Hatched—and Believed," *Boston Globe*, November 4, 1994, p. 17.

3. Paul Mooney, *Race* (Stepsun Music, 1993).

4. It is likely that the most common racial hoax is intraracial. These, however, do not attract the same degree of media attention as interracial hoaxes. Newspaper reports of crime hoaxes do not usually state the race of the perpetrator and victim.

5. *See, generally,* Dan Carter, *Scottsboro: A Tragedy of the American South* (Louisiana State University Press, 1969). The Scottsboro injustices were addressed in *Powell v. Alabama*, 287 U.S. 45 (1932), which outlined the parameters of the Sixth Amendment.

6. *See* Michael D'Orso, *Like Judgment Day* (Berkeley, 1996).

7. While the women were on the lawn outside the party, one of the party-goers, apparently upset that the women had not stripped, told them to thank their grandfather for his cotton shirt.

8. The bands were available on the website http://www.debt-pro.org/duke_wristband_order_form.pdf (accessed January 17, 2008).

9. Quoted in Roni Rabin, "Hoax Fed on Prejudice: Frightened by Notes, Neighbors Suspected Black Family," *Newsday,* October 10, 1990, p. 3.

10. *Id.*

11. Douglas H. Palmer, mayor of Trenton, New Jersey, press release, January 12, 1995.

12. 505 U.S. 377 (1992).

13. 508 U.S. 476 (1993). After viewing the movie *Mississippi Burning,* a young Black man and some of his friends discussed one of the scenes. In the scene, a White man beat a young Black boy who was praying. After this conversation, they decided to "move on some white people." They then severely beat a White boy who was walking down the street.

14. *Id.* at 488.

15. *Id.*

16. Frederick Lawrence refers to the free-speech-versus-bias-crime debate as a "false paradox": "the apparent paradox of seeking to punish the perpetrators of racially motivated violence while being committed to protecting the bigot's right to express racism is a false paradox. Put simply, we are making this problem harder than it needs to be. We must focus on the basic distinction between bias crimes—such as racially motivated assaults or vandalism—and racist speech." Frederick Lawrence, "Resolving the Hate Crimes/Hate Speech Paradox: Punishing Bias Crimes and Protecting Racist Speech," *Notre Dame Law Review* 68 (1993): 673, 676.

17. This is an updated version of Justice Oliver Wendell Holmes's pronouncement that one does not have the right to "shout fire in a crowded theatre." *Schenck v. United States,* 249 U.S. 47, 51 (1919).

18. 538 U.S. 343 (2003).

19. "An Act Concerning False Reports to Law Enforcement Authorities," State of New Jersey, Senate (212th Legislature, 1995), No. 1505, (amends N.J.S. 2C: 28-4).

20. Mari Matsuda, "Public Response to Racist Speech," in Mari Matsuda, Charles Lawrence, Richard Delgado, and Kimberlé Crenshaw, eds., *Words That Wound* (Westview, 1993), 36.

21. Marc Fleischauer, "Review of Florida Legislation, Teeth for a Paper Tiger: A Proposal to Add Enforceability to Florida's Hate Crimes Act," *Florida State University Law Review* 17 (1990): 697, 706n. 34.

22. Lawrence, "Resolving the Hate Crimes/Hate Speech Paradox," 698.

23. Ludwig Wittgenstein, *Philosophical Investigations,* 3rd ed., trans. G. E. M. Anscombe (Macmillan, 1968), 146e.

24. Fleischauer, "Review of Florida Legislation," 703.

25. Charles Lawrence, "The Id, the Ego, and Equal Protection: Reckoning

with Unconscious Racism," *Stanford Law Review* 39 (1987): 317, 322 (citations omitted).

26. William Raspberry, "Automatically Suspect," *Washington Post*, November 5, 1994, p. A19.

NOTES TO CHAPTER 7

1. Richard Delgado, "Rodrigo's Eighth Chronicle," *Virginia Law Review* 80 (1994): 503.

2. *See, e.g.*, Eyal Press, "The Way We Live Now," *New York Times Magazine*, December 3, 2006, p. 20 (discussion of immigration and crime rates included focus on Latinos and Haitians, but there was no reference to White immigrants).

3. Gary Kamiya, "Toni Morrison Tells the Publishers They Reinforce 'Racial Half-Truths,'" *San Francisco Examiner*, April 28, 1994.

4. The five journals are *Criminology, Justice Quarterly*, the *Journal of Research in Crime and Delinquency, Criminology and Public Policy*, and the *Journal of Criminal Law and Criminology*. The first two journals were selected because they are the official publications of the two largest professional organizations of criminologists, the American Society of Criminology and the Academy of Criminal Justice Sciences. The remaining three were chosen because of their wide readership and rank in the field of criminology. The search for articles on White crime and Black/African American crime was based on a review of the title, abstract, and full text.

5. Edwin Sutherland, *White Collar Crime* (Dryden, 1949), 6.

6. Francis Cullen and Michael Benson, "White-Collar Crime: Holding a Mirror to the Core," *Journal of Criminal Justice Education* 4 (1993): 325, 334.

7. *Id.*

8. *Id.* at 332.

9. Hate Crimes Statistics, 2006 Uniform Crime Report (2007), available online at www.fbi.gov/ucr/hc2006/dowloadfiles.html (accessed January 15, 2008).

10. Andrew Hacker, "Caste, Crime, and Precocity," in Steve Fraser, ed., *The Bell Curve Wars* (Basic Books, 1995), 97.

11. Marvin Wolfgang and Bernard Cohen, *Crime and Race: Conceptions and Misconceptions* (Institute of Human Relations Press, 1970).

12. Bureau of Labor Statistics, "Current Population Survey," available online at http://www.bls.gov/cps/cpsaat11.pdf (accessed January 17, 2008).

13. For a more detailed discussion of the role of the Black criminologist, see Katheryn K. Russell, "The Development of a Black Criminology and the Role of the Black Criminologist," *Justice Quarterly* 9 (1992): 667.

14. C. Wright Mills, *The Sociological Imagination* (Oxford University Press, 1959), 178.

15. James Q. Wilson, "Crime, Race, and Values," *Society* 30 (November/December 1992): 90, 91.

16. *Id.*

17. *Id.*

18. *See, e.g.,* Wesley Skogan, "Crime and the Racial Fears of White Americans," *Annals of the American Academy of Political and Social Sciences* (May 1995).

19. *Id.*

20. Jesse Jackson's complete statement was, "There is nothing more painful for me at this stage of my life than to walk down the street and hear footsteps and start to think about robbery and then look around and see it's somebody white and feel relieved. How humiliating." Quoted in John DiIulio, "My Black Crime Problem, and Ours," *City Journal* (spring 1996): 14.

21. *See, e.g.,* George Will, "A Measure of Morality," *Washington Post*, December 16, 1993, p. A25; Susan Estrich, "Race in the Jury Room," *Washington Post*, September 11, 1996, p. A23.

22. Steven D. Levitt and John J. Donohue, "The Impact of Legalized Abortion on Crime," *Quarterly Journal of Economics* 116 (2001): 379.

23. Quoted in Brian Faler, "Bennett Under Fire for Remark on Crime and Black Abortions," *Washington Post*, September 30, 2005, p. A5.

24. Andrew Hacker, "Malign Neglect: The Crackdown on African Americans," *Nation*, July 10, 1995, p. 49.

25. *See, e.g.,* Frankie Bailey, "Race, Law and 'Americans': A Historical Overview," in Michael Lynch and Britt Patterson, eds., *Race and Criminal Justice* (Harrow and Heston, 1991), 12.

26. *See, e.g.,* Derrick Bell, *Race, Racism, and American Law,* 3rd ed. (Little, Brown, 1992), 29 (quoting speech given by Benjamin Franklin).

27. *See* Hacker, "Malign Neglect," 45. Hacker recounts a hypothetical exercise he uses with his White students. He gives them the choice between having $300 in their wallets and having it taken by someone White or having $100 in their wallets and having it taken by someone Black. The majority of students selected the first choice: "They would gladly play the extra $200 to avoid a black assailant" (p. 46).

28. *Id.*

29. The photos with their captions can be viewed at the Snopes.com website, http://www.snopes.com/katrina/photos/looters.asp (accessed January 17, 2008).

30. Presumably referring to Blacks, in a discussion on the reaction to the verdict in the LAPD/Rodney King trial, Wilson comments, "The racist bigotry now being directed at the Ventura County jurors by people who did not sit through the trial or read the transcript is appalling." Wilson, "Crime, Race, and Values," 90–91.

31. Derrick Bell, *And We Are Not Saved* (Basic Books, 1987), 245, 246.

NOTES TO CHAPTER 8

1. *See, e.g.,* Elijah Anderson and Douglas Massey, "The Sociology of Race in the United States," in Elijah Anderson and Douglas Massey, eds., *Problem of the Century: Racial Stratification in the United States* (Russell Sage, 2001), 3–4.

2. 350 F. 2d 445 (D.C. Cir. 1965).

3. Judith Shapiro, "From Sociological Illiteracy to Sociological Imagination," *Chronicle of Higher Education*, March 31, 2000, p. A68.

4. *See, generally,* Katheryn Russell-Brown, "The Myth of Race and Crime," in Robert Bohm and Jeffery T. Walker, eds., *Demystifying Crime and Criminal Justice* (Oxford University Press, 2005); Matthew Robinson, "The Construction and Reinforcement of Myths of Race and Crime," *Journal of Contemporary Criminal Justice* 15 (2000): 133.

5. *See* Project Implicit website, www.implicit.harvard.edu (accessed January 17, 2008).

6. Malcolm Gladwell, *Blink* (Little, Brown, 2005).

7. 347 U.S. 483 (1954).

8. See Kiri Davis's website, www.kiridavis.com (accessed January 17, 2008).

9. Derrick Bell, *Faces at the Bottom of the Well: The Permanence of Racism* (Basic Books, 1993).

10. Quoted in Channing Joseph, "Police Chief Says He Exaggerated Post-Katrina Crime," *New York Sun*, August 21, 2006.

11. *See, e.g.,* Cheryl Harris and Devon Carbado, "Loot or Find: Fact or Frame?" in David Troutt, ed., *After the Storm: Black Intellectuals Explore the Meaning of Hurricane Katrina* (New Press, 2006).

12. Katheryn Russell-Brown, "While Visions of Deviance Danced in Their Heads," in Troutt, *After the Storm.*

13. "Racism, Resources Blamed for Bridge Incident," *CNN.com*, September 13, 2005 (accessed April 13, 2008).

14. *Tracy Dickerson, et al., v. City of Gretna, et al.,* Civil Action No. 05-6667 (E.D. La. 2005).

NOTES TO APPENDIX A

1. Only sections 2, 4, and 5 are reprinted here.

NOTES TO APPENDIX B

1. For a detailed discussion of racial hoaxes, see chapter 6.

Selected Bibliography

Addis, Adeno. (1993). "'Hell Man, They Did Invent Us': The Mass Media, Law, and African Americans." *Buffalo Law Review,* 41: 523.

Alfieri, Anthony V. (1997). "Lynching Ethics: Toward a Theory of Racialized Defenses." *Michigan Law Review,* 95: 1063.

———. (1995). "Defending Racial Violence." *Columbia Law Review,* 95: 1301.

Alpert, Geoffrey, Roger G. Dunham, and Michael R. Smith. (2007). "Investigating Racial Profiling by the Miami-Dade Police Department: A Multimethod Approach." *Criminology and Public Policy,* 6: 25.

Asim, Jabari. (2007). *The N Word: Who Can Say It, Who Shouldn't and Why.* Boston: Houghton Mifflin.

———. (2002). *Not Guilty: Twelve Black Men Speak Out on Law, Justice, and Life.* New York: Amistad.

Austin, Regina. (1995). "Beyond Black Demons and White Devils: Anti-Black Conspiracy Theorizing and the Black Public Sphere." *Florida State University Law Review,* 22: 1021.

———. (1994). "Deviance, Resistance, and Love." *Utah Law Review,* 179: 1994.

———. (1992). "The Black Community: Its Lawbreakers, and a Politics of Identification." *Southern California Law Review,* 65: 1769.

Banks, R. Richard, Jennifer Eberhardt, and Lee Ross. (2006). Symposium on Behavior Realism: Discrimination and Implicit Bias in a Racially Unequal Society." *California Law Review,* 94: 1169.

Barnes, Mario. (2006). "Black Women's Stories and the Criminal Law: Restating the Power of Narrative." *UC Davis Law Review,* 39: 941.

Barnes, Robin. (1996). "Interracial Violence and Racialized Narratives: Discovering the Road Less Traveled." *Columbia Law Review,* 788: 96.

Bell, Derrick. (1992). *Faces at the Bottom of the Well: The Permanence of Racism.* New York: Basic Books.

———. (1992). *Race, Racism, and American Law.* Boston: Little, Brown.

———. (1987). *And We Are Not Saved: The Elusive Quest for Racial Justice.* New York: Basic Books.

Belton, Don. (1995). *Speak My Name: Black Men on Masculinity and the American Dream.* Boston: Beacon.

Blumstein, Alfred. (1993). "Racial Disproportionality of U.S. Prison Populations Revisited." *University of Colorado Law Review*, 64: 743.

Bonilla-Silva, Eduardo. (2003). *Racism without Racists: Color-Blind Racism and the Persistence of Racial Inequality in the United States.* Lanham, MD: Rowman and Littlefield.

Brady, Surrell. (2002). "A Failure of Judicial Review of Racial Discrimination Claims in Criminal Cases." *Syracuse Law Review*, 52: 735.

Brophy, Alfred. (2002). *Reconstructing the Dreamland: The Tulsa Riot of 1921.* Oxford: Oxford University Press.

Brown, Michael, Martin Carnoy, Elliott Currie, Troy Duster, David Oppenheimer, Marjorie Shultz, and David Wellman. (2003). *Whitewashing Race: The Myth of a Color-Blind Society.* Berkeley: University of California Press.

Browne-Marshall, Gloria J. (2007). *Race, Law, and American Society: 1607 to Present.* New York: Routledge.

Browning, Sandra Lee, Francis Cullen, Liqun Cao, Renee Kopache, and Thomas Stevenson. (1994). "Race and Getting Hassled by the Police." *Police Studies*, 17: 1.

Brown-Scott, Wendy. (1994). "The Communitarian Law: Lawlessness or Reform for African-Americans?" *Harvard Law Review*, 107: 1209.

Bushway, Shawn, and Anne Morrison Piehl. (2001). "Judging the Judicial Discretion: Legal Factors and Racial Discrimination in Sentencing." *Law and Society Review*, 35: 733.

Butler, Paul. (2004). "Much Respect: Toward a Hip-Hop Theory of Punishment," *Stanford Law Review*, 56: 983.

———. (1995). "Racially Based Jury Nullification: Black Power in the Criminal Justice System." *Yale Law Journal*, 105: 677.

Carbado, Devon, and Rachel Moran, eds. (2008). *Race Law Stories.* New York: Foundation Press.

Carter, Dan. (1969). *Scottsboro: A Tragedy of the American South.* Baton Rouge: Louisiana State University Press.

Carter, William. (2004). "A Thirteenth Amendment Framework for Combating Racial Profiling." *Harvard Civil Rights–Civil Liberties Review*, 39: 17.

Cole, David. (2000). *No Equal Justice: Race and Class in the American Criminal Justice System.* New York: New Press.

Cole, Johnetta Betsch, and Beverly Guy-Sheftall. (2003). *Gender Talk: The Struggle for Women's Equality in African American Communities.* New York: Ballantine.

Collins, Patricia Hill. (2004). *Black Sexual Politics: African-Americans, Gender, and the New Racism.* New York: Routledge.

Crenshaw, Kimberlé, Neil Gotanda, Gary Peller, and Kendall Thomas, eds. (1995). *Critical Race Theory.* New York: New Press.

Crutchfield, Robert. (2004). "Warranted Disparity? Questioning the Justification of Racial Disparity in Criminal Justice Processing." *Columbia Human Rights Law Review*, 36: 15.

Cullen, Francis, and Michael Benson. (1993). "White Collar Crime: Holding a Mirror to the Core." *Journal of Criminal Justice Education*, 4: 325.

Culp, Jerome McCristal, Jr. (1993). "Notes from California: Rodney King and the Race Question." *Denver University Law Review*, 70: 199.

Daly, Kathleen. (1994). "Criminal Law and Justice System Practices as Racist, White, and Racialized." *Washington and Lee Law Review*, 51: 431.

Darder, Antonia, and Rodolfo Torres. (2004). *After Race: Racism after Multiculturalism*. New York: New York University Press.

Davis, Angela J. (2007). *Arbitrary Justice: The Power of the American Prosecutor*. New York: Oxford University Press.

———. (1997). "Race, Cops, and Traffic Stops." *University of Miami Law Review*, 51: 425.

Davis, F. James. (1991). *Who Is Black? One Nation's Definition*. University Park: Pennsylvania State University Press.

Davis, Peggy. (1989). "Law as Microaggression." *Yale Law Journal*, 98: 1559.

Dawsey, Darrell. (1996). *Living to Tell about It: Young Black Men in America Speak Their Piece*. New York: Anchor Books.

Delgado, Richard. (1996). *The Rodrigo Chronicles: Conversations about America and Race*. New York: New York University Press.

———. (1994). "Rodrigo's Ninth Chronicle: Race, Legal Instrumentalism, and the Rule of Law." *University of Pennsylvania Law Review*, 143: 379.

Deloria, Philip J. (2004). *Indians in Unexpected Places*. Lawrence: University Press of Kansas.

DiIulio, John. (1996). "My Black Crime Problem, and Ours." *City Journal*, 6: 14.

D'Orso, Michael. (1996). *Like Judgment Day*. New York: Berkley.

Du Bois, W. E. B. (1967). *The Philadelphia Negro*. New York: Schocken Books.

Dulaney, Marvin. (1996). *Black Police in America*. Bloomington: Indiana University Press.

Dyson, Michael Eric. (2006). *Come Hell or High Water: Hurricane Katrina and the Color of Disaster*. New York: Basic Books.

Edwards, Harry. (1995). "We Must Let O.J. Go: Separating Fact from Image." *Sport*, 86: 80.

Ellison, Ralph. (1947). *Invisible Man*. New York: Vintage Books.

Feagin, Joe. (2001). *Racist America: Roots, Current Realities and Future Reparations*. New York: Taylor and Francis.

Finkelman, Paul. (1993). "The Crime of Color." *Tulane Law Review* 67: 2063.

———, ed. (1992). *Race, Law, and American History, 1700–1990: The African American Experience*. New York: Garland.

Fleishauer, Marc. (1990). "Review of Florida Legislation; Comment: Teeth for a

Paper Tiger: A Proposal to Add Enforceability to Florida's Hate Crimes Act." *Florida State University Law Review,* 17: 697.

Foner, Eric. (1988). *Reconstruction: America's Unfinished Revolution, 1863–1877.* New York: Harper and Row.

Gabbidon, Shaun. (2007). *Criminological Perspectives on Race and Crime.* New York: Routledge.

Gates, Henry Louis, Jr. (1998). *Thirteen Ways of Looking at a Black Man.* New York: Vintage Books.

Georges-Abeyie, Daniel, ed. (1984). *The Criminal Justice System and Blacks.* New York: Clark Boardman.

Gibbs, Jewelle Taylor. (1996). *Race and Justice: Rodney King and O. J. in a Divided House.* San Francisco: Jossey-Bass.

Gomez, Laura. (2007). *Manifest Destinies: The Making of the Mexican American Race.* New York: New York University Press.

Goodell, William. (1968). *The American Slave Code.* New York: Negro University Press.

Guinier, Lani. (1998). *Lift Every Voice: Turning a Civil Rights Setback into a New Vision of Social Justice.* New York: Simon and Schuster.

Gutierrez-Jones, Carl. (2001) *Critical Race Narratives: A Study of Race, Rhetoric, and Injury.* New York: New York University Press.

Hacker, Andrew. (1992). *Two Nations: Black and White, Separate, Hostile, Unequal.* New York: Scribner.

Hagan, John, and Celesta Albonetti. (1982). "Race, Class, and the Perception of Criminal Injustice in America." *American Journal of Sociology* 88: 329.

Harris, David. (2002). *Profiles in Injustice.* New York: New Press.

Herrnstein, Richard, and Charles Murray (1994). *The Bell Curve: Intelligence and Class Structure in American Life.* New York: Free Press.

Higginbotham, A. Leon, Jr. (1996). *Shades of Freedom: Racial Politics and Presumption of the American Process.* New York: Oxford University Press.

———. (1978). *In the Matter of Color: Race and the American Legal Process.* New York: Oxford University Press.

Higginbotham, A. Leon, Jr., and Anne F. Jacobs. (1992) "The 'Law Only as an Enemy': The Legitimization of Racial Powerlessness through the Colonial and Ante-Bellum Criminal Law of Virginia." *North Carolina Law Review,* 70: 969.

Hindus, Michael. (1980). *Prison and Plantation: Crime, Justice, and Authority in Massachusetts and South Carolina, 1767–1878.* Chapel Hill: University of North Carolina Press.

Ifill, Sherrilyn. (2007). *On the Courthouse Lawn: Confronting the Legacy of Lynching in the Twenty-First Century.* Boston: Beacon.

Jackson, John L., Jr. (2008) *Racial Paranoia: The Unintended Consequences of Political Correctness.* New York: Basic Civitas Books.

Johnson, Paula. (2003). *Inner Lives: Voice of African American Women in Prison.* New York: New York University Press.

Johnson, Sheri L. (2001). "Racial Derogation in Prosecutors Closing Arguments." *Petit Apartheid in the Criminal Justice System.* Durham, NC: Carolina Academic Press.

———. (1998). "Unconscious Racism and the Criminal Law." *Cornell Law Review,* 73: 1916.

Kappeler, Victor, Mark Blumberg, and Gary Potter. (1993). *The Mythology of Crime and Criminal Justice.* Long Grove, IL: Waveland.

Kennedy, Stetson. (1959/1990). *Jim Crow Guide.* Boca Raton, FL: Florida Atlantic University Press.

Klein, Stephen, Susan Martin, and Joan Petersilia. (1988). "Racial Equality in Sentencing." Santa Monica, CA: Rand.

Lawrence, Charles, III. (1987) "The Id, the Ego, and Equal Protection: Reckoning with Unconscious Racism." *Stanford Law Review,* 39: 317.

Lawrence, Frederick. (1993). "Resolving the Hate Crimes/Hate Speech Paradox: Punishing Bias Crimes and Protecting Racist Speech." *Notre Dame Law Review,* 68: 673.

Lee, Cynthia Kwei Yung. (1995). "Beyond Black and White: Racializing Asian America in a Society Obsessed with O. J." *Hastings Women's Law Journal,* 6: 165.

Lee, Orville. (2001). "Legal Weapons for the Weak? Democratizing the Force of Words in an Uncivil Society," *Law and Social Inquiry,* 26: 847.

Lemelle, Anthony, Jr. (1995). *Black Male Deviance.* Westport, CT: Praeger.

Lenhardt, R. A. (2004). "Understanding the Mark: Race, Stigma, and Equality in Context." *New York University Law Review,* 78: 803.

Levitt, Steven D., and John J. Donohue. (2005). *Freakonomics: A Rogue Economist Explores the Hidden Side of Everything.* New York: HarperCollins.

Loewen, James. (2005). *Sundown Towns: A Hidden Dimension of American Racism.* New York: New Press.

López, Ian F. Haney. (1996). *White by Law: The Legal Construction of Race.* New York: New York University Press.

Lynch, Michael, and Britt Patterson, eds. (1991). *Race and Criminal Justice.* Guilderland, NY: Harrow and Heston.

MacLean, Brian, and Dragan Milovanovic, eds. (1990). *Racism, Empiricism, and Criminal Justice.* St. Augustine, FL: Collective Press.

Maclin, Tracey. (1990). "Seeing the Constitution from the Backseat of a Police Squad Car." *Boston University Law Review,* 70: 543.

Magee, Rhonda V. (1993). "The Master's Tools, from the Bottom Up: Responses to African-American Reparations in Mainstream and Outsider Remedies Discourse." *Virginia Law Review,* 79: 863.

Mann, Coramae Richey. (1993). *Unequal Justice: A Question of Color*. Bloomington: Indiana University Press.

Marable, Manning. (2006). *Race, Reform and Rebellion: The Second Reconstruction and Beyond in Black America, 1945–2006*. Jackson: University Press of Mississippi.

Markovitz, Johnathan. (2004). *Legacies of Lynching: Racial Violence and Memory*. Minneapolis: University of Minnesota Press.

Matsuda, Mari, Richard Delgado, Charles Lawrence III, and Kimberlè Williams Crenshaw, eds. (1993). *Words That Wound: Critical Race Theory, Assaultive Speech, and the First Amendment*. Boulder, CO: Westview.

Mauer, Marc. (2007). "Racial Impact Statements as a Means of Reducing Unwarranted Sentencing Disparities." *Ohio State Journal of Criminal Law*, 5: 19.

Mauer, Marc, and Tracy Huling. (1995). "Young Black Americans and the Criminal Justice System: Five Years Later." Washington, DC: Sentencing Project.

Mauer, Marc, and Ryan King. (2007). "Uneven Justice: State Rates of Incarceration by Race and Ethnicity." Washington, DC: Sentencing Project.

Mayer, Jane, and Jill Abramson. (1994). *Strange Justice: The Selling of Clarence Thomas*. Boston: Houghton Mifflin.

McIntyre, Charshee. (1998). *Criminalizing a Race*. Queens, NY: Kayode.

McNeilly, Maya. (1995). "Effects of Racist Provocation and Social Support on Cardiovascular Reactivity in African American Women." *International Journal of Behavioral Medicine*, 2: 321.

Merida, Kevin, and Michael Fletcher. (2007). *Supreme Discomfort: The Divided Soul of Clarence Thomas*. New York: Doubleday.

Miller, Jerome. (1996). *Search and Destroy: African American Males in the Criminal Justice System*. New York: Cambridge University Press.

Mills, C. Wright. (1959). *The Sociological Imagination*. New York: Oxford University Press.

Mincy, Ronald B. (2006). *Black Males Left Behind*. Washington, DC: Urban Institute Press.

Morris, Thomas. (1996). *Southern Slavery and the Law, 1619–1860*. Chapel Hill: University of North Carolina Press.

Morrison, Toni, ed. (1992). *Race-ing Justice, Engendering Power*. New York: Pantheon Books.

Moynihan, Daniel P. (1965). *The Negro Family: The Case for National Action*. Washington, DC: U.S Government Printing Office.

Myers, Samuel L., and Margaret Simms, eds. (1988). *The Economics of Race and Crime*. Edison, NJ: Transaction.

Myrdal, Gunnar. (1944). *An American Dilemma: The Negro Problem and Modern Democracy*. New York: Pantheon Books.

Neal, Mark Anthony. (2005). *New Black Man*. New York: Routledge.

Nelson, Jill. (2001). *Police Brutality: An Anthology*. New York: Norton.

Nelson Mandela Foundation. (2005). *A Prisoner in the Garden: Photos, Letters and Notes from Nelson Mandela's 27 Years in Prison.* New York: Penguin.

Onwuachi-Willig, Angela, and Mario Barnes. (2005). "By Any Other Name? On Being 'Regarded as' Black, and Why Title VII Should Apply Even If Lakisha and Jamal Are White." *Wisconsin Law Review,* 2005: 1283.

Pager, Devah. (2003). "The Mark of a Criminal Record." *American Journal of Sociology,* 108: 937.

Parent, Anthony S., Jr. (2003). *Foul Means: The Formation of a Slave Society in Virginia, 1660–1740.* Chapel Hill: University of North Carolina Press.

Patterson, Orlando. (1998). *Rituals of Blood: Consequences of Slavery in Two American Centuries.* New York: Basic Civitas Books.

Peterson, Ruth, Lauren Krivo, and John Hagan, eds. (2006). *The Many Colors of Crime.* New York: New York University Press.

Pew Research Center. (2007). "Optimism about Black Progress Declines: Blacks See Growing Values Gap between Poor and Middle Class." Washington, DC: Pew Research Center.

Raper, Arthur. (1933). *The Tragedy of Lynching.* Chapel Hill: University of North Carolina Press.

Reitzel, John, and Alexis Piquero. (2006). "Does It Exist? Studying Citizens' Attitudes of Racial Profiling." *Police Quarterly,* 9: 161.

Roberts, Dorothy E. (2004). "The Social and Moral Cost of Mass Incarceration in African American Communities." *Stanford Law Review,* 56: 1271.

———. (1994). "Deviance, Resistance, and Love." *Utah Law Review,* 179: 180.

Ross, Thomas. (1997). *Just Stories.* Boston: Beacon.

Russell, Katheryn K. (1997). The Development of a Black Criminology and the Role of the Black Criminologist." *Justice Quarterly,* 9: 667.

———. (1994). The Racial Inequality Hypothesis: A Critical Look at the Research and an Alternative Theoretical Analysis" *Law and Human Behavior,* 18: 305.

Russell-Brown, Katheryn. (2006). *Protecting Our Own: Race, Crime, and African Americans.* Lanham, MD: Rowman and Littlefield.

———. (2004). *Underground Codes: Race, Crime, and Related Fires.* New York: New York University Press.

Schafer, Judith K. (1986). "The Long Arm of the Law: Slave Criminals and the Supreme Court in Antebellum Louisiana." *Tulane Law Review,* 60: 1247.

Sheley, Joseph F. (1993). "Structural Influences on the Problem of Race, Crime, and Criminal Justice." *Tulane Law Review,* 67: 2273.

Sherman, Lawrence. (1993). "Defiance, Deterrence, and Irrelevance: A Theory of the Criminal Sanction." *Journal of Research in Crime and Delinquency,* 30: 445.

Skogan, Wesley. (1995). "Crime and the Racial Fears of White Americans." *Annals of the American Academy of Political and Social Sciences,* 539: 59.

Smith, J. Clay. (1994). "Justice and Jurisprudence and the Black Lawyer." *Notre Dame Law Review,* 69: 1077.

Stampp, Kenneth. (1988). "Chattels Personal." In *American Law and the Constitutional Order: Historical Perspectives*. Ed. Lawrence M. Friedman and Harry N. Scheiber. Cambridge, MA: Harvard University Press.

———. (1956). *The Peculiar Institution*. New York: Knopf.

Steele, Claude M., and Joshua Aronson. (1995). "Stereotype Threat and the Intellectual Test Performance of African Americans." *Journal of Personality and Social Psychology*, 69: 797.

Steinberg, Stephen. (1995). *Turning Back: The Retreat from Racial Justice in American Thought and Policy*. Boston: Beacon.

Sulton, Ann, ed. (1994). *African American Perspectives on Crime Causation, Criminal Justice Administration, and Crime Prevention*. Englewood, CO: Sulton Books.

Sutherland, Edwin. (1949). *White Collar Crime*. New York: Dryden.

Tassel, Emily F. (1995). "Only the Law Would Rule between Us." *Chicago-Kent Law Review*, 70: 873.

Tillman, Robert. (1987). "The Size of the 'Criminal Population': The Prevalence and Incidence of Adult Arrest." *Criminology*, 25: 561.

Tonry, Michael. (1994). *Malign Neglect: Race, Crime, and Punishment in America*. New York: Oxford University Press.

Troutt, David Dante, ed. (2007). *After the Storm: Black Intellectuals Explore the Meaning of Hurricane Katrina*. New York: New Press.

Ungarte, Francisco. (2006). "Reconstruction Redux: Rehnquist, *Morrison*, and the Civil Rights Cases." *Harvard Civil Liberties–Civil Rights Review*, 41: 481.

U.S. Bureau of the Census. (1986). *Historical Corrections Statistics in the United States, 1850–1984*. Washington, DC: U.S. Government Printing Office.

———. (1975). *Historical Statistics of the United States, Colonial Times to 1970, Bicentennial Edition, Part 2*. Washington, DC: U.S. Government Printing Office.

———. (1969). *Negro Population, 1790–1915*. Washington, DC: U.S. Government Printing Office.

U.S. Department of Labor, Bureau of Labor Statistics. (2005). *Current Population Survey: Employed Persons by Detailed Occupation, Sex, Race, and Hispanic of Latino Ethnicity, 2005*.

U.S. House of Representatives. (2006). *A Failure of Initiative: Final Report of the Select Bipartisan Committee to Investigate the Preparation for and Response to Hurricane Katrina*. Washington, DC: U.S. Government Printing Office.

U.S. Sentencing Commission. (1995). *Cocaine and Federal Sentencing Policy*. Washington, DC: U.S. Government Printing Office.

Verdun, Vincene. (1993). "If the Shoe Fits, Wear It: An Analysis of Reparations to African Americans." *Temple Law Review*, 67: 597.

Walker, Nancy, Senger, J. Michael, Villarruel, Francisco, and Angela Arboleda. (2004). *Lost Opportunities: The Reality of Latinos in the U.S. Criminal Justice System*. National Council of La Raza.

Wang, Lu-in. (2006). *Discrimination by Default*. New York: New York University Press.

Weitzer, Ronald, and Steven Tuch. (2006). *Race and Policing in America: Conflict and Reform*. New York: Cambridge University Press.

Wells-Barnett, Ida B. (2002). *On Lynchings*. New York: Humanity Books.

———. (1969). *On Lynchings: Southern Horrors, a Red Record, Mob Rule in New Orleans*. New York: Arno.

West, Cornel. (2004). *Democracy Matters*. New York: Penguin.

Wheatherspoon, Floyd. (2007). "The Mass Incarceration of African-American Males: A Return to Institutionalized Slavery, Oppression, and Disenfranchisement of Constitutional Rights." *Texas Wesleyan Law Review*, 13: 599.

White, Brent. (2006). "Say You're Sorry: Court-Ordered Apologies as a Civil Rights Remedy." *Cornell Law Review*, 91: 1261.

Wideman, Daniel, and Rohan Preston, eds. (1996). *Soulfires: Young Black Men on Love and Violence*. New York: Penguin.

Williams, Patricia. (1998). *Seeing a Color-Blind Future the Paradox of Race*. New York: Farrar, Straus, and Giroux.

———. (1987). "Spirit-Murdering the Messenger: The Discourse of Fingerpointing as the Law's Response to Racism." *University of Miami Law Review*, 42: 127.

Wilson, James Q. (1992). "Crime, Race, and Values." *Society*, 91.

Wilson, William J. (1987). *The Truly Disadvantaged: The Inner City, the Underclass, and Public Policy*. Chicago: University of Chicago Press.

Wingate, Keith C. (1995). "The O. J. Simpson Trial: Seeing the Elephant." *Hastings Women's Law Journal*, 6: 121.

Wolfgang, Marvin, and Bernard Cohen. (1970). *Crime and Race: Conceptions and Misconceptions*. New York: Institute of Human Relations Press.

Worden, Robert, and Robin Shepard. (1996). "Demeanor, Crime, and Police Behavior: A Reexamination of the Police Services Study Data." *Criminology*, 34: 83.

Wu, Frank. (2002). *Yellow: Race in America beyond Black and White*. New York: Basic Books.

Zatz, Marjorie S. (1987). "The Changing Forms of Racial/Ethnic Biases in Sentencing." *Journal of Research in Crime and Delinquency*, 24: 69.

Index

About the Author

Katheryn Russell-Brown is Professor of Law and Director of the Center for the Study of Race and Race Relations at the University of Florida's Levin College of Law. She is the author of several other books, including *Protecting Our Own: Race, Crime, and African Americans* (2006) and *Underground Codes: Race, Crime, and Related Fires* (2004). Professor Russell-Brown received her undergraduate degree from UC Berkeley, her law degree from UC Hastings, and her Ph.D. from the University of Maryland. Katheryn Russell-Brown, who is from Oakland, California, now resides in Gainesville, Florida, with her family.